From the Lookout

From the Lookout

Memories of Peninsula State Park's Summer Camp for Girls

Kathleen Harris

WISCONSIN HISTORICAL SOCIETY PRESS

Published by the Wisconsin Historical Society Press
Publishers since 1855

The Wisconsin Historical Society helps people connect to the past by collecting, preserving, and sharing stories. Founded in 1846, the Society is one of the nation's finest historical institutions.
Join the Wisconsin Historical Society: wisconsinhistory.org/membership

Front cover illustration adapted from a 1941 Camp Meenahga brochure. Back cover photo courtesy of Grace Lanier Brewer; postcard courtesy of Lynn Matke.

Printed in the United States of America
Cover design by Kristyn Kalnes
Typesetting by Integrated Composition Systems
24 23 22 21 20 1 2 3 4 5

Library of Congress Cataloging-in-Publication Data
Names: Harris, Kathleen (Naturalist), author.
Title: From the lookout : memories of Peninsula State Park's summer camp for girls / Kathleen Harris.
Description: [Madison] : Wisconsin Historical Society Press, [2020] | Includes bibliographical references and index.
Identifiers: LCCN 2019046355 (print) | LCCN 2019046356 (e-book) | ISBN 9780870209383 (paperback) | ISBN 9780870209390 (e-book)
Subjects: LCSH: Clark, Alice Orr. | Mabley, Fanny (Frances Louise) | Camp Meenahga (Fish Creek, Wis.)—History. | Camps—Wisconsin—Fish Creek—History. | Camps for girls—Wisconsin—Fish Creek—History. | Peninsula State Park (Wis.)—History.
Classification: LCC GV194.W52 H37 2020 (print) | LCC GV194.W52 (e-book) | DDC 796.5409775/63—dc23
LC record available at https://lccn.loc.gov/2019046355. LC e-book record available at https://lccn.loc.gov/2019046356.

∞ The paper used in this publication meets the minimum requirements of the American National Standard for Information Sciences—Permanence of Paper for Printed Library Materials, ANSI Z39.48–1992.

To my sons, Brendan and Cole

My life flows on in endless song,
Above earth's lamentation.
I hear the clear, though far off hymn
That hails a new creation. . . .
Through all the tumult and the strife,
I hear that music ringing.
It finds an echo in my soul.
How can I keep from singing?

—From the traditional hymn
"My Life Flows On"

Contents

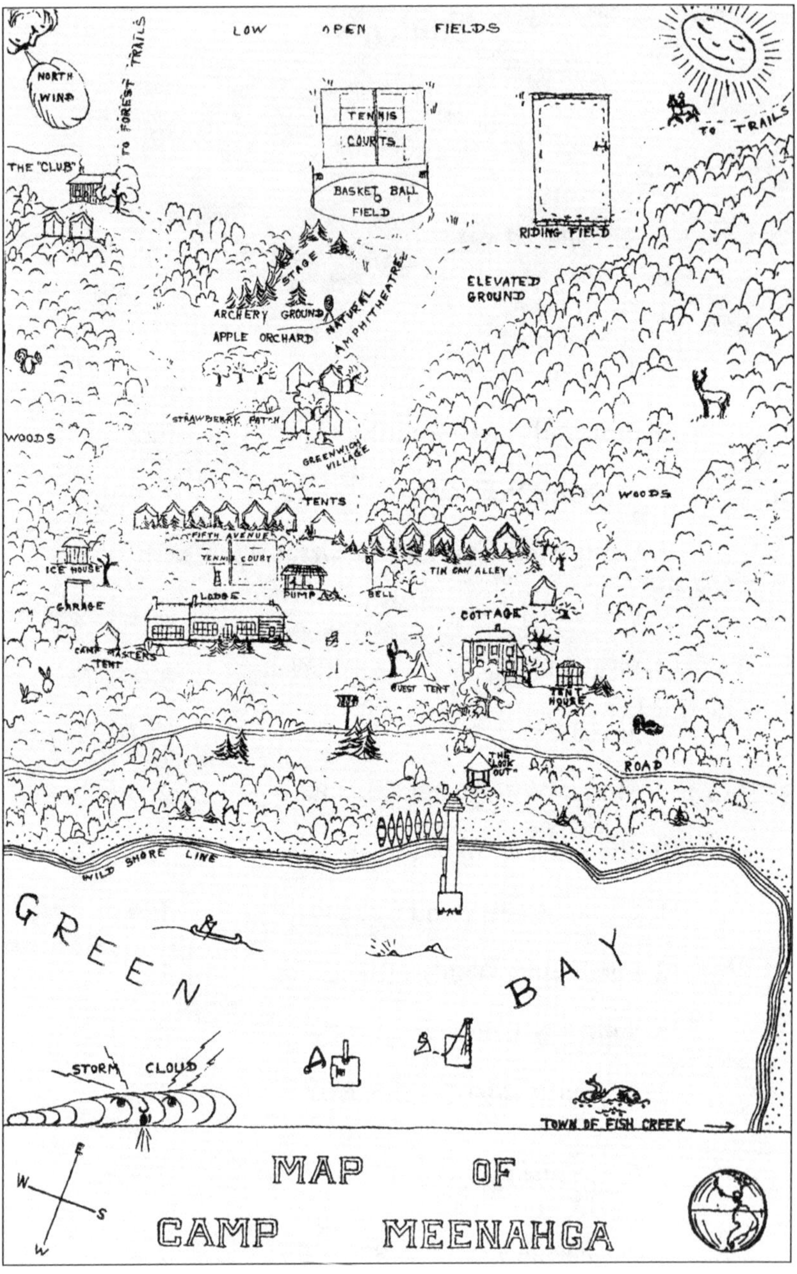

Map of Camp Meenahga. COURTESY OF THE WISCONSIN DEPARTMENT OF NATURAL RESOURCES

Introduction

In 1916, a summer camp for girls opened in Door County, Wisconsin, within the boundaries of Peninsula State Park. Both the camp and the state park were new at the time, signs on a changing rural landscape of an American culture and economy in transition. *From the Lookout* tells the story of Camp Meenahga, the dedicated proprietors and staff who ran it, its campers and counselors, and perhaps more significantly, the memories made there. Set against the shore of Lake Michigan's Green Bay in a place known to some as the "Cape Cod of the Midwest," Camp Meenahga affected the lives of those who knew and loved it best in lasting and meaningful ways. This book reveals what life was like at Camp Meenahga, how twentieth-century history shaped camp for better or worse, and more subtly, how a new state conservation agency did its best to manage Camp Meenahga and the public land around it.

In 1990, during the first summer I worked in Peninsula State Park, I knew little about Camp Meenahga. That year, a lanky, athletic older woman introduced herself to me at the park's nature center. "I'm Evelyn Katz," she said. Then she proudly added, "I'm a Meenahga girl." I smiled kindly, not knowing then what I know now.

A decade later, I was working as Peninsula State Park's full-time naturalist. Katz still occasionally dropped by to say hello. During that time, I created a small display at the nature center about Camp Meenahga. I remember Katz bristled when she read its title: "Privilege in the Park." She continued to visit, though, for a few more summers and was always friendly to me when I saw her. Then she was gone.

I never learned anything more about Katz. I skimmed camp rosters that I located among park records, hoping to find her name. The name Evelyn appears a few times in the records, but there is no mention of an Evelyn Katz, suggesting that Katz was probably not her maiden name. As time went on, Katz remained a mystery to me—and an inspiration. Over the years, with support from Peninsula State Park managers and a small grant from the Cliff and Clara Herlache Foundation, park staff and I have tracked down and interviewed nearly two dozen Meenahga campers and Door County residents with knowledge of the camp. The memories and valuable information they shared have made this book possible.

Camp Meenahga operated every summer from 1916 to 1948. Neither two world wars nor a global economic crisis—the Great Depression—kept it from welcoming campers for the summer. The effects of war and economic collapse affected camp and campers' lives, however. Accounts gathered through interviews with and letters from Meenahga girls similar to Katz convey perspectives that reveal how people living on a small strip of land in Lake Michigan felt the world change around them during times of war and economic uncertainty. A Meenahga director, for example, recalled dealing with butter shortages during World War II. Butter shortages forced the kitchen staff to use margarine colored with orange dye. Serving yellow margarine in Wisconsin was a crime in those days, punishable by imprisonment or fines. At one point, a sign was posted in the camp dining room that read, "We do not serve real butter all the time, and some that looks like butter isn't."[1] The Meenahga yearbook, called *Pack and Paddle,* recorded the rhythms of camp life in essays, songs, and poems written by campers. The pages of *Pack and Paddle* often captured how campers experienced historical trends and events. Entries were predictably sentimental, but many contained references to places and ideas far from Door

County. Girls wrote about Sigmund Freud, minstrel shows, and the atomic bomb. Campers also put in *Pack and Paddle* the names of those who lived in Peninsula State Park, the summer artists and farmers who called the park home for a few months a year or for a lifetime. The names, however, of the carpenters, groundskeepers, cooks, and many others who built and maintained Camp Meenahga, received little mention. Nearly forgotten Wisconsin Conservation Commission correspondence and ledgers, yellow carbon copies of typed documents stashed away in a park file cabinet, yielded crucial information about these people.

Approximately 1,300 different girls attended Meenahga during its thirty-three-year history. Most came from affluent, even very wealthy, Midwestern families. Some campers traveled by train from faraway places such as Texas, Kentucky, and Park Avenue in New York City. One girl, Kathy Hinch, arrived as a refugee from England during World War II. Others came by steamship from Chicago or Milwaukee.

At Camp Meenahga, girls from some of America's largest cities lived in a rustic landscape with modest amenities, in a state park nestled between two coastal villages on the eastern shore of Green Bay in Lake Michigan. Campers stayed six to eight weeks, for the most part without electricity or running water. Many were sent to camp, as thousands of other boys and girls were elsewhere across the United States, to escape the rigors and supposedly unhealthy influences of crowded cities and urban life. At camp, adults, including Camp Meenahga co-founders Alice Orr Clark and Frances Louise "Kidy" Mabley, organized regimented activities designed to keep campers fit and to take advantage of everything that the natural setting around them had to offer. Archery, horseback riding, hiking, swimming, sailing, and canoeing were all popular pastimes at Camp Meenahga.

Meanwhile, northern Door County youth, most living in small lakeside villages or on farms, had no money to attend summer camps like Meenahga. These children explored the woods and beaches around Door County on their own, when they weren't working in the fields, pulling fishing nets, looking after their younger siblings, or helping at their parents' hotels. A few worked at Camp Meenahga. *From the Lookout* tells some of their stories as well.

Camp Meenahga was located on a former farm within Peninsula State Park. The camp encompassed about seventy of the park's 3,776 acres. The waterfront, part of Peninsula State Park's eight miles of Lake Michigan shoreline, was Meenahga's most prominent natural feature. White cobblestones lined the waters of Green Bay then as they do now. Looking west from camp, a chain of small islands, the Strawberry Islands, broke up the horizon. A dock with a fleet of green canoes stretched into the water. Beyond the dock, a diving raft with a metal slide invited swimmers into water that might warm to seventy degrees each summer. A round, stone gazebo stood near the shore. Called the Lookout, this gathering place was perched atop a beach ridge, one of many ancient shorelines in Door County formed by changing water levels since the last glaciers retreated from the region around twelve thousand years ago.

Camp buildings were easy to see from the waterfront. Decades before Camp Meenahga opened for business in 1916, big pines, maples, and cedar trees had been harvested during the heyday of logging in northern Wisconsin. With the land cleared, immigrants, many from Scandinavian countries, moved into the region to farm. By 1909, when the state of Wisconsin established Peninsula State Park, about thirty homesteads, including a few summer cabins, dotted the open landscape. Creating the park meant asking families to either sell their land to the state or opt for a life lease. Some families sold and others chose to stay.

One deserted farm, once owned by Simon and Emily Evenson, became Camp Meenahga. A barn, transformed into the One-Hundred-Foot Lodge, stood on a rise about forty yards east of the waterfront. It contained a dining hall, kitchen, and gathering room. A farmhouse, refurbished to house the camp directors and named the Cottage, was nearby. A road, visible today as a service road, cut between the two buildings.

Girls slept in rows of canvas tents erected on wooden platforms. Tents were raised east of the Lodge near a tennis court and organized into groups by age. Each group of tents was assigned a different name. The youngest girls, ranging from ages eight to eleven, slept in a row called Tin Can Alley. Twelve-year-olds camped at Fifth Avenue, and teenagers camped in Greenwich Village. Girls slept five to a tent, with one counselor per tent. Counselors, usually college-aged and former Meenahga campers, also resided in a refurbished building called the Villa, the Club Rosa (shortened to the Club). Kitchen staff and camp masters, the young men hired to do seasonal manual labor at Meenahga, lived in separate tents on the north side of the Lodge. Other structures at camp included an ice house, garage, nurse's tent, and many outhouses.

Past the tents, at the bottom of a steep slope, was the riding ring. The site had once been an apple orchard. By 1944, Meenahga's American Saddlebred horses were kept in a stable named Coronaga. Pecan shells brought in from the southern United States improved the terrain, while hay, harvested from the Kodanko farm, still operating at the time on Middle Road within park boundaries, kept the horses well fed.

In addition to hiking, canoeing, sailing, and horseback riding, campers staged plays, such as *Anne of Green Gables*, in Meenahga's outdoor amphitheater. Girls also tramped through the woods to park locations such as Tennyson Bay, where there was an abandoned farm once owned by a Civil War veteran. They picked fresh raspberries, then built fires for roasting wienies and frying cornpone. Campers often ventured four miles north to the village of Ephraim for ice cream sundaes, ambling along Eagle Trail and passing white cliffs soaring more than 150 feet skyward. Or they hiked south past Fish Creek, once stopping to converse in French with neighboring Belgian farmers or to have lunch at the nearby Alpine Resort.[2] Along the way, Meenahga campers snapped photographs of Door County scenery with Kodak "Brownie" cameras, later selling the pictures to tourists to raise money for war orphans. In the evening, girls sometimes enjoyed moonlit horse-drawn hayrides to places such as Eagle Terrace, a park overlook still loved by countless visitors. More often, campers sat, as campers in Peninsula State Park still do, cross-legged before outdoor fires, surrounded by dense black above and around, their faces lit by the flickering glow of orange and red embers.

Then as now, Peninsula State Park offered campers a compelling backdrop. The bluffs have always been there, pushing upward across the land in a long, undulating rock ridge. Where once birch trees lined trails and roads, tall maples and red oaks grow in abundance. Meenahga girls heard whippoorwills and probably meadowlarks, but few cardinals. Today, a flashy red cardinal singing its clear whistle song is a common sight and sound in the park. White-tailed deer were not so abundant then as they are now. In fact, deer were so uncommon between 1927 and 1935 that the Wisconsin Conservation Commission prohibited deer hunting during five of those years. Wildflowers grew plentiful. Slipper-shaped orchids as yellow as the sun, and amethyst asters, sculpted like daisies, were easily spotted. Given what campers had around them, a summer at Meenahga involved direct, authentic, and even healing encounters with Wisconsin's natural world.

Over the decades, shelter buildings, roads, parking lots, and electric lines were introduced to Peninsula State Park. As a result, Meenahga became less and less isolated and more and more crowded. Additionally, some of Camp Meenahga's old-fashioned facilities began to appear worn and in need of repair. In contrast with other youth camps in America, which had begun to manufacture wilderness and simulate outdoor experiences according to professional standards, Meenahga looked out of date. In the late 1940s, when the Wisconsin Conservation Commission secretly tried to persuade the Girl Scouts of the USA to take over running Meenahga, the plan floundered. Girl Scouts representatives inspected Meenahga's antiquated structures and quickly passed, choosing instead a site near Baileys Harbor known today as Camp Cuesta.

If Camp Meenahga resisted change, it did so because its purpose never wavered. From 1916 onward, founders Clark and Mabley made it their mission every summer to prepare Meenahga campers for what lay ahead of them. "We [Clark and Mabley] are trying to teach our girls to THINK," Clark wrote in the 1935 Camp Meenahga brochure. "Each girl," wrote Clark, "has her place, her individuality, and as such she must learn to take her part in the great whole. She must realize her responsibility, first to herself and then to others; what she must contribute, and what she must get out of . . . community life."[3] Clark's niece Katherine Orr said that what Clark gave campers was "the wise loving of us," a generosity of spirit, an unsparing forgiveness of failures, and a "clear understanding of what is real in us."[4]

Many of the girls who attended Camp Meenahga were among the Greatest Generation, those who grew up during the Great Depression and lived through or served in World War II. At Meenahga, they were fun-loving and sometimes silly, exuberant or maudlin. They paddled canoes over Green Bay by moonlight or tricked friends into nighttime snipe hunts in the park cemetery. *From the Lookout* emphasizes that what girls did at Camp Meenahga inspired and precipitated greatness in their lives and the lives of others. It is this connection, an arc between a summer camp founded and run by St. Louis socialites, and the generation who grew up to alter the trajectory of the twentieth century, that is Camp Meenahga's most enduring legacy.

1

Up to Me

> *It is only after doing one's best in one's own sphere, be it home, school, or camp that one is fitted for playing a greater part in service to the world.*
>
> —Marian Wickham, 1921 *Pack and Paddle*

The world seemed a bewildering place to Alice Orr Clark in 1915. Unexpectedly, she found herself living with her sisters in the family home in St. Louis, Missouri, with two children in tow. The war in Europe was a muddle and race riots in East St. Louis a possibility. Then, on August 20, 1915, the River des Peres ran swiftly over its banks onto the streets of St. Louis. Rainfall from a tropical storm had swelled the river to its flood stage. Sewage flowed alongside rainwater, swirling past the white marble columns of the new Jefferson Memorial before cutting a mile-wide path through industrial neighborhoods. Devastation surrounded anyone with the courage to face it.[1]

Clark could relate to those who suffered terrible losses in the flood. A great wave of destructive change had recently swept through her own life. Clark's husband, Warren Clark, had abandoned Clark and their two children and moved to New York City. For Clark, the separation was as embarrassing as it was financially devastating. Her life looked nothing like it had the decade before, when she was the affluent Mrs. Clark—wife, mother, and proud member of St. Louis society. Clark, like St. Louis, had been so sure of herself in those years. In 1904, the city hosted the Louisiana Purchase Exposition, informally called the St. Louis World's Fair, in magnificent fashion. For seven months, St. Louis entertained travelers and dignitaries from around the world, where they were introduced to the architectural, technological, and scientific wonders of the new and extraordinary twentieth century—and cotton candy. A box of "fairy floss" cost an extravagant twenty-five cents, and nearly seven thousand boxes were sold.

Forest Park, the site of the fair, was hit hard by the flooding. By autumn, however, much of the mess had been cleaned up. Clark, too, was by autumn ready to salvage the wreckage of her world. It was, she believed, a matter of mind over matter, a willingness to see her need as a blessing. Clark knew she had to imagine a different life for herself and her children. By October, the path forward seemed clear to her. It ran northeast, from her home in St. Louis on Lafayette Street all the way to Door County, Wisconsin, through farmlands and small towns toward the picturesque shoreline of the Door County peninsula. Clark had decided to open a summer camp for girls.

She found a ready business partner in a friend, Frances Louise "Kidy" Mabley, and the pair got to work. They never looked back. For the next three decades, Clark and Mabley welcomed more than 1,300 young women to Camp Meenahga in Peninsula State Park. There campers lived in canvas tents, swam in and paddled across the waters of Green Bay, explored Door County, told campfire stories, took afternoon tea, wrote poetry, and more than anything, made memories that would last a lifetime.

WOMEN ALONE

Serendipity made it all possible. On a Tuesday evening in October, less than three months after the flooding in St. Louis, Clark found herself on Washington Avenue to see the Veiled Prophet Parade. Festive horse-drawn floats and noisy brass bands attracted the attention of onlookers.[2] Clark and Mabley were among the crowd gathered to watch. They were brought together by their young children who knew each other from school. Clark and Mabley exchanged pleasantries and, after some time, began to talk about their futures.

Both women came from families with deep roots in St. Louis. Clark, born October 27, 1875, was the ninth child of William Campbell Orr and Mary Dorothy Orr. William Orr owned the Orr and Lindsey Shoe Company, a successful enterprise. Hard financial times were on the Orr family horizon, however. The business eventually declined. By the time Clark's father died when she was twelve years old, there was little money left. She did not regain any sort of financial security until she married Warren Clark, who had inherited a successful grocery business in 1899, the same year in which Clark's mother passed away. Yet when Warren Clark left for New York and a new woman, he left his wife; his daughter, Alice; and his son, Benjamin (called Benno), without financial resources or any assurances they would be cared for.

Like her friend Clark, Mabley came from a prosperous St. Louis family. Born September 30, 1869, Mabley grew up as Fanny Woodward in a comfortable middle-class home. Her father, Calvin Milton Woodward, was a Harvard-educated professor of mathematics and applied mechanics at Washington University in St. Louis, where he was also the dean of engineering. Woodward had achieved international fame for developing the public-school program for manual training, known widely as shop class. Mabley's husband, Harold Clifton Mabley, was a physician from Ohio, where Mabley lived with him and their three daughters. Tragically, her husband died in 1924 from tuberculosis. Eight years earlier, he had entered a sanatorium for treatment. By the end of 1915, Mabley and her daughters, Frances (called Fanny), Hilda (Hilly), and Elaine, had returned to St. Louis to live near her parents because Harold Mabley's poor health prevented him from earning a living.

The two would-be entrepreneurs were finding it hard to make ends meet. If Warren Clark sent money to care for his wife and children, it was not enough for her to keep the family household on Lafayette Street going. Clark had to generate some revenue. Many years after Clark founded Camp Meenahga, she wrote, "It was certainly up to me to find some work I could do, for there I was with my two children and no income."[3] Mabley found herself in a similarly tight situation financially. She worked as the head of the McKinley High School cafeteria, but she was always short on cash.

Above the din of the parade, the conversation between Clark and Mabley moved beyond polite inquiries and platitudes toward the serious problem of financial independence that both women were trying their best to solve. When Clark told Mabley about her idea for a summer camp for girls, Mabley knew immediately that she had found in Clark what she was looking for—an opportunity for herself and her daughters.

Many years later, Mabley's granddaughter, Judy Clark Stephens, recalled the first meeting between Clark and Mabley in this way: "When my grandmother and Mrs. Clark got the idea of taking their children up to Door County for the summer, they began to think it would be a good idea to take some other daughters and charge them so that they had financial backing. And that is how it all started."[4]

ST. LOUIS LADIES

Clark and Mabley did not cut figures that one might assume to be at home even in the relatively hospitable scenery of Peninsula State Park. Clark was slender and petite, standing less than five feet two inches tall in size three and a half shoes, which more often than not were red. She was almost forty, and the blond curls of her youth had begun to turn silver. Mabley was also short in stature, though her outgoing nature complemented Clark's more reserved personality. Mabley was funny, too, with a wonderful sense of humor that both delighted people and put them at ease. More than six years older than Clark, Mabley was nevertheless considered "very active and very vivacious."[5]

That their plan was audacious and out of the ordinary was not lost on Clark and Mabley. They were women raised during the Victorian era, when Queen Victoria reigned in the United Kingdom from 1837 to 1901. It was a time of strict social mores in America, when ladies were expected to evince the best qualities of discipline, obedience, and impeccable values. Clark and Mabley cared deeply about what they had been taught and saw to it that their campers did the same. Clark, for instance, often welcomed girls to tea to teach them proper deportment and decorum. She also awarded a felt pine tree to girls with straight posture and strong ideals. She was, in every way, "a lady born and bred," wrote her grandson Laurence Day, "to the purple, so to speak."[6] Mabley, for her part, was fond of saying, "Do it girls, because it's good for your character."[7] To be sure, labor of most kinds was not the sort of thing ladies did to build character or refine their manners. Day summed it up when he wrote, "Except for the normal common labor that women were participating in at that time—and many did—it was not an accepted thing for women to start a business or be physicians, lawyers, or in the professions. There were those that were, but few and far between."[8]

It is probably safe to guess, then, that during the best of times in their marriages to Warren Clark and Harold Mabley respectively, neither Clark nor Mabley thought that one day they would need to work for money. In their time, marriage, not achievement in business, was the yardstick that measured a woman's success. How happy and fulfilled a woman was in her marriage was determined by motherhood, not bank accounts. Separation and divorce were painful and shameful public admissions of a woman's failure to make a good home for her husband and family. Divorce had terrible social consequences as well, as Day noted, "If one transgressed in such fashion, one was ostracized." It is easy, then, to understand why throughout her life, though her divorce was finalized in 1923, Clark presented herself as a widow.[9]

When Clark and Mabley opened Camp Meenahga in 1916, they were women on their own. By following a dream, they were transgressing rigid societal norms they had respected and abided by all their lives. They were not young, and what they had in age they lacked in business experience. But they had each other. And they had something even more important—purpose.

THE "ME" IN MEENAHGA

In the months that followed their chance encounter at the parade, Clark and Mabley enjoyed a thrilling and happy exit from the debris of lost dreams as they entered a realm of new possibilities. The business partners went ahead with all the confidence in the world, believing Camp Meenahga would generate income and provide a healthy place for their children to spend the summers. Each woman brought different talents to the table. Clark had clear ideas on how to prepare girls to meet the challenges of a changing world. Mabley understood the practicalities of setting up a kitchen and supervising staff. Both were resourceful problem solvers—and both reckoned they were first among equals.[10] Without a hint of envy or jealousy, Mabley claimed that "Mrs. Clark and I worked hand-in-hand for seventeen years, each one thinking she put the 'me' in Meenahga, but we never discussed it, just went ahead with the little hidden secret."[11]

The question might be asked: Why Door County? In order to attract campers from the Midwest, Clark and Mabley decided the camp needed to be within two days travel by train from St. Louis. One of Clark's closest friends and bridesmaids, Elizabeth Chittenden Crunden, knew of such a place. Crunden told Clark that Door County offered a mild climate, lovely beaches, and warm hospitality. Many prominent residents of St. Louis summered there, she told Clark, including herself.

If it was good enough for Crunden, it was good enough for Clark and Mabley. They decided to go north and find a place for their camp, set among small fishing villages, summer retreats, and awe-inspiring sunsets.

2

Scouting for a Camp

It is the opinion of the ladies that they have the most beautiful site in the world for their camp.

—*Door County Democrat*, Sturgeon Bay, Wisconsin, July 14, 1916

Elizabeth Crunden endorsed her friend Alice Orr Clark's idea to open a summer camp for girls in Door County. She and her husband, Frank, had summered there for years. In 1898, they built an estate on a Fish Creek country lane named Cottage Row. As boys, Frank Crunden and his brother Fred had summered in the area because of the reputed relief it offered allergy sufferers. Kidy Mabley's father was one of their summer tutors.

With her plans in tow, Clark went to Door County in April 1916. To say that by that time the Crundens were well-established summer residents would be an understatement. They were Democrats, entertaining the likes of the famous labor lawyer Clarence Darrow when he was in the region. They gave memorable parties, where Elizabeth, barely five feet tall, made grand entrances. In contrast, Frank stood six feet four inches and weighed close to 285 pounds. The unmatched pair often danced to their honeymoon song, "La Paloma," on their outdoor rock patio, sprinkled with cornmeal to make the Latin-style pivots easier.[1]

Crunden appreciated the rougher features of Door County's natural beauty. She hired local stonemason Henry Eckert to fashion walls, benches, and grottos using only native dolostone with no cement. Some rock came from a quarry that today is an overflow parking lot near Nicolet Beach. In time, Crunden "sculpted" the length of Cottage Row, leaving a visual legacy that is distinctly Door County. Unfortunately, that legacy is now eroding. Many stone fences and grottos have crumbled away, abandoned as nothing more than piles of rubble to be replaced by fabricated materials.

BLUEBERRIES

In 1916, Crunden's rock walls still stood straight. Behind them, she helped her friend Alice put ideas into practice. Like Clark and Mabley, Crunden knew how to organize people and tasks. At the time, she was rallying Red Cross relief efforts for the Great War in Europe and was as well at work helping to organize the first birth control advocacy group in St. Louis. Crunden was also an invaluable source of information about Door County and its residents, the perfect person to connect Clark and Mabley with the right people.

When Crunden heard that Clark had contacted Door County proprietors and planned to build her summer camp near Sawyer, a village twenty-five miles south of Fish Creek and annexed to Sturgeon Bay in 1891, she spoke frankly to her friend. "No, I won't let you go there," she told Clark. "It is low, hot, and on the central canal between Green Bay and Lake Michigan. It is one mosquito hole."[2] Clark was glad for the advice but told Crunden that she and Mabley had already chosen a name for their camp, Meenahga, because of the blueberries that grew at the site near Sawyer. They had even purchased china embossed with the letter *M* from a defunct shipping line.

Why Meenahga? The answer was obvious in 1916. In those days, schoolchildren were often required to memorize poetry. One popular selection was Henry Wadsworth Longfellow's *The Song of Hiawatha*. The poem includes this stanza:

> By the river's brink he wandered,
> Through the Muskoday, the meadow,
> Saw the wild rice, Mahnomonee,
> Saw the blueberry, Meenahga . . .[3]

Crunden remained undeterred. She insisted her friend inspect a different place, one more emblematic of Door County's scenic beauty and temperate summer climate.

She knew just how to make it happen.

THE DOOR PENINSULA

A unique interplay between landscape and memory creates extraordinary places. Such has happened on a slice of land in northeast Wisconsin. The Door County landscape shaped Camp Meenahga—memory sustained it.

Door County encompasses most of the seventy-five-mile-long finger of land that extends from central Wisconsin northeastward into Lake Michigan. The width of the peninsula is about twenty-five miles at its widest, narrowing northward until the land explodes in a spray of islands at its tip. A rocky corridor snakes around the shoreline of the peninsula, formed over 420 million years ago when the land was at the edge of an inland sea. Impressive linear precipices offer seasonal views of migrating eagles, ducks, and songbirds, all of which use the bluffs and surrounding waters of Green Bay as a migration corridor.

Lake Michigan surrounds the landform. For centuries, Native Americans and Euro-Americans traveled across the lake over trade routes connecting the western Great Lakes to the East. The lake was central to the lucrative Great Lakes fur trade. Ships also carried lumber and iron ore from Wisconsin to industrial centers across the Midwest, from which goods and materials made their way around the globe. Lake travel could be treacherous, especially through the shallow passage between the tip of the Door Peninsula and Washington Island. Early French explorers heard Native people warn of the strait's hidden shoals and windy weather and experienced the danger there firsthand. They called the passage Porte des Mort, which was later translated as Death's Door. When citizens in the region organized Door County in 1861, they named it after the legendary water crossing.

Long before any Euro-Americans were in Door County, however, the land was the ancestral home of many Native Americans, in particular the Potawatomi Nation. Native homes were threatened as Americans moved westward during the nineteenth century. The Potawatomi Nation ceded all its lands between Wisconsin and Ohio, forced to do so by the US government through treaties. The largest land cession, one of five million acres, occurred as a result of the Chicago Treaty of 1833. Treaties like it, as well as passage of federal legislation such as the 1830 Indian Removal Act, opened Door County to Euro-American intrusion. As settlers began migrating to the area, territorial expansion became an excuse to remove Indians from their lands. The US government ordered the Potawatomis to leave their homes and travel, often by walking, to designated territories west of the Mississippi River, a march known today as the Potawatomi Trail of Death. By 1850, most Potawatomis had been forced out of the region. Many resisted, however. A few unpublished family histories allude to the presence of small clans in Door County throughout the nineteenth century.[4]

After Wisconsin became a territory in 1836, then a state in 1848, adventurers looking for a good living found their way to the peninsula. Increase Claflin, a native of New York State and a veteran of the War of 1812, was the first to purchase land in what would become Door County. Claflin lived and was later buried on property that became Peninsula State Park. He and his wife, Mary Ann, homesteaded in a cozy harbor just north of a stream he named Fish Creek because of its abundant catch. When he needed to travel, Claflin, like his neighbors, routinely did so by boat rather than try his luck on mucky, nearly impassable roads. In summer, this meant sailing fourteen miles west across Green Bay to resupply in the little towns of Marinette and Menominee. In winter, Claflin got across the lake on an ice skiff. Every so often, he walked seventy-five miles south to Green Bay. Other settlers, including Door County mail carriers and ministers, did the same.

While Claflin was settling future park land, other fishermen were busy with seasonal work on Rock Island at the tip of the Door Peninsula. The island was a familiar port to sailors. The federal government had built a lighthouse, Pottawatomie Lighthouse, on Rock Island in 1836, the first on Lake Michigan. A few hardy, intrepid anglers and coopers made the island their year-round home. Residents organized Door County's first township on the island in 1851. Yet, as the fishing industry declined in the early twentieth century and lifestyles changed accordingly, the island lost its economic appeal and its residents moved to nearby Washington Island. Rock Island became a state park in 1965.[5]

All the while, immigrants, many from western European countries, were moving in alongside Yankee anglers. For the most part, they were landlubbers seeking rich farmland, and many purchased inland parcels in what would become Peninsula State Park.

By the 1880s, the logging industry had harvested the valuable white pine and hardwoods in Door County. Logging left a "cutover region" open to farming and development. The limestone soil, scraped and thinned by glaciations, made farming difficult but not impossible. Peas grew well for a time. Fruit trees fared better. In 1892, a member of the State Board of Agriculture visited the peninsula after a trip to the Wisconsin State Fair, where he had tasted some Jonathan apples grown by a Door County farmer. During his visit, he noted that "the modifying influence of the waters and ice of Lake Michigan and Green Bay" makes spring in Door County last longer than usual, causing fruit tree buds to develop slowly. The water surrounding the Door Peninsula also helps create air movement beneficial to certain fruits. Lake breezes diminish frost on developing buds. During Door County's growing season—which is long enough for crops such as cherries and apples but too short for peaches—carbohydrates (starches) in fruits slowly break down into tasty sugars.[6]

Door County bedrock, the parent material for soil, is largely dolomitic limestone formed by ocean sediment deposited hundreds of millions of years ago. Door County's limestone bedrock is part of a 650-mile bowl-shaped landform called the Niagara Escarpment. The edge of the escarpment extends in a roughly circular pattern northeast through Canada's Bruce Peninsula all the way to Niagara Falls.

In addition to fruit trees, Door County's landscape supports species of flora that are unique and lovely. Inland, away from high cliffs and foaming whitecaps, acres of snow-white apple and cherry blossoms interrupt an undulating, pastoral topography. Yellow lady's slipper orchids and pearly white trilliums blossom between fiery red oaks and wispy-needled hemlock trees. Fringed gentians, colored in Dresden blue, are scattered across edges of abundant wetlands. It is no wonder, then, that seasonal fisherman, lumberjacks, and fruit pickers often returned to Door County with family and friends during the nineteenth and early twentieth centuries. They eventually gave way to tourists, as proprietors transformed rustic cabins at old work camps into quaint resorts and, later, upscale condominiums.

At first, shrewd hotel owners advertised Door County as a place free from pollen, where people with allergies (such as Frank and Fred Crunden) could find relief. When antihistamine medications became available in the 1930s, that flawed marketing ploy slowly disappeared.[7] But the tourists did not, coming in greater numbers each year. By 1910, hospitality commerce had become more lucrative than commercial fishing and other industries in northern Door County. Yet, even as increasing numbers of tourists vacationed in the region, the number of year-round residents did not change much. In 1910, Door County had 18,711 year-round residents. A century later, the year-round population had grown to only 27,785.[8] Today, more than two million annual visitors move in and out around permanent Door County residents, drawn to the area by the same allure of natural beauty and charm that has attracted people to it for centuries.

PENINSULA STATE PARK

Wisconsin lawmakers recognized the need to preserve the natural beauty of the Door Peninsula long before Clark saw fit to open a summer camp there. On June 9, 1909, Wisconsin Governor James O. Davidson signed a bill creating a system of state parks. Peninsula State Park was the first state park opened under the new system. Tucked between the picturesque villages of Fish Creek and Ephraim, the 3,776-acre park features 150-foot bluffs and eight miles of spectacular, sun-drenched Green Bay shoreline. Narrow dirt roads zigzag through a northern hardwood forest, stitching together what was in 1909 a patchwork of family farms and summer cottages. Most of the thirty-odd individuals who owned land in the park were paid an average of twenty dollars per acre to move out. Their abandoned cabins were later leased by summer residents, some of whom became friends of Camp Meenahga. Lifelong leases were granted to those who did not sell and vacate.

In 1913, Albert E. Doolittle became the first superintendent of Peninsula State Park. A trained forester, Doolittle saw a hodgepodge landscape when he looked at what he was in charge of maintaining and protecting. Much of it had been recently logged. On the farms still operating within the park, potatoes, cabbage, and raspberries were common crops. Some farms had dairy cows, sheep, and pigs. Apple and cherry orchards also grew on park property, including on a section of land that in time became part of the park's golf course.

Hjalmar Holand, a founder of the Door County Historical Society and a vehement opponent of Peninsula State Park, owned that particular piece of land. Before the park opened, Holand wrote scathing letters to local newspapers in which he warned that the park would lead to economic and environmental calamities. Holand believed that wolves would hide in Peninsula State Park's woods and emerge to kill valuable livestock. He also foresaw a landscape charred by crackling forest fires, along with untilled fields choked with weeds. When state workers felled four- and five-foot diameter hemlock and pine trees near Eagle Tower—built in 1914—as part of a 1917 Wisconsin Conservation Commission timber harvest plan, Holand again put pen to paper to air his grievances. This time Holand's efforts paid off, and the timber harvest stopped. When it did, it was up to Doolittle to pacify a suspicious public.[9]

Holand was not alone in his distrust of the Commission. When local families were displaced from their land in order to create a state park, a rift opened between the state and the community around Fish Creek. Doolittle, savvy and strong-willed, made a smart decision that relieved some of the tension. He recognized that employing local laborers might soften hard feelings. Hometown men, Doolittle thought, could build amenities desired by park visitors. Laborers from nearby villages and farms were quickly hired and assigned to construction details.

It was not the first time that Doolittle proved his worth as a capable park superintendent. Nor would it be the last. During his thirty-year tenure, Doolittle remained constantly productive. Under his direction, local men used horses, sleighs, wagons, hand tools, and plenty of muscle to transform miles of wagon-rutted park trails into passable roads. Nearly all of the modern park roads have been laid over those either improved or built by Doolittle and his teams. Work on them was no small thing, and Doolittle's daughter Ruth noted in a 2006 interview that "I think the roads that my father built were one of the accomplishments he was most proud of."[10]

Away from the roads, nearly all of Peninsula State Park still bears Doolittle's signature. He directed the expansion of hiking and riding trails, the clearing of scenic overlooks, and the construction of two fire watch towers, one at Sven's Bluff and the other at Eagle Bluff (the latter built on land owned by Holand). Doolittle brought modern conveniences to Peninsula State Park, running telephone lines into the park in 1916 and lines for electricity in 1925. Doolittle also reforested much of what had been a cutover region in 1913, overseeing the planting of more than forty thousand trees at two dozen plantations.

Needless to say, Doolittle was a man who cared a great deal about Peninsula State Park and the community around it. He was also a man who knew a good opportunity when he saw one. When Doolittle heard about Clark and Mabley's idea for their camp, he predicted immediately that it would provide a boost to the local economy and improve the strained relationship between the local community and the state.

He was right on both counts.

OILING THE WHEELS

Crunden knew Doolittle well enough to know that he liked the idea of a summer camp for girls in his park and that he was the man who could help turn Clark and Mabley's plan into reality.

Thinking it a good idea, Crunden steered her friend Clark toward Doolittle. She paid for Clark's lodging at the Thorp Hotel in Fish Creek during Clark's trip to Door County in April 1916, and she personally arranged an outing with the park superintendent. Years later, Clark wrote:

> In making the trip to Fish Creek to talk to Mr. Doolittle, I found that Miss Elizabeth had oiled all the wheels. She gave me money for the train tickets, wrote to a driver, Mr. Vorous, to meet me at the station in Sturgeon Bay, and arranged for him to take me to Thorp's Hotel. She asked Mr. Doolittle to meet me at the hotel, and with Mr. Vorous, arranged for a tour of the area, driving anywhere we wanted to go. Mr. Doolittle, Mrs. Thorp, and I were driven [all] over the park for two days.[11]

During her tour of the park, Clark noticed the abandoned Simon and Emily Evenson farm on Shore Road, about a mile from the park's entrance. In her mind, the old farm appeared to have everything she was after. There was a large threshing barn that Clark envisioned as a dining room and recreational hall. The farm cottage would make adequate living quarters for Clark and Mabley and their families, with an office and sitting room upstairs where the partners could work and welcome guests.[12] Clark asked to see the farm more than once. Doolittle was happy to oblige, as he kept in mind the economic good Clark and Mabley's camp would do for the area. Doolittle said as much to Clark, who delayed a final decision until discussing with Mabley what she had seen in Door County.

When Clark returned to St. Louis, she immediately met with Mabley. They then sent a telegram to Doolittle expressing their wish to locate Camp Meenahga in Peninsula State Park. On May 31, 1916, the *Door County News* reported: "A party or organization of St. Louis, Mo. young ladies, who wrote to this city some time ago in regard to a suitable camping site for a large party of girls, have chosen the Peninsula State Park from the many places suggested."[13] Doolittle drafted a fifty-year lease. It was renewable every five years and required no fee the first year. Annual payments would be charged thereafter for camp maintenance.

The Crundens gave Clark $1,000 (almost $24,400 in 2019) to get things started, asking her to keep the gift a secret, which she did. Clark and Mabley talked about and planned how to spend the money. Before long, they had a list of items to order from Sears, Roebuck and Company. Clark remembered getting "tents, four I think, kitchen utensils, a kerosene stove, and one dozen potties." The potties in particular surprised Clark and Mabley. "When we unpacked at camp," Clark recalled, "we found the potties were baby size. We never stopped laughing over those."[14]

LOCALS LEND A HAND

Doolittle found local carpenters to restore the Evenson farm. First, men converted the threshing barn into what came to be called the One-Hundred-Foot Lodge. A kitchen and dining room were built on one side of the Lodge, while workers extended a 50-by-25-foot screened-in porch along its opposite side.[15] In 1923, carpenters added a large framed wing to be used for reading, sewing, and assemblies, then connected it to the

Lodge with archways to finish off a 4,600-square-foot space. Inside, a stonemason from Michigan crafted an impressive fireplace with Door County dolostone and granite, which workers topped with a raw-hewn oak mantel. For the mantelpiece, Doolittle chose a thirty-six-inch propeller from the steamboat *Pilgrim*, painting it green to look like a shamrock. Albert Zahn, an ironsmith from Baileys Harbor, forged andirons to cradle long and heavy logs. The Lodge also had a reading room, where Clark and Mabley placed white wicker furniture purchased from Door County resident Arthur Bissell. Game tables and a piano were added later, as were long wood-hewn dining tables with log legs and decorative birch branch details.[16]

Outside the Lodge, a wooden eagle twirled lazily atop a windmill. Purple martin houses were perched aloft on high poles, as was the American flag. The camp bell, its brassy signal resounding across Lake Michigan and through the woods, clanged commands to change activities, including gathering for "dear old mail."[17] One camper wrote of the bell:

> And through it all the ruler of our day
> Remains unchanged, and with its rusty smile
> It clangs its warning note with n'er a change
> Whether we curse or smile.[18]

Workmen also remodeled the farmhouse. Called the Cottage, it was a suitable home for the Clark and Mabley families. From the Cottage, an expansive clearing extended to the shore. Near the edge of the water, on the circular stone base of an old lime kiln, was the Lookout, a lovely roofed gazebo perfect for watching sunsets and the northern lights.[19]

East of the Lodge, crews constructed three-foot-high wooden platforms to support thirty-two tents. Yards of heavy canvas hung over the tent frames. Each tent had six cots. Evelyn Bhirdo

Franke began work in Camp Meenahga's kitchen in 1927 and stayed with other local girls in the tent reserved for hired help. She remembered the tents having "flaps on the sides. When it was nice, you could roll them up and when it wasn't nice, they came down. You fastened them on the corners."[20] Mosquito netting was in good supply, too. By the late 1930s, so was Rutgers 612 lotion, an early insect repellant. Camp Meenahga girls smeared it on their bed sheets to deter no-see-ums. Still, mosquitoes found a way to bother campers. One Camp Meenahga girl, Dorothy Sherman, wrote in 1922, "How the playful mosquito manages to get inside the netting, ready to lead campers in a merry game of tag, no one knows."[21] Mice also visited the tents. Mary Orr Williams advised girls to respond in the following brutal way when spotting a mouse: "If you see a mouse / Don't bother what I've said, / Just grab a stick and do be quick / And bash it on the head."[22]

Not all girls dealt with animals or insects in the same harsh way. At least one Meenahga camper expressed affection for the harvestman, or daddy longlegs, an arachnid cousin to the cellar spider:

Dear old Daddy Long Legs
You've swarmed about my tent,
There were millions of you
On mischief always bent.
I'd go to bed at night
With you tickling my toes,
And wake up in the morning
With you walking o'er my nose.
Oh! Daddy's on the ceiling,
And Daddy's on the floor,
You surely love the tent flaps
As you ne'er did before.

Some folks will not miss you,
They'll leave you with great glee,
But dear old Daddy Long Legs,
Your name spells "tent" to me.[23]

Workers quickly added more amenities. They built a diving raft and a tennis court. As time went on, a baseball diamond, basketball hoops, and a riding ring were made available for use. Trees and brush were cleared from a sweeping hollow to make an amphitheater. Cone-shaped evergreens served as stage decor. Cow sheds were converted to cold storage buildings, and a new garage was raised to house camp vehicles.

Johnnies were also built. The grandest johnnie of them all was a five-seater installed several years after Camp Meenahga opened. It was, according to Elizabeth Lanier DeRamus, a camper and later a counselor at Meenahga, a "serial outhouse, down the lane near senior camp. You had to walk down there with your flashlights. There were five stalls and you sat, and there was a pit down below, and it went well down there. There was a sign on the door that read, 'Roses are red. Violets are blue. Please pump ten times when you are through.'"[24] Today, an astute observer will see a similar outhouse northwest of the tennis court. Four rusty vaults in crumbling concrete proudly stand amidst creeping poison ivy and Pennsylvania sedge.

After months of planning and weeks of frenzied work, Clark and Mabley were ready to welcome their guests. On July 12, 1916, less than three months after Clark's April visit to Door County, Camp Meenahga opened for business.

3

Beautiful Place, Beautiful Country

> *Once there was a beautiful place in a beautiful country. There were great trees, a lake, a fine climate, and peace and beauty everywhere. Now, some very discerning people, having seen this place, decided that it was the best place in the world for a girls' camp. Many girls came; some because their parents, being older and wiser, knew it would be good for them; and others, who knew already the customs and joys of outdoor life, thought they might teach and help others to love it with them.*
>
> —Betty Fairfield, 1919 *Pack and Paddle*

On a cool June evening in 1916, Alice Orr Clark, Kidy Mabley, and their families arrived at a wooded notch along Peninsula State Park's cobblestone shore. Clark and her children, Alice and Benno, then Mabley with daughters Fanny, Hilly, and Elaine, tumbled out of a cab, wide-eyed at what to them was a wilderness. Carl Stephenson and his wife, Olive, accompanied the children and their mothers. Stephenson, a history professor hired as head camp master, was a colleague of Mabley's father at Washington University in St. Louis.

From the shore, the Clarks, Mableys, and Stephensons

watched the sun set beneath the western shore of Green Bay. Years later, Elaine Mabley recalled the scene:

> I remember well the first trip over the rough primitive road from Fish Creek to the chosen camp site, a park road full of holes and bumps which literally made us hold on. The first thing we did was of course to explore the grounds, and with squeals of joy we fell to picking strawberries, once farm cultivated, but now small and wild. I, a city girl, had never encountered them before. Where they grew was soon to become a basketball court, a dancing green, and a riding ring.[1]

NATURE AS REFUGE

Clark and Mabley chose Peninsula State Park for several reasons in addition to its natural beauty. One was that the park promised safety from the urban decay and moral dangers that parents feared. Less than a decade earlier, Wisconsin Assemblyman Thomas Reynolds had used a similar argument to justify the creation of Peninsula State Park. Reynolds claimed that, "Away from the dust and filth of the city [people] can breathe in the clear, pure, invigorating air fresh from the waters of Green Bay."[2]

As they were in other large American cities during the early 1900s, public services in St. Louis were old, inadequate, and becoming increasingly overwhelmed by a growing population. America's transformation from an agrarian to an industrial economy was in full swing. With industrialization and rising populations in urban centers came a proportional rise in disease. Although medicine had advanced to treat illness and cities such as St. Louis had working sanitation facilities, the spread of life-threatening illnesses remained a major concern. Tuberculosis, for example, killed one in seven people in the early 1900s.[3]

Outbreaks of polio were also common. In fact, Meenahga campers and counselors occasionally stayed with St. Louis friends on Cottage Row during polio scares.[4]

In addition to worries about disease, parents such as Clark and Mabley worried that life in the city offered their daughters too many chances to fall into bad behaviors or to do something disreputable. Conversely, Door County was a world away from St. Louis, Chicago, and Milwaukee, a place where young ladies and their reputations would be safe from harm. The camp brochure put it plainly:

> Camp life, with its regularity, its good food, healthy activity, and long hours of sleep has rapidly become the right kind of summer for the schoolgirl. Our aim at Camp Meenahga is to give a limited number of girls, from the ages of twelve to twenty, a wholesome, happy and winsome leadership. . . . Camp Meenahga is the emblem of loving comradeship, gentleness, and courtesy, as well as promptness and neatness.[5]

Clark and Mabley relied on careful persuasion and endorsements from friends in high places to assure anxious parents that their daughters would stay safe. Activities, they promised, would foster qualities essential to healthy womanhood and service to others.

One way that Clark and Mabley promoted good health was to endorse physical activity and sports. When it came to athletics, they let their campers do the talking. "The road to strength is by way of physical perfection," wrote Mabley's daughter Hilly in an early edition of *Pack and Paddle*, Camp Meenahga's yearbook and most effective marketing tool. Hilly Mabley added that "the road to fortitude and endurance is by way of deep-rooted conceptions of courage, fairness, and decision. And these qualities in a woman are best attained during girlhood through wholesome athletics, under wholesome conditions, amidst wholesome companions."[6]

Comradery meant more than competition, and winning meant less than self-improvement. The idea was to help girls grow into capable and confident family caretakers. To that end, Clark and Mabley initially restricted each camper to "one strenuous activity a day"[7] so as not to risk their girls losing any appearance of femininity. Exercise supplemented with summer lessons in the social graces and optional academic learning were enough to convince skeptical parents that a summer at Camp Meenahga would be good for any young woman of social standing.

To care for their campers, Clark and Mabley hired a camp doctor, a "resident physician who cooperates with the director in maintaining healthful conditions and promoting the physical well-being of the girls." Among other duties, the doctor oversaw "facilities for sun baths . . . given under the supervision of the camp physician."[8] Even with a doctor looking on, sometimes sunbathing did campers more harm than good. One camper warned others of the sun's harmful effects in a poem in *Pack and Paddle*:

Be careful of my shoulders,
They're burnt and awfully hot,
And if you know what's good for you,
Touch them you will not.

Oh gee, my legs are peeling,
And they're getting awfully sore.
And if I know what's good for me,
I will burn no more![9]

THE CAMPING MOVEMENT

Camp Meenahga was one of the first residential camps for girls in the Upper Midwest, and the first such camp in Wisconsin. Meenahga and camps like it were established during an era that saw the rise of national youth camping and scouting movements, when, for example, Ernest Thompson Seton helped start the Boy Scouts of America in 1910. Two years later, Juliette Low founded the Girl Scouts of the USA. By the 1920s, as many as one million children were enrolled at more than one thousand overnight camps across America.[10]

Yet camp was not for everybody. "In the 1920s," wrote Door County native Duncan Thorp, "such camps were the 'in' thing, and only for the upper classes. They could pack their sons and daughters in a carefully supervised institution with plenty of exercise, food, shelter, dramatics, hiking, nature study, even dancing lessons. The kids flocked to the camps in summer while parents cruised, toured abroad, and worried not."[11]

Play was a central part of the movement and understood at the time as "a moral force no less than work and prayer." Play, especially in nature, was a necessary antidote to the perceived inert, soul-deadening bricks and mortar of cities. "There is no religion of greater social force than the unconscious religion of the open," wrote author and attorney Henry Wellington Wack. "God's voice is the voice of Nature." Summer camps trained the imaginations of countless youth, fostering in them an ability to take on the future no matter what the circumstances. Camp, it was thought, created a positive and dynamic adult, "the only kind of citizen who can serve the public well."[12] Such beliefs, essential to Camp Meenahga, reflected ideas related to the purpose and justification for the recently established system of state parks in Wisconsin, that physical and moral health as well as happiness were to be found in scenic places around the state.[13]

NOT IF, BUT HOW

For the girls at Camp Meenahga, sports may have been as much a draw as being miles away from protective parents. Their childhoods were in many ways shaping up to be very different from their mothers.'

"Formerly," wrote a Meenahga camper in 1918, "the world had no great or immediate need for the mentality of women, but the modern day finds women and even girls confronting the duties of men and with like necessity the strength and fortitude of men."[14] By the 1920s, strict Victorian-era gender norms had begun to have decreasing influence. Where once domesticity and fragility defined femininity, now resiliency and competency beyond marriage and motherhood distinguished the so-called New Woman of the twentieth century.[15] America's entry into the Great War, the onset of the Great Depression, and eventually World War II all lowered a drawbridge between home and community that many women eagerly crossed. The question was no longer *if* middle- and upper-class white women should venture from the realm of domesticity but *how* they should do so.

Changing ideals were made apparent in camp athletics. Horseback riding, steeped in tradition and long embraced by elite women with leisure time, was front and center. Meenahga hosted its own derby, a grand August event that people throughout Door County were invited to attend. Clark and Mabley also allowed campers to play basketball, a new American sport, but required that girls do so in private where the public was not allowed to watch.

At Meenahga, currents of social and societal change affected more than what sports girls were allowed to play. In 1916, for example, though neither Clark nor Mabley could vote, they nevertheless took patriotism very seriously. Campers raised the American flag every day, participated in patriotic pageants, and contributed to war relief efforts with the Red Cross. When camp closed thirty-two years later, girls still posted the colors daily, but Meenahga's last generation of girls were among the first to grow up with voting rights in America. Some of these same girls followed their big sisters to the battlefields of World War II, not only as nurses and ambulance drivers, but also as mechanics and pilots.

4

Traveling to Camp

> *Isn't it wonderful how moonlight and a tiny star*
> *Show us so clearly the beauty of things as they are?*
>
> —Helen Jean "Pete" Simpson,
> 1928 *Pack and Paddle*

On July 12, 1916, cars from Harry Dana and Frank Anderson's Yellow Cab and Transit Company in Sturgeon Bay coasted down the Fish Creek hill carrying thirty girls from St. Louis, the very first Meenahga campers. Dressed for their trip, girls typically wore calf-length dresses or skirts sashed at the waist, with billowy buttoned blouses pleated at the shoulders (corsets were still worn but becoming less rigid). Younger girls wore sailor-style collars and neckerchiefs. Jackets hung to the hips, and by the time of the Great War, button epaulettes and snappy belts accessorized outwear. Campers traveled in style to Meenahga until the camp closed, though by the 1940s, dress hemlines had begun to creep daringly upward.

Counselors served as chaperones and met campers at train stations, where daughters waved goodbye to their parents and hopped aboard. One Kentucky camper recalled boarding the Louisville L & N Railroad at four o'clock in the morning, alone, and arriving in Chicago. She met other Meenahga girls who had taken the Chicago and Alton Railroad overnight. All boarded specially chartered Pullman cars (Alice Orr Clark contracted as many as six Pullman sleepers and a dining car for campers)[1] and traveled overnight again to Appleton, Wisconsin. The cars were then hooked and attached backward to a freight train,[2] which chugged northward up the Door Peninsula toward Sturgeon Bay. "How we younger ones loved sleeping on a train, whether in an upper or a lower berth," recalled Clark's daughter, Alice Clark, many years later, adding they could never afford the luxury of an expensive stateroom.[3]

The next day usually included a nonstop cacophony of ukuleles, gossip, card playing, snoring, and eating.[4] Clark's son, Benno, who was eleven years old when Meenahga opened in 1916, likened the ruckus to "days and days of jabbering" that "finally simmered down some." He added that "at night there is one continuous giggle."[5]

Counselors did what they could to quiet the giggling. So did Clark and Mabley when they selected their roster of campers. Unless applicants were known by Clark or Mabley, would-be campers had to be vouched for by "responsible references (three) who know her [an applicant] to be the kind of girl whom we desire in camp."[6] If a girl acted unruly, she and her parents would hear about it. If the same girl misbehaved again, Clark and Mabley reserved the right to withdraw her from camp without issuing a refund.[7]

With the campers, two other people likely traveled in the reserved Pullman cars. An African American couple named Bill and Adell Davis from St. Louis worked as handyman and cook at Camp Meenahga from the time it opened until about 1926. It seems the Davises were long-time employees of the Orr family. The 1870 census lists Frank Davis, age thirty, as William Orr's carriage driver. Bill Davis was likely a descendent of Frank. Even during an era of racial segregation, the Davises were allowed to sit with the group in a private car. If they ate meals in the dining car, the Davises sat at a table at the end nearest the kitchen. Other African Americans on the train were porters, maids, and cooks.[8]

A few girls traveled by steamship instead of train. They boarded in Chicago and Milwaukee and docked at either Fish Creek or Ephraim. If it was Ephraim, a cannon boomed on Folda's Island when the steamship *Carolina* rounded Welcker's Point. The ship's captain answered the blast with three piercing horn blows as the boat puffed toward Anderson Dock. Once campers disembarked, they were taken by private car to Meenahga.

ONE HUNDRED ELEVEN TRUNKS

During Meenahga's early years, when the camp was still new, the girls' arrival set Door County abuzz. "On July 4, in the evening," reported the *Door County Democrat* in 1917, "special Pullman cars will leave St. Louis bound for the Door County state park. The special cars will carry a party of fifty young ladies who will spend the summer at the park at Camp Meenahga, enjoying physical and mental training."[9] A few days later, the *Door County Advocate* told readers: "Young ladies from St. Louis, who are to camp in the state park, and who have named their camp as Camp Meenahga, arrived on the train Thursday evening, coming directly from the southern city. They will leave for the north by stage Friday morning."[10]

For many, each year's arrival was a happy déjà vu that brought with it dreamy images of summer escape. When cars carrying campers stopped at top of the Fish Creek hill high above Green Bay, girls and counselors always broke out in song:

Just what White Sox means in baseball
Just what Tiffany means in rings,

Just what home-made means in pie crusts,
So with Heinz and pickled things,
Just what Hershey's means in nut bars,
Just what tungsten means in lamps,
Just what sterling means in silver,
Meenahga means in camps![11]

Voices grew to a crescendo as cars rolled down the hill toward a village street less crowded than today and with unobstructed views of the water and docks. When the cars turned right at the base of the hill, everyone knew Meenahga was just three miles away.

Traveling north along Route 17 (now State Highway 42), the cars turned west into Peninsula State Park after driving over a little bridge above Fish Creek. The narrow dirt road, oiled for the camping season, followed the Green Bay shoreline. From the cars, girls saw a solitary log cabin, a frame house, and a tawny marsh alive with red-winged blackbirds. They passed Mengelberg Lane, another cottage, then the Lookout. A gazebo, the Lookout stood twenty feet or so from the water, perched on a stony beach ridge. A four-sided roof peaked in the middle. Supporting beams were balanced on a knee-high circle of large limestone rocks. Meenahga campers and staff gathered at the Lookout for waterfront activities as well as quiet moments with special friends.

When the cars finally stopped, girls were reminded not to leave the grounds without permission and to do so only when accompanied by a counselor.[12] Campers ran up a slope toward the Lodge, where cooks had a meal waiting for them. Campers also rang the bell, the sound of which marked the beginning of their time at camp. "We . . . rang and rang the old ship's bell," remembered Clark's daughter, Alice. "This bell woke us up, summoned us to all three meals, to morning drill and swimming.

How we campers could distinguish what all these ringing bells meant, but we did!"[13]

Bags, usually steamer trunks, were then unloaded. During one summer, 111 trunks were "hauled to the northern part of the county Friday morning by the Yellow Cab Company," reported the *Door County News* in 1920, "requiring several large trucks to transport the baggage, practically all of which were for the girls of the camp."[14]

YEAR-ROUND RECRUITING

Meenahga's first campers were relatives and friends of Clark and Mabley. Both knew, however, that if their business was going to turn a profit, they needed to advertise and recruit wherever and whenever possible. They were limited in where they could advertise and did not have much money for marketing, but they did create a high-quality camp brochure, illustrated with professional photographs. Soon, girls were arriving not only from St. Louis but from Milwaukee, Chicago, Louisville, and Detroit. In time, they came from New York City, Buffalo, Dallas, and Canada.

Camp fees reflected the affluence of most Meenahga campers. In 1921, a nine-week session cost $300 (about $7,000 in 2019) with special rates for two or more campers from the same family. In 1935, during the Great Depression, fees for an eight-week session dropped to $275, but several activities required a surcharge. A single riding lesson cost $1.75, for example, but ten could be had for $15.

Because it cost so much to attend Camp Meenahga, most campers came from very privileged backgrounds. Alice Hotz, from a wealthy family in Chicago, attended Camp Meenahga when it opened in 1916. Her father, Ferdinand Hotz, was a diamond merchant known in Chicago as the Diamond King. In the late 1920s, cousins Nancy and Mary Kimberly, whose family owned part of the Kimberly-Clark Corporation, attended camp. Katherine and Janet Turnbull, whose father became the first president of the Green Bay Packers in 1923, were campers at the same time. Signs of wealth were often obvious. Evelyn Bhirdo Franke worked in the camp kitchen. She remembered that campers' parents "would come to see their children, and the chauffeur would be standing there. He always had to open the doors for them and everything. He had a real uniform on, you know. Well, they were very rich."[15]

Cincinnati camper Mousie Stix alluded to the wealth of Meenahga's clientele in the 1927 *Pack and Paddle*:

> Probably you have all been frequently annoyed by the well-worn parental saying: "It's not what you *want* to do, dear, that must count, but what's *best* for you!" And—if you think over summer resorts, hotel life, touring with the family, Western excursions, European traveling—and are honest you will admit that camp, with its wholesome life, its well-ordered activities, its inimitable good times, *is* best for you. You will have few finer opportunities in life offered you of living absolutely without pretense, of giving your most admirable self, of knowing and loving those about you. What are you missing by coming to camp? A few dances—a few shows—a few dates—a few clothes. You can have them all when you return in September; and they will seem all the more attractive for your short absence from them. Even the presence of the "he" whom you most adore begins to pall upon you if presented for too steady a diet. Come to Meenahga—she wants you very much! And undoubtedly—you need her badly.[16]

Not all Meenahga girls were well-to-do. Ruth Doolittle Steinseifer, daughter of Peninsula State Park superintendent

Albert E. Doolittle, attended camp at no charge beginning in 1920. She remembered being very aware of the differences between her and the rest of the campers:

> I was about nine. I went there about three years and the fourth year Mrs. Clark called me and wanted me to come again . . . and I said, "No. I don't want to go." Those people were wealthy people and I was not. I didn't have the things that they had and I felt out of place. I think they were more sophisticated. Because we had uniforms, the clothes didn't matter, except for the shoes. I remember not having very good shoes . . . I think I was pretty bashful and it was hard for me to mix with those people.[17]

RED COWS AND PIE-BEDS

Looking after the campers were the camp counselors. Clark called them her "girls," and they largely made the success of Camp Meenahga possible. Counselors worked tirelessly and cheerfully for very little pay. Most attended prestigious colleges and universities such as Smith, Vassar, Bryn Mawr, and Northwestern, returning to Meenahga during the summer.[18] Many were accomplished swimmers, equestrians, and dancers. Most were from privileged families, and several counselors became so enamored with Door County that they purchased summer homes in the area. Libby Tatman, who worked as a tennis instructor at camp during the 1930s, was one. She married Spencer Gould, who later led efforts to refurbish the famous Peninsula State Park totem pole in 1970.

Many counselors were known by their nicknames. Among them were Pete, Mousie, Shoestring, and Peanuts. Counselors taught lessons and supervised campers six days a week, from sun up to sun down. They offered a shoulder to cry on when homesickness or disappointment were too much to bear. Many were fearless in the woods. As one camper wrote:

> If you can swat flies with real enjoyment
> And still not seek elsewhere for employment,
> Or keep tent inspection on your mind
> And yet to your two-legged charges be kind,
> You're a counselor at Meenahga.[19]

Each counselor bunked with five campers in a canvas tent built on a wooden platform. Pranks such as short-sheeting bed linen (pie-beds) were standard fare. Two campers penned the following limerick after tricking some counselors:

> There once was a nice pie-bed sheet
> And the pie-bed was made very neat.
> The victim got stuck
> Said, "Curses, what luck!
> I find there's no room for my feet!"[20]

Counselors responded in turn with something called "red cows":

> Red Cows! What a fascination in the term "Red Cows," suggesting green pastures and daises. But no! You are wrong, not an innocent bossie, merely the dastardly revenge of a group of merciless counselors upon defenseless girls. The cowardly people crept silently upon them while they slept and branded each nose with iodine. When the morning dawned pale and grey the victims appeared with adhesive strips covering the incriminating marks.
>
> Why all this ado, you ask, why this torture? Merely because of a few innocent pie-beds made by the mischievous

> darlings, with perhaps a few cracker crumbs, pepper, or rotten apples mixed in. What a thirst for revenge some people have![21]

Unsuspecting campers were sometimes talked into midnight frolics away from counselors. One camper recalled a figure in a bathrobe leaning over her bed, murmuring, "Be as quiet as you can, put something on, and come down to the Lookout."[22] When this happened, girls were warned not to wake the counselors. Girls crept off creaking cots, trying to be stealthy.

Down by the water, forty-five girls whispered and wondered while the two who had woken them all up hissed that they be quiet. Suddenly, Fatté, Clark's daughter Alice's Highland terrier, woofed an alarm from the Cottage, just across Shore Road. The girls huddled closer. One revealed that in the end the campers did not fool anyone:

> At last . . . we all trailed to the Lodge. There, in the dark and quiet of night, fudge was passed, and we all felt wicked and devilish. Suddenly, a light was seen in a far corner of the Lodge, then another, until they were all over. The counselors. There were screams, apologies, explanations, but no one paid the least bit of attention, because someone had discovered that the counselors knew all about the plan. In other words, it was a "put up job."[23]

BRAINS AND BRAWN

Each summer, Clark hired three or four college-aged men to handle work she considered too strenuous for the counselors. They were called camp masters, and they arrived a few weeks before camp opened and stayed after Meenahga closed, setting up and taking down tents, racking canoes, anchoring the diving raft, and cleaning buildings. In addition, they prepared the ice shed for the winter harvest. Camp masters also hauled water and food, lit fires, split wood, and made evening rounds to secure the camp, giving fair warning to tents grouped by age with shouts such as "Coming up Greenwich!" before entering different sections of camp. Nightly patrols included cleaning, filling, and lighting nearly fifty kerosene lanterns in the Lodge, Cottage, and tents.[24] A few camp masters taught woodcraft and athletics. Wally Cole, Elizabeth Crunden's grandson, taught sailing.

In 1935, the year his three sisters enrolled at Meenahga, Robert Wollaeger worked as a camp master at Meenahga. Wollaeger was seventeen years old at the time. "We always had to go collect the mail," he recalled. Mail call created a flurry of activity, since girls hoped for a letter from home or from a suitor. Wollaeger considered himself "a rather quiet guy usually" but admitted that "[Camp Meenahga] brought me out a bit." He remembered long conversations under starry skies with different counselors, all from St. Louis, on Meenahga's pier.[25] Wollaeger's experience was not unique. Sam Frank, a member of the Kappa Alpha House at Washington University in St. Louis, was the inspiration for a 1930 poem penned by the counselors for the annual Meenahga banquet:

> I'm Sam, a glutton for drill,
> Of this I know you've had your fill;
> I've tried a mustache,
> And think it's quite dash,
> To give all the counselors a thrill.[26]

The most famous camp master to work at Camp Meenahga spent the summer of 1927 taking care of the grounds and campers. Clark McAdams Clifford came from St. Louis. He was handsome and witty, and he spoke with a gentle southern lilt. At age thirty-seven, he enlisted in World War II and became a navy captain. After the war, Clifford became a naval advisor, then special counsel and principal speech writer for President Harry S. Truman, a fellow Missourian. Clifford then served as the Democratic liaison for the transition of power between the Eisenhower and Kennedy administrations before Lyndon Johnson appointed him Secretary of Defense in 1968. Later, Clifford established a prominent law practice in Washington, DC, while still advising presidents when they sought his counsel. During Jimmy Carter's administration, Clifford served as Special Emissary to India. Through it all, Clifford never forgot Camp Meenahga and kept in touch with Clark throughout her life. As a young man, Clark's grandson Laurence Day met Clifford on several occasions, describing him as "the epitome of integrity, wisdom, and caution" and "Mr. Cool personified with a quick wit and sense of supreme dignity."[27]

5

Camp Meenahga and the Great War

From our little world, we look out on one big one that is whirling by with a rapidity that at times frightens us, yet intrigues us all at the same moment. We are frightened because we do not see how our simple lives are involved in that big world of affairs. We must realize that each one of us, in her little circle, by laboring in an altruistic spirit, is playing her part.

—MARIAN WICKHAM, 1921 *PACK AND PADDLE*

When Camp Meenahga opened in 1916, Alice Orr Clark relied on staff to fetch mail in Fish Creek, three miles from camp. Local farmers William and Amelia Zachow delivered supplies for Kidy Mabley's kitchen, bringing fresh produce and heavy, five-gallon aluminum milk cans by wagon. Horses strained to pull the load up the steep hill to the Lodge.[1] A year later, things changed when Clark bought a car. Convenience and independence offset worries about bewildering mishaps. The first time Clark parked in front of Lundberg's dry goods store in Fish Creek, she returned from her shopping to find boys and men under the chassis and peering inside the car. The new, shiny black Model T was quite a sensation, one of the first seen in Fish Creek.[2]

That summer, camp masters drove to town for supplies and mail. On occasion, they also chauffeured passengers in the boxy "queer apparatus" with its piece of "black goods" stretched over the top. Six or seven people sat on seats and the floor, "packed like sardines." The driver set the fuel mixture and ignition timer gears manually, then walked to the front of the vehicle to turn a hand crank and start the motor. It did not always work. "We try to get it started," Clark's daughter, Alice, lamented in the 1917 *Pack and Paddle,* "and one poor victim uses up all her strength trying to crank it. First the cook is called to the rescue, and then the yard man. As a last resort, we all get out and give a grand push." That usually did the trick. With a lurch, the car would start down Shore Road. Campers would chase the Ford and then pile in again, out of breath. It was worth it to them, as they felt of the Model T that "we should be lost and helpless without it."[3]

Clark's car carried more than people. It also hauled baggage from steamships to Meenahga. Flat-topped steamer trunks (wardrobe trunks were not allowed) contained things that campers needed. Clark and Mabley advertised that campers should have two pair woolen bloomers, one pair khaki bloomers, three white middy blouses, four unbleached middy blouses, one yellow silk tie (one of the camp colors), one pair high waterproof boots for hiking, one raincoat and nor'wester hat, three suits of light underwear and some heavy underwear, and one pair heavy stockings.[4] By 1935, a flashlight, a metal drinking cup, a hot water bottle, and two good books to donate to the camp library were added to the list.[5] By the 1940s, campers were bringing bobby pins, sweaters, records, radios, stuffed toys, and Baby Ruth candy bars. Silk stockings and party dresses were not allowed, but directors asked campers to pack one simple summer dress. They labeled clothing with "name tape" and inked names on shoes and even tennis balls (a rare commodity during World War II because rubber went toward the war effort), then packed it all into steamer trunks. Duffle bags held extra blankets.

Meenahga's first "regulation costume" consisted of olive-colored bloomers, knee-high stockings, and white middies. Green corduroy shorts later replaced the bloomers. On Sundays, girls sported white or tan shorts. By the 1940s, campers could wear a shirt of choice on Wednesdays. A local woman cleaned clothing, stockings, and bed linens for an extra charge. Some campers washed their undergarments in the waters of Green Bay.[6]

IN THE TRENCHES

Clark heard from Arthur Doe, a former camp master, that women drove ambulances around the Western Front in Europe. After the 1917 summer season, Doe spent several months driving ambulances in France after Congress had declared war on Germany that April. American "doughboys" shipped out to join Allied troops in Europe. Doe wanted to see the action, and he did. When he returned to Camp Meenahga the next year, his descriptions of the war, according to one writer, "brought before our minds again the dreadful suffering that exists, which only can be done away with by each one of us doing all we can."[7]

During the war, Elizabeth Crunden served as president of the St. Louis chapter of the American Fund for the French Wounded. In that capacity, Crunden supervised Red Cross knitting and sewing projects at Meenahga. Campers picked cherries at local orchards, too, turning any money earned over to the Red Cross. The money added up quickly, as Meenahga raised over $200 "to support three French orphans."[8] In addition to picking cherries, Meenahga campers made or raised items for the war relief effort, including muslin slings and washrags.[9]

Girls dedicated the 1918 yearbook "To Our Loved Ones 'Over

There.'" In the same issue, they wrote, "In these stirring times, when the whole world seems to be upset and full of distress, there is something worthwhile for each one of us to do, and it is necessary to do not only 'our bit' but 'our best.'" That summer, head camp master Carl Stephenson gave accounts of the daily war movements at the close of the day. On Sunday nights, everyone gathered in the Lodge to sing "The Star-Spangled Banner," which President Wilson had recently ordered to be played at official military occasions.[10]

Camp Meenahga continued to raise money even after the Armistice was signed in November 1918. During the following summer, Meenahga invited the public to attend a dance drama based on the Greek story of Persephone and her descent into the underworld, charging the public admission. Counselors also collected tent inspection fines, made and sold Kewpie[11] pillows, and sold photographs of Peninsula State Park scenery, all in the name of war relief efforts. Counselors planned a "jitney party" as well. Jitney was once common slang for low-value coins. At this fundraiser, girls sold ice cream cones and popcorn balls for a nickel. The campers worked hard to raise as much as they could because "The Belgian babies must have their money" decreed that year's *Pack and Paddle*.[12]

THE PATRIOTIC PAGEANT

In 1918, campers performed *The Sentiments of War* at Meenahga's amphitheater. Actors posed mute and motionless, depicting historical scenes in a style called tableau vivant.[13] A narrator described each scene. During "Immigrants," a voice proclaimed, "You came here seeking freedom. You must help to preserve it." During "The Trail of the Hun," girls posed as Belgian orphans helped by the Red Cross.[14] Later, actors silently changed poses.

One girl posed as Liberty awakening in 1917 to preserve Democracy.[15] The narrator declared:

> Shall an ultimate nation, God's own child,
> Arise and rule and never conquered be,
> Untouched by time because all undefiled,
> She makes His ways her ways eternally![16]

The 1918 Armistice ended fighting, but peace was not official until the following June with the signing of the Treaty of Versailles. Peninsula State Park's annual picnic in August seemed the perfect venue to reprise Meenahga's patriotic pageant. Albert E. Doolittle invited the public to bring "basket dinners" to a Peace Day Celebration at Eagle Terrace. The event attracted more than four thousand people and featured speeches, bands, baseball games played on the golf links, stands selling items such as coffee and soda, and a reprisal of Meenahga's patriotic tableau vivant from the year before.[17]

In one scene, girls representing Prosperity and Liberty held evergreen branches and wore garlands of maple leaves. When Liberty's draperies began slipping off, someone whispered, "My kingdom for a safety pin!" Everyone stifled giggles. Fanny Mabley, quiet and motionless, crouched at the foot of a girl representing Peace. Mabley remembered that,

> I could see neither the crowd of people nor the other girls in the tableau. After staring at the dry leaves on the ground for perfect ages, my curiosity got the better of me and I lifted my head slowly and took a look around. The dove of peace was perched on Wynne's wrist over my head, and it struck me as being terribly funny. Kath Gardner, Prosperity, standing there draped in a flag, and looking so stately, suggested under her breath that we should all "shimmy" and we simultaneously burst.[18]

Suddenly, riders wearing spotless jodhpurs and polished black boots emerged from the woods on shining American Saddlebred horses. Girls carried flags of the Allied nations, creating what Doolittle remembered years later as "the most beautiful thing I have ever seen. . . . It showed the Allies working together, and everyone who saw it was so impressed they were choked with tears."[19]

CAMP MEENAHGA AND ITS NEIGHBORS

Pageants were just one of the ways that Meenahga campers and counselors made themselves part of the Door County community. Clark and Mabley stressed to their girls that it was important to be on good and friendly terms with their neighbors. When the girls took the Model T to Fish Creek, they passed an assortment of summer residences and those of "homers," the name Meenahga girls gave to year-round residents. If some of these folks disliked what they saw when the girls drove by, they said something. During the camp's first few summers, for example, residents thought girls should wear skirts in town instead of bloomers, or worse, shorts. After hearing as much from their neighbors, Clark and Mabley insisted that their girls not "roll bloomers up as high as they would go" when going into town.[20]

Two St. Louis teachers, sisters Lilia and Lidia Dyer, kept a summer residence near Meenahga. The sisters lived in a hand-hewn, chinked pioneer cabin located between the entrance to Peninsula State Park in Fish Creek and the park manager's residence. Poppies, larkspur, and lilies adorned their front yard. The Dyers had no indoor plumbing or electricity, but they kept their cabin clean and tidy with help from Fish Creek children such as Irene Krause. Her father, Herman, worked as a teamster in the park. Irene dusted the log walls, carefully pulling splinters from the dust rag.[21]

Charles and Meta Lesaar leased a cottage adjacent to Weborg Campground in Peninsula State Park. Carl Friedrich Meyer, born in Emmerich, Germany, immigrated to Canada and then the United States in 1913, when, fearing anti-German sentiment, he changed his name to Charles Lesaar and his birthplace to Belgium.[22] Lesaar gave painting lessons to Meenahga campers, including Helen Stern, who later became one of the first and most prominent women in American interior design. Clark eventually hired Stern to work as an art counselor. Among other things, Stern taught graphic arts skills by helping campers create posters for events such as the horse derby.[23]

Lesaar once attempted to paint a portrait of Clark's daughter, Alice, but could not do so successfully. Alice recalled that Lesaar came to camp with paints and easel, "setting up shop way back where the old golf house used to be." She was fifteen at the time and remembered that "it was a hot day. Before Mr. Lesaar had sketched the outline of my head, I promptly fainted. He never tried again. I had never fainted before, nor have I since!"[24]

The Carlson brothers, Bill and Al, lived on the north side of Weborg Campground. They would eventually be the last tenants to leave Peninsula State Park. Their house and barn stood on the east side of Shore Road, just north of the Thorp-Claflin Cemetery. They farmed eighty acres there and fished throughout the year. Bill was Al's guardian, and Bill's partner, Gertrude Lund, was their housekeeper. Their buildings were destroyed in 1974. Today, pilings from the Carlsons' pier, low mounds along the shore, are barely discernable.[25]

NEIGHBORS TO THE NORTH

Farther along Shore Road lived three sisters, all in separate homes. The first, Louise, leased a cottage at the intersection of Shore Road and Mengelberg Lane. Her daughter Marjorie married Clark's son, Benno, during World War II. The second Bach sister, Viola, summered on Strawberry Island. The third sister, Marie Gatter, a weaver at the prestigious Latin School in Chicago, leased a cottage closer to Meenahga, just north of the intersection of Shore Road and Middle Road. The rambling summer home was known as the Owl's Nest because of Gatter's collection of owl bric-a-brac.[26]

Gatter's dear friend Agnes Kuechler, a professional pianist from Evanston, Illinois, leased Sven Anondsen's former cabin. It stood downslope from the spectacular Sven's Bluff overlook. Kuechler likely saw a pair of bald eagles soaring overhead most days, at least through the 1950s.[27] "Near Sven's Tower," recalled Alice Clark, "our most proud and beautiful neighbor was an American eagle. It was a quietly wild place in 1916."[28]

The Weborg sisters, Joanna, Vida, and Ella, if not eccentric, were certainly colorful to city-bred Meenahga girls. Their father, Peter Weborg, had arrived in Door County in 1853. He built a log home for his wife, Oluffa, and their children on a rise along Shore Road, a bit south of the base of Sven's Bluff. In time, the Weborg sisters owned land known today as Weborg Point, having purchased it from the Claflins. As young girls in the 1880s, the sisters picked strawberries on Adventure Island to make jam. As adults, they often walked to town, for the women had no car. Sometimes they would stop at camp and ask for a ride. "They were very chatty," wrote Alice Clark. "I think Ella was the last survivor. I recall seeing her walking by on one crutch. What guts she had."[29]

Two miles north of camp stood Eagle Bluff Lighthouse. William and Julia Duclon raised seven sons in the brick dwelling. Alice Clark recalled of Duclon, "He was a white-haired old gentleman who drove a horse and buggy on Shore Road in front of camp to get his mail and supplies in Fish Creek. He would wave his horse whip as he drove by."[30] Duclon retired in 1918.

Peter Coughlin served as lighthouse keeper until 1926 when the light was automated.

During Camp Meenahga years, many former homesteads were leased for the summer, including the lighthouse's stable and barn. Hjalmar Holand leased a cottage along the south end of Eagle Trail. As a child, Gladys Taber summered well past the north end of Eagle Trail. She became a prominent columnist for *Ladies' Home Journal*.

Others who called Peninsula State Park home did so briefly. Around 1929, state game farm keepers raised and released three thousand pheasants near Nicolet Bay. Between 1935 and 1937, young men in the Civilian Conservation Corps (CCC) lived at Camp Peninsular, located east of Meenahga. The camp and the young men who worked and lived there were absolutely off limits to Meenahga campers and counselors. During the 1940s, German prisoners of war were briefly held in Fish Creek near Evergreen Road, close to the main entrance to Peninsula State Park.

Meenahga began and ended in an era of hospitality that seems extraordinary today. Peninsula State Park's first fifty years saw an assortment of artists, authors, and teachers taking up residence at one time or another. In 1964, upon the death of tenant Thade "Ted" Cornils, all leases that had been granted since the creation of the park in 1909 came to a formal end, and eventually the last of the old tenants passed away. Many are buried in Blossomburg Cemetery, located within the boundaries of Peninsula State Park.

MORE THAN A NEIGHBOR

Of all the people who lived nearby, Doolittle was the most beloved by Camp Meenahga campers, counselors, and owners. Tall and handsome, Doolittle was viewed either as a visionary or as a bull-headed adversary. Photos show him sporting a derby hat and smoking a cigar. Clark called him "a lifesaver." Doolittle's enthusiasm and support for Clark never wavered, and they remained lifelong friends. Girls dedicated the 1917 *Pack and Paddle* to Doolittle, "whose untiring efforts and sympathetic interests" were "great factors in ensuring the success of" Camp Meenahga.[31]

If Clark was the dreamer, Doolittle was the doer. He had the practical know-how needed to make Clark and Mabley's venture succeed. Doolittle not only hired laborers to improve and maintain Camp Meenahga but also made important purchases such as firewood, lamp oil, and cold storage ice for camp.

The Doolittles lived on Shore Road, then a narrow dirt lane. Doolittle and his wife, Lettie, along with seven children, had a vegetable and flower garden as well as a milk cow. Their chicken coop was later converted to a residence for the assistant superintendent of Peninsula State Park.[32] A fresh spring provided drinking water. The spring no longer runs, but the stone grotto that once caught water from it still remains.

Doolittle was born in Plymouth, Wisconsin, on January 15, 1870, to John Franklin Doolittle and Frances Ellen Skinner. Before his appointment in 1913 as Peninsula State Park's first superintendent, Doolittle worked as a state forest ranger. He also managed the Trout Lake Fish Hatchery while owning and operating the Rocky Reef Resort, both of which were in Vilas County, Wisconsin. Doolittle's professional life prepared him not only to get the park up and running amidst a swirl of contentious public opinion and raw feelings from landowners pushed out of the park, but also to help Clark and Mabley run their business the way it needed to be run.[33] Alice Clark remembered that without Doolittle, her mother "wouldn't have known what to do. He had a delightful . . . sense of humor and loved telling tales—on himself mostly—of his experiences in the lumber camps."[34]

Doolittle held Clark in high esteem as well. He told campers and guests at a 1942 banquet held at Meenahga, "It has been a great privilege for me to know Mrs. Clark and see what she has accomplished. . . . Ever since 1916, when Mrs. Clark came up here, and looked at this Lodge, which was then just a threshing barn, she has seen possibilities I never would have seen."[35]

6

Rise and Shine

When you return to the dear camp in the woods after the clamor and the crowds of the city, Meenahga seems like heaven. When you look at the little white tents nestled among the trees, a wave of thankfulness comes over you.
—LILY ANNE PECK, 1929 *PACK AND PADDLE*

A cease-fire silenced the guns in Europe, but it did not end fear in America. Starting in 1918, influenza became the new nemesis, killing more people during a global pandemic than had died in the Great War. Adults ages twenty through forty were especially vulnerable.[1]

Less frightening was the passage by the US Congress of the Nineteenth Amendment in 1919. While Alice Orr Clark and Kidy Mabley prepared to open Camp Meenahga in July of that year, in June a parade of suffragettes holding yellow parasols rode in motor cars through downtown St. Louis, celebrating women's suffrage.[2]

Meenahga's isolated setting kept flu and politics at bay but extinguished neither. German immigrants Herman and Henrietta Welcker held a life lease on a large tract of parkland known today as Welcker's Point. Herman was a Milwaukee physician. The Welckers built Welcker's Casino, a health spa in

Fish Creek that today is the Whistling Swan. Guests, many of them German Americans, often walked along Shore Road past camp, speaking their native language. "With World War I going on," remembered Clark's daughter, "we thought they might be spies! What imagination girls had."[3]

Devil's Pulpit, referred to in German as *Teufel Kanzel,* was a favorite hiking destination for the Welckers' guests and is still found along a less-traveled path in Peninsula State Park. Meenahga girls hiked there, too. They clambered up a low bluff along Hemlock Trail to rest on Balsam Bench with its "tree top view of the bay and Fish Creek," then turned east. "We have been there several times but never have found 'Der Teufel' on his job," wrote Aimee Hollister in the 1917 *Pack and Paddle.*[4]

A NEW DAY

In war or peace, good health or bad, Clark and Mabley had a camp to run. They designed a program based on those that worked effectively at girls' camps in the Northeast, where group and individual athletics and artistic pursuits ordered the day. The camp bell did as much as Clark or Mabley ever could to keep camp moving and to keep girls on schedule. One camper wrote of the bell's everyday influence:

> Ding dong! Ding dong! goes that bell!
> What a command it does tell;
> All the things it does demand—
> Wake up, drill, go back and dress,
> Tent inspection—clean up the mess;
> Assembly, baseball, swimming, dinner,
> Rest hour, swimming, then dear old mail
> Next to supper—eat again;

Call to lodge; lights-out sounds—
All this the duty of our bell.[5]

Some mornings it was not the bell that woke girls from their beds but scratching sounds outside their tents. Out of bed, campers looked for the porcupine they knew to be nearby, an animal that inspired one camper to write: "Poor little porky trapped in a tree / Being pelted with apples by Page-o and me."[6]

Days began with an early morning dip in the chilly waters of Green Bay. Down one side of the Meenahga dock and up the other girls went, braving the shocking cold of the water seven days in a row, even when the temperature dropped to as low as forty degrees in the morning.[7] Katherine Elizabeth Turnbull wrote about what it took to make the plunge:

You wake up in the morning
And the sky is cold and gray,
Your counselor is shouting,
"Come on, be on your way."
The morning breeze is chilly
And the water's caked with ice;
You really can't help thinking
That your bed is warm and nice.
And you shiver and you quiver
As down to the Bay you slip.
Oh! it's nice to get up in the morning
For that early morning dip![8]

Afterward, it was back to the tent to slip off wet swimsuits and dress in uniforms. Maggie Woodbury, from Kansas City, made her morning swim a point of pride, preferring it to staying in her bed alongside timid tent mates. If any camper who saw Woodbury's fingers shaking and teeth chattering asked, "Was the water really cold?" she had an answer for them:

"Dear, no!" you fondly answer
With a calmness you think wise,
My teeth, of course, *do* chatter,
But they need the exercise.
Why, the water was steam heated—
As warm as buttered toast—
We had to jump right out again
For fear we all would roast![9]

Girls might avoid the cold waters of Green Bay in the morning, but they could not avoid the morning tent inspection. Counselors checked to see if the wooden floors of the tents had been swept clean of sand and other debris. Clothes and toiletries had to be neatly stored in steamer trunks. Bedsheets had to be stretched tight and smooth over mattresses. Counselors were demanding. Campers sometimes had to make their beds more than once. Campers whose tents and beds passed inspection were awarded a star. Two campers borrowed Rudyard Kipling's poem "If—" to advise others on how to get a counselor's star:

If you can make a perfect bed
So not a wrinkle shows,
If you can keep a tidy trunk
With room for all your clothes,
If you can crowd ten sweaters
On a board that's two by four
With nothing hanging o'er the sides
And room for things galore,

If you can rid a brush of hair
And pick up all the straws,
And neatly roll the tent flaps
So counselors can't find flaws,
If you can do all this, my dear,
And finish not too late,
Why then you'll pass inspection
And maybe get an eight.[10]

After tent inspection, girls assembled on the west side of the Lodge for leg and arm exercises. They did arm circles and touched their toes to improve their breathing and balance. Signe Gundersen Schroeder recalled preferring swimming to calisthenics, claiming, "If I had my druthers, I'd [swim] rather than go exercise."[11] A flag raising followed, after which camp leaders announced activity options for the day and reinforced camp rules. Finally, all gathered inside the Lodge for breakfast, usually toast with jam, eggs, and pancakes or oatmeal. When they finished eating, campers cleared dishes and set tables for the next meal, passing the time singing chants such as this one:

Hi ro hi, hi ro hee,
Glasses, glasses don't you see!
Silver, silver sis boom ba,
Dirty dishes rah, rah rah![12]

GRACE NOTES

Whether clearing dishes, exercising, or when gathered for assembly, girls at Camp Meenahga sang original songs whenever and wherever they could. Memorizing song lyrics that none but Meenahga campers and counselors knew was a rite of passage. Camp songs often reflected the camp values of comradery and good manners, while singing created and reinforced strong feelings of belonging and trust.[13] In 1916, the first Meenahga campers bonded over an original rendition of "Moonlight Bay," their voices jarring up and down as they traveled over bumpy dirt roads in sight of Lake Michigan:

> As we were drifting along on Ephraim Bay
> You could hear our comrades calling
> They seemed to say—
> Oh, we have paddled enough so let us stay
> And at Cedar Springs we'll camp
> On Ephraim Bay—On Ephraim Bay.[14]

Professional musicians from the Midwest and elsewhere visited Camp Meenahga more than once. Rudolph Reuter, of the American Conservatory of Music, came to Meenahga and entertained its campers in August 1917, as did Arthur Bissell of the Chicago Opera Club. Later, in the 1930s, members of the Chicago Lyric Opera sang in Huber Theater, the pavilion at Weborg Point that has long since been dismantled. In the opposite direction, in a leased cottage on Skyline Road, Agnes Kuechler played classical melodies on a grand piano, sometimes reading music by light from candelabras because her cottage had no electricity.[15] Meenahga campers enjoyed the thrill of listening to opera singers and appreciated classical music, but for the most part, they favored popular tunes. Campers reimagined, for example, a popular 1916 song of lost love in France called "Roses of Picardy." In sentimental tribute to Meenahga, girls sang

> Meenahga, we'll ever be true to you,
> We will cherish you day by day—
> Meenahga, we'll ever remember you—
> In our hearts, there's a place you'll stay.

And our memories will always be happy ones—
Not a tear or a single regret,
For the days that we spent there as comrades all
Are the ones that we'll never forget.[16]

LITTLE TALKS

After breakfast, campers listened to an inspirational thought or two from Clark. Girls who summered at Meenahga remembered Clark's daily messages decades later, recalling Clark to be a wise person who emphasized the best in people. Clark "instilled campers with good thoughts, good manners, and generally set a high tone with inspirational messages," said Barbara Becker Glass, adding that Clark's words were not particularly religious but more about being good citizens.[17] Counselors did their best to emulate Clark's words of wisdom, often repeating, "Don't get your blood in a bubble." Clark's daughter frequently repeated a popular adage her mother was fond of: "Is it true? Is it kind? Is it necessary?"[18]

Elizabeth Lanier DeRamus remembered that Clark shared her thoughts on marriage more than once. DeRamus noted that Clark's advice was met with some skepticism at home. "My mother made a rather snide remark but I can't mention it," DeRamus recalled. "Mother said, 'I don't know how she can talk about that. She's divorced.' Mrs. Clark said one of the most important things in a marriage was that you had to like him. I think that was a rather perceptive remark. I think that is why I remembered it all these years."[19]

THE UNEXPECTED HAPPENS

When morning assembly ended, girls split into groups. After lunch at the Lodge, they napped on cots or sunbathed on warm days. In the afternoon, campers enjoyed water sports and team games. Some, whose families paid extra for the privilege, took riding lessons. When it rained, girls went into the Lodge to play Ping-Pong or to their tents to play jacks. Others spent time in the craft cabin, where they put birdhouses together.

Occasional surprises interrupted the tranquility of life at Meenahga. In 1917, the captain of the lake steamer *Carolina* invited Camp Meenahga on an overnight voyage to Mackinac Island, about ninety miles northeast of the Door Peninsula.[20] In 1919, a harsh and unknown droning sound cut through the evening calm just before supper. A plane flew above Meenahga before landing in Green Bay just off the Lookout. Girls rushed to the shore, shrieking with excitement. Camp master George "Bud" Dyer and another man, the father of Meenahga camper Jocelyn Marks, paddled a canoe toward the plane and extended its passengers an invitation to dine. Marks knew the men in the plane, who agreed to have supper at Meenahga, but not before they flew across Lake Michigan to Marinette to retrieve their bathing suits and other supplies.

A few hours later, when the camp bell sounded the call to supper, the men in the plane had not yet returned. At around eleven thirty the next morning, however, "the belated guests arrived and the girls suffered many more thrills," wrote a camper in *Pack and Paddle*, "for after performing several stunts, the hydroplane landed and the aviators came ashore." The pilots squeezed their way to dinner at the Lodge while girls snapped photos, and "some of the young and foolish asked for their autographs." The men left shortly afterward, flying just above camp several times before turning west across Green Bay. A crowd watched from shore as the plane dwindled to a tiny speck on the horizon. "No one got a ride," lamented a camper in *Pack and Paddle*.[21]

THE WEDDING

One day in 1920, the camp bell rang with a steady rhythm that was neither maddening nor tiresome. The strange and unfamiliar toll of the bell sounded more sublime. At five o'clock, girls hurried to the Lodge to watch their friend and counselor Eleanor Gaik get married during the late summer of Meenahga's fifth season.

Guests sat facing the grand fireplace that doubled as an altar. When counselors carrying sprays of goldenrod bedecked with yellow ribbons entered and formed a center aisle, all turned to watch. A quartet sang, "Oh promise me, you will be true to me," to the tune of a song popular at the time. Flower girls and ring bearers arrived, then bridesmaids Alice Clark and Hilly Mabley. Ida Maney, from Kentucky, was maid of honor. Each carried a bouquet designed by Charles Lesaar. One camper wrote of the wedding: "Miss Gaik made a darling bride in a white organdy dress with a wreath of white flowers about her head. After a most impressive ceremony the blushing bride was smothered with kisses and tears. The wedding supper was lovely, but the most fun was showering the happy pair with rice as they jumped into the car which was laden with old shoes and a sign 'Just Married.'"[22]

Others were married at Camp Meenahga during the 1920s. When camp opened in 1916, Mabley's oldest daughter, Fanny, was eighteen. Four years later, Fanny and two girlfriends went into business, opening the Orange Tea House in Fish Creek in a cottage owned by Ferdinand Hotz and leased by Mabley.

Tearooms in the 1920s were fashionable, sometimes rustic, places where women gathered to socialize and make plans for their futures. Women with business sense and culinary skills could earn money running a tea house. Tea houses often served popular lunch entrees, including fresh tomatoes stuffed with cucumber mayonnaise, diced apples and chopped walnuts, and peppery cabbage and carrot slaw. Desserts such as rhubarb upside-down cake and cherry kuchen incorporated local produce. The Orange Tea House advertised in *Pack and Paddle* from 1921 to 1925, and campers from Meenahga were loyal customers.[23]

Three years after she opened the Orange Tea House, Fanny Mabley married Frederick Leonard Hall. She later gave up her business for married life, and the Orange Tea House became the Mabley family's summer retreat. One of Clark's children married during the 1920s as well. Her son, Benno, married Atwood McVoy in 1927. Their brief marriage ended in divorce, but Benno married again years later, this time to Marjorie Bach in 1942.

LIGHTS OUT

On most nights, evening paddles close to shore, special parties, or dancing (excluding Sundays during Meenahga's early years) were the norm. When the fun ended at dusk, a bugler played "Taps" while campers lowered the American flag and girls walked to their tents. On clear and calm nights, campers rolled up their tent walls to invite in the night sky and cool breezes. Sometimes the clear whistle of a whippoorwill cut through the falling stillness. Emily Arnold, from Fort Benning, Georgia, wrote of the view from her tent: "You look out at the stars and know that you are safe and loved."[24] At nine o' clock, camp masters extinguished the kerosene lanterns hanging along camp trails, while counselors announced lights out. Older girls were allowed an extra half-hour to talk and gossip. As soon as counselors heard the steady, slow breathing of campers, they went quietly from their tents to the Lookout. There they scanned the sky for a glimpse of the northern lights or perhaps rendezvoused with a camp master.

On nights when it rained, campers closed up their tents and slept to the sound of raindrops on canvas. Wrote two young ladies in *Pack and Paddle*:

When the rain comes at night
And the wind howls and blows,
We rush out to the line
And gather up our clothes.
We put down the tent flaps
And hurry back to our beds
And stub our toes or bump heads.
And in the morning when the rain is gone
We put up our tent flaps with a song
And make our beds with cheerful smile.
We like it to rain a little while.[25]

SUNDAY TRADITIONS

Sundays were special days at Meenahga. Campers still went swimming in the morning, but at breakfast they enjoyed a special treat—deep-fried sour cream donuts topped with fresh applesauce.

After breakfast, girls attended church services in Fish Creek. One camper remembered that on Sundays some "girls would dress up in white dresses and gloves and walk downtown into Fish Creek to attend the church of their choice."[26] The girls who stayed in camp participated in a noon Sunday assembly. A Bible reading, several hymns, and a recitation of the Lord's Prayer opened the assembly, followed by an "open discussion of constructive subjects conducive to right living" often led by Clark.[27] Clark was a member of the Church of Christ, Scientist,[28] a relatively new religion established in 1879. Mabley's religious affiliation is unknown. Meenahga advertised as nonsectarian and, given its Midwest location, mostly attracted girls raised in Christian households, but at least a few Jewish campers and counselors also attended camp. Dinner followed Sunday assembly, served by the counselors because kitchen workers had the afternoon off.[29] Campers then spent the afternoon sunbathing, reading, or sewing dresses for the final banquet.

Campers also took a weekly bath on Sundays according to a schedule prepared by counselors. All were obliged to bathe and shampoo their hair before six thirty in the evening. Meenahga had neither electricity nor plumbed hot water for most of its history, so girls either washed in the bay or brought buckets of water to their tents. Campers were then weighed and had their fingernails and toenails inspected so that all were fresh and clean for Sunday supper.[30]

Every girl wore a Sunday uniform to supper. The uniforms were not always flattering or a pleasure to wear. In 1944, Carol Mansfield Moore said of Meenahga's Sunday attire:

> You've all heard a great deal about the green bloomers of the old days. I'd like to say a word about the white Sunday bloomers, which I feel have been neglected. Besides being as voluminous as the green ones, they were made of about the heaviest material you can imagine. We used to think that each year Mrs. Clark and Mrs. Mabley sold the old tent flaps to McCarthy Simon Company, who in turn made up the season's supply of Sunday bloomers.[31]

Sunday suppers included table settings complete with finger bowls.[32] Pleck's Ice Cream and Dairy Company from Sturgeon Bay stopped by on Sundays as well, driving up to the kitchen door with "gallons and gallons of ice cream."[33] Afterward, campers gathered for what they called "Literary" around the massive stone fireplace in the Lodge. Besides writing letters home, girls wrote and recited essays and poems.

No one phoned home. Meenahga relied on the telephone in Lundberg's dry goods store in Fish Creek until Doolittle extended the park line to the Cottage sometime in the 1930s. Everyone knew to telegram urgent or celebratory news to Lundberg's store. Alice Lundberg kept careful track of telegrams in a unique and efficient way: "[she] often pinned the telegram on her ample bosom, and would hand it over if the person came in."[34]

MEENAHGA ADJUSTS CONVENTION

From sunrise to sunset, girls at Camp Meenahga lived a routine that celebrated and imbued in campers the values of individuality, community, resiliency, and kindness.[35]

The model Clark and Mabley developed blended tradition with modernity, a departure to varying degrees from Victorian social mores. On the one hand, campers learned to accept simplified constructions of affluent, white femininity. They were expected to understand and act on their roles as prominent women in society, to care for and serve others. On the other hand, campers were introduced to and expected to excel within a masculine framework of individual achievement in sports and recreation. Neither were girls isolated from local communities as they were at other summer camps. Campers were free to roam nearly everywhere in a large state park as well as in Fish Creek and Ephraim along Peninsula State Park's southern and northern boundaries.

Meenahga campers were also some of the first group of young people to live extended childhoods in America. During the early decades of the twentieth century, middle- and upper-class Americans had more collective leisure time. Compulsory public education went through high school,[36] and the shift from agriculture to industrialization brought with it more free time for some. Suddenly, there was purpose in play and summer vacation. Researchers first put the value of play on scientific footing before promoting new theories about childhood stages of development independent of gender. At the same time, "nature" became a coveted place to play, doubly so for young people living in big cities. Books such as Anna Botsford Comstock's *Handbook of Nature Study* provided unschooled and urbanized adults a useful teaching template they could put into practice.[37]

As the number of summer camps for youth ballooned to nearly seven thousand by the 1930s, many of them began to implement standards proposed by professional camping organizations.[38] Camps became more gentrified and comfortable in the process, a symbol of which were neatly notched log cabins where campers spent their summers.[39] Other camps manufactured a wilderness or sought to brand it with newly built structures to make play in nature less dangerous.[40] Camp Meenahga, however, never followed the same trend. It remained rustic, even austere, throughout its history, never trading its canvas tents for anything. Meenahga also operated in a *recovering* landscape, surrounded by authentic beauty that remains legally protected from development and exploitation. More *of* than *over* the landscape, Meenahga blended in with the land and its history. A lime kiln became the Lookout, a logged clearing became the riding ring, and an old barn became the Lodge. Stone fences, symbols of Door County's rich agrarian past then and now, were left intact.

Camp Meenahga co-founder Alice Orr Clark, ca. 1920. COURTESY OF ADELINE PEIL AND LYNN MATKE

Camp Meenahga co-founder Frances Louise "Kidy" Mabley in front of the Lodge, ca. 1920. COURTESY OF SIGNE GUNDERSEN SCHROEDER/EPHRAIM HISTORICAL FOUNDATION

Frank and Elizabeth Crunden. The Crundens were longtime friends of Alice Orr Clark and were instrumental in helping Clark and Mabley start Camp Meenahga. COURTESY OF BILL GUENZEL

A young camper pumping water in 1916, the year Camp Meenahga opened. For much of its history, Camp Meenahga had no running water. Campers had to pump water from wells. COURTESY OF SIGNE GUNDERSEN SCHROEDER/EPHRAIM HISTORICAL FOUNDATION

Bloomers like the ones worn in this photo were part of the Camp Meenahga uniform for many years. COURTESY OF SIGNE GUNDERSEN SCHROEDER/EPHRAIM HISTORICAL FOUNDATION

A view of the Lodge printed in the 1928 camp brochure. COURTESY OF THE WISCONSIN DEPARTMENT OF NATURAL RESOURCES

A look inside the Lodge. COURTESY OF JANE CHIVVIS MOORE

Alice Orr Clark walks toward the Cottage. COURTESY OF THE WISCONSIN DEPARTMENT OF NATURAL RESOURCES

Tents were arranged in rows and organized into groups by age. This photo of tents was taken in 1919 and appeared in *Pack and Paddle*. COURTESY OF THE WISCONSIN DEPARTMENT OF NATURAL RESOURCES

The diving raft was often crowded. This photo shows a camper diving into Green Bay while others watch, ca. 1926. COURTESY OF AGNES JOHNSON AND ROY GAUGER

Four Meenahga campers on the diving raft in 1919. COURTESY OF SIGNE GUNDERSEN SCHROEDER/ EPHRAIM HISTORICAL FOUNDATION

Campers gathered at the pier and Lookout, ca. 1926. COURTESY OF AGNES JOHNSON AND ROY GAUGER

The Lookout was in many ways the symbol of Camp Meenahga. In this photo, campers are arranged at the Lookout in the shape of the letter *M*. COURTESY OF GRACE LANIER BREWER

The Lookout in a photo from 1929. COURTESY OF THE WISCONSIN DEPARTMENT OF NATURAL RESOURCES

Bill and Adell Davis worked at Camp Meenahga during its earliest years. They are among the many African Americans who worked in Door County during an era of racial segregation. COURTESY OF AGNES JOHNSON AND ROY GAUGER

Portrait of Albert E. Doolittle. Doolittle was a tireless supporter of Alice Orr Clark and Camp Meenahga. COURTESY OF THE DOOLITTLE FAMILY

Most campers arrived to Camp Meenahga by train. This map, printed in the 1928 camp brochure, shows the distances in miles from Camp Meenahga to several major Midwestern cities. COURTESY OF THE WISCONSIN DEPARTMENT OF NATURAL RESOURCES

Camp masters often drove to Fish Creek to collect mail and supplies. Camp masters are shown here parked in front of the Lodge. COURTESY OF GRACE LANIER BREWER

7

Fit as a Fiddle

> *Do you like beach breakfasts, beach suppers, and impromptu picnics? Do you like surprise swims by moonlight on a warm night? Would you like an early morning canter ending up with breakfast five miles away? You would soon realize that you were on a glorious vacation, and school life left far behind.*
>
> —*Meenahga Camps for Girls*, 1935

After the Great War, the American economy wobbled into a brief depression. Returning soldiers found work hard to come by. Jobs supported by military expenditure and production vanished, and declining trade with a ruined Europe made problems worse. Federal spending dropped from $18.5 billion to $3.3 billion between 1919 and 1922.[1] At first, Camp Meenahga went along as usual against the economic headwinds. In 1920, 118 campers and 22 counselors attended camp. In 1921, when US unemployment was at 11.7 percent, 144 campers and 9 counselors registered for a summer at Meenahga.

On August 12, 1921, thirty acres of cutover forest caught fire north of Fish Creek's Gibraltar School. The fire spread to Peninsula State Park. Campers and counselors went into action to help Doolittle and a hundred or so firefighters contain the blaze. High winds, however, nursed tiny flames overnight, and embers flared again the next day. Another thirty acres of second-growth balsam, pine, and juniper burned until surplus army trucks hauled water to the fire. Camp Meenahga escaped without damage.[2]

Nevertheless, economic instability was not so different from those smoldering embers likely to start a new fire at any moment. In 1922, the realities of economic hardship throughout the country set in at camps across the country. Enrollment at Camp Meenahga plunged to thirty-one campers and eight counselors. The following year, however, financial markets and economic forecasts improved.[3] Enrollment rebounded to 126 campers and stayed high through the 1920s, bolstered briefly by the addition of a separate junior camp for younger girls, which Clark and Mabley opened near Nicolet Beach in 1923. The junior camp ultimately proved too costly to maintain and was closed in 1925.

GOOD SPORTS

Alice Orr Clark and Kidy Mabley came of age when everyone from doctors to academics wondered if athletics and Victorian-era womanhood were compatible. In the 1870s, a respected Harvard physician argued that vigorous exercise and competitive sports damaged a young girl's womb.[4] His widely read paper was seen as evidence that physical activity was bad for young women, a theory that took decades to debunk.

By 1916, however, people had begun to recognize and accept the benefits girls gained from strenuous exercise and outdoor leisure. Outdoor sports such as croquet and lawn tennis were popular games played by women. A few upper- and middle-class ladies were even bold enough to participate in rougher sports, such as basketball. Fashion responded to changes in female athletics by loosening and elasticizing the corset, and May

Thorpe's Millinery Parlors of Sturgeon Bay started advertising athletic corsets in the 1920 *Pack and Paddle*.

Clark and Mabley were among a growing number who advised young women to balance competition with more traditional ladylike behaviors. Athletics and femininity did not need to be mutually exclusive, as progressive educators argued that sports increased stamina, cultivated courage, and developed expert hand-eye coordination, all necessary skills in the domestic sphere.[5]

Writing about the campers at Meenahga, the *Door County News* reported in 1919 that "the physical development of the girls is very marked" and that many looked twenty pounds heavier since arriving at camp. Mindful always of safety, Clark and Mabley promised any worried parents that all physical activity would take place under proper supervision. Whether they were horseback riding, swimming, playing tennis, or knocking croquet balls across the lawn, girls would do so with someone watching over them. Whatever the sport, Clark and Mabley linked the benefits of athletics to the greater good, often in *Pack and Paddle* essays written by their daughters. Hilly Mabley, for instance, wrote in *Pack and Paddle* that "the keynote to modern efficiency is coordination, and we may interpret this as coordination between our mental and physical activities. . . . Natural and habitual release of physical energy is necessary to avoid a state of over-strained mentality."[6]

YELLOWS AND PURPLES

Accounts of competition filled the pages of *Pack and Paddle*. Winning was important to campers, but directors and counselors rewarded sportsmanship more than final scores. Campers were awarded a felt *M* when they demonstrated as much effort as proficiency, be it in athletics or the arts. To avoid looking boastful, if a camper received multiple *Ms*, she might sew one on a uniform shirt and put the others away as keepsakes.

Girls were organized by age and ability into two teams: the Yellows and the Purples. Divisions between the two were not to be taken lightly. "The two 'teams' [Yellows and Purples] were bitter rivals," remembered counselor Elizabeth "Joe" Paine. "From year to year you stayed on the same team and hoped that the *new* girls would measure up to the *high* standards of *your* team." Moreover, during "the last week of camp," recalled Paine, "the charts [used for scorekeeping], which had been available for avid counting by all concerned all season, were taken down and brought to the directors' office."[7] Teams earned felt stars for initiative, fair play, and comradery. Doing one's best was more important than being the best. At the final banquet, everyone cheered when Clark revealed which team had earned the most stars.

Directors and counselors could take stars away when infractions occurred. "Oh, sorrow ineffable!" remembered Paine. "One year . . . *I whispered during rest hour*—terrible sin—my counselor, who was the arbiter of such actions decreed that I had bothered her, that I should have a star off. I don't know that my psyche was permanently damaged but, these many years later, I can still recall the desperate social shame!"[8] Team loyalty was fierce, if mostly in good fun. Team spirit created feelings of belonging—a feeling quintessential to camp life. "How can you make a Purple change color?" teased one writer in the 1923 *Pack and Paddle*. "Tell her she's Yellow."[9]

FIVE STROKES OUT, FIVE STROKES IN

Perhaps more than any other activity, swimming, no matter how chilly the water, was enormously popular at Meenahga. Campers gathered for lessons near the Lookout before trotting down stone steps toward the wooden pier. Sometimes, before jumping into the water, they rhythmically pumped arms, practiced the front crawl, and repeated:

> Five strokes out and five strokes in
> Makes a girl healthy, peppy, and thin![10]

If a girl could swim 150 yards, she was allowed to try to swim toward a floating raft anchored beyond the pier. The raft had a spring diving board and a metal slide. Diving lessons were taught every afternoon. Girls who could not dive when camp opened for the summer often excelled at it by the time camp closed for the season.[11]

Many girls came to Meenahga from landlocked cities and suburbs and from places with undeveloped waterfronts. Nor were public pools common until well after Camp Meenahga opened. Clark and Mabley thought it necessary to teach swimming given the unpredictable and strong currents in Green Bay. Additionally, any camper who wanted to go on an overnight canoe trip or long-distance sailing trip had to pass the Red Cross Basic Lifesavers Skills test. To pass, a camper had to swim three hundred yards, demonstrate aptitude in at least five different strokes, and make four perfect dives. The ACE test was even more challenging, adding four additional strokes, a twenty-five-minute endurance crawl swim (in the bay's choppy waters), and a lifesaving test. ACE swimmers received a felt award cut in the shape of a clover. Notably, swimming at Meenahga was also significant because, by and large, it showcased the competency and relevancy of camp counselors and masters. They taught children something that in many cases their parents could not.

Given the popularity of swimming at Meenahga, swimwear was no small thing among its residents. Initially, girls swam in sleeveless, long-skirted woolen suits with knickers and black tights. On their heads, they wore aviator-style caps made of a rubbery material. Girls could not bring just any swim cap to Meenahga, however. The 1921 camp brochure advised girls "not to bring colored bathing caps or ties, as caps and ties are ordered to fit our requirements."[12] Bathing suits were available for purchase at camp.

When wet, the wool swimsuits retained warmth but were cumbersome. As a result, campers sometimes went without. "On picnics, hikes, and canoe overnights," recalled Elaine Mabley, "we swam without our suits in Green Bay waters, far from the public eye." Meenahga girls called this "going à la Venus, and how we loved the feel of it, sometimes in the path of moonlight in the water." In later years, skinny dipping stopped because of the increasing number of tourists, whom Meenahga girls "scorned."[13] Wool suits eventually gave way to colorful two-piece apparel made of different materials. The bare midriff style covered the belly button and most cleavage. Meenahga girls never wore bikinis.

PADDLING ADVENTURES

Canoeing was also a common pastime at Meenahga. To canoe away from the pier, even for a moonlit paddle over calm waters, girls had to demonstrate that they could maneuver a canoe safely around Green Bay. Campers had to know the difference between the bow and the stern, how to grip a canoe paddle correctly, and how to row a swamped, or water-filled canoe, to shore. The wood and canvas canoes weighed about eighty pounds. Lighter aluminum canoes were not manufactured until after 1945.

Eleanor Beach described the canoe test in *Pack and Paddle*. Dressed in a petticoat, middie (a cotton shirt that hung straight from the shoulders to the hips), shoes, and stockings, Beach paddled toward the middle of Green Bay. Then the instructor told her to leap into the water, climb back into the canoe, and rock it back and forth. Eleanor leaned to the side and fell overboard. From the shore, she could hear shouts urging her to take her heavy clothes off, including her shoes. Beach wrote that, after a struggle, "nothing remained to be tackled but my middie (pesky thing)." Then the instructor told Beach to push the canoe toward shore. It was not an easy thing to do. Beach wrote, "I felt as though it were a battleship. Reaching land in safety after all my escapes from a watery grave, I thanked my lucky stars I had passed the test."[14]

Unpredictable wind and weather changes on Lake Michigan sometimes turned what were intended to be short canoe trips into more harrowing adventures. In 1917, canoeists from Meenahga arrived at Cedar Springs at half past noon. Named for the spring that emerges near the golf course from the base of Eagle Bluff, Cedar Springs (sometimes called Crystal Springs) was a Peninsula State Park campground that was later abandoned when the golf course expanded. After dinner, girls paddled back toward camp. By the time they reached Shanty Bay, storm clouds were visible on the western horizon and the campers had another mile to go. "Matters were quite thrilling for a while," reported one canoeist in *Pack and Paddle*, but all made it safely back to Meenahga.[15]

An overnight canoe trip in 1938 brought an encounter with Chicago landscape architect Jens Jensen, who had recently established a folk school called The Clearing in Door County. "Hark to us you land lubbers," girls sang to the children's tune "Johnny Rebeck." Their song described a stop in Ephraim for ice cream, a lamb chop dinner at "Pebbly Beach," and a paddle to Ellison Bay, where they camped overnight. "We met a man named Jensen / He talked from six to ten / We stumbled down the inky path / Upon the beach, and then—" cooked a hasty supper, is how one camper remembered things. The next morning, some girls swam on "little ledges" of the escarpment while four others walked to Ellison Bay to discover "the town was not alive." The paddle back to Meenahga was fiercely sun drenched, with everyone wearing shirts and laying towels across their knees.[16]

Sunset brought less variation between land and air temperatures, causing winds to diminish. Many evenings, camp canoes glided quietly near shore, weaving between glistening reflections of white birch and shaggy pine. "Shimmering gold path of the moon," wrote a 1926 *Pack and Paddle* poet, "Moan of the waves breaking too soon."[17]

THE COURTS

Tennis, an exclusive sport traditionally associated with the kind of affluence most Meenahga campers enjoyed, was a fixture at camp. Players practiced strokes to music from "the wireless," a battery-operated radio. By the mid-1920s, drop shot and volley thwacks signaled doubles and singles matches, watched by cheering camp friends.

Girls played on two courts, one of which remains. The courts were originally grass, but later the grass was replaced with clay. Camp masters rolled and packed the uneven ground all summer. One year, in 1928, camp masters gave up the court to weather after nonstop rains. That year, players christened the clay court "Mississippi Mud." The tennis courts served an additional purpose as well. On clear nights, campers unrolled sleeping bags over them and slept under the stars.[18]

On less exclusive courts, Meenahga girls shot hoops. Basketball was very popular, though not nearly as socially acceptable as tennis. Since amateur athletic organizations advised against girls playing in public, deeming aggressive competition between women unbecoming, those who spectated courtside at the tennis and basketball courts were of a different breed, according to one *Pack and Paddle* account: "We cannot help wondering what all the deer . . . thought about such a clamor as was heard on the nights we had a tournament."[19]

SPORTING WITH CAMP NEIGHBORS

Camp Meenahga made it a point of pride to schedule athletic competitions with nearby camps. In 1922, Clark and Mabley invited girls from Camp Kewahdin, on Chambers Island about seven miles west of Meenahga in Green Bay, to a day of athletic tournaments.[20]

In 1927, two Meenahga girls played a doubles tennis match against two boys from Camp Wildwood. Girls greeted their Fish Creek neighbors by assembling on the lawn in the shape of the letter *M*. Meenahga campers cheered and sang songs while boys from Wildwood watched the Yellows and Purples compete. The boys toured the camp and even got a look inside the tents.

The following Tuesday, the campers from Camp Meenahga visited the boys at Camp Wildwood. The girls were surprised and disappointed to learn that their male counterparts kept clean and orderly tents. "We felt our tents had been very neat," reported one camper in *Pack and Paddle*, "and that mere boys could never achieve such order." To the contrary, the neatness of the tents at Wildwood "was such as we had never dreamed existed." The boys at Wildwood were gracious and smug enough to give the girls from Meenahga a few pointers.[21]

Adventure Island Camp for Boys, Meenahga's closest neighbor, was a mile northwest on Adventure Island in Green Bay. Industrial arts teacher Charles A. "Skipper" Kinney established the original camp on Chambers Island in 1923. Within two years, he had purchased Adventure Island, the largest of the Strawberry Islands, and relocated his camp to it. Kinney, of slight build and stature and with a visible limp, planned to arrive at his new camp in extravagant style during the summer of 1925. He and his youth crew built a thirty-six-foot replica of a Viking sailing ship. Christened *Serpent of the Sea*, it was driven over the water by sail and up to twenty-eight rowers. In July, Kinney and his boys cast off from a Chicago port and sailed two hundred miles north, around Death's Door, then south toward Adventure Island. Or so went the story.

In truth, *Serpent*'s maiden voyage was very nearly its only voyage. Kinney used his personal forty-foot cruiser yacht, *Dream Girl*, to tow *Serpent* north. A motor boat and "tons of camp luggage" were crammed inside the gaudily striped but otherwise ineffectual Viking ship. Ten boys, ages ten to fifteen, accompanied Kinney, along with George Gleixner, a sailor. The yacht passed Sheboygan sometime after midnight, just as a fierce squall blew in. Lightning flashed all around the two ships, and three inches of rain fell around the would-be Norsemen. *Dream Girl* made her way toward Manitowoc, finally docking at about four in the morning. Drenched boys were taken to the boiler rooms of a Goodrich steamship to dry out. According to Kinney, the boys "behaved like sailors." When everyone was dry and ready to set sail again, Kinney and his crew boarded *Dream Girl* for the final leg of the journey.[22]

APPLES AND ORANGES

Although the summer camp for boys on Adventure Island and Camp Meenahga were separated by only about a mile of water, they were as different as apples and oranges. Where, for example, Clark and Mabley oversaw their girls as benevolent monarchs encouraging structure and conformity, Skipper Kinney acted more as a facilitator, a leader who largely rejected authority and regimentation. As a progressive educator, Kinney embraced spontaneity and work with a purpose.[23]

Where Meenahga had a riding ring with gorgeous American Saddlebred horses, Adventure Island had a darkroom. Girls at Meenahga took cheerleading lessons, played the piano, and whacked Ping-Pong balls across the table in the Lodge. Adventure Island had a makeshift but seaworthy Viking ship. Meenahga allowed only a few dogs at camp, in particular Fatté, Clark's daughter's Highland terrier. In contrast, any boy could bring his dog to Adventure Island, and many did. Boys could fish for black bass any time, too, and some built their own kayaks to fish the nearby shoals. Girls such as Nancy Chilson, from Green Bay, fished only now and then. "Fishing is my favorite sport," she wrote during Literary. "All I need is a hook of some sort. A cork, a leader, a line, a sinker and I'm ready to go."[24]

Normalized expressions of masculinity and femininity marked differences between the camps as well. Meenahga campers assembled birdhouses in a cabin called the Woodpecker Tent. Additionally, they embellished art with birch bark and tried their hand at block printing. For other arts and crafts, campers painted coasters and crafted leather moccasins, belts, rings, toothbrush holders, and cigarette cases. "I made a leather bracelet," recalled Janice Chamberlaine Pierce, "and clothespin dolls."[25] One year, art counselor Mary Ann Courtenay brought two small table looms to camp along with "lovely pre-war thread."[26] Another summer, counselor Jean Dicks hosted stage makeup classes.[27]

The boys on Adventure Island were asked to do more with their hands. Hard work, often in the form of manual labor, was part of the day. "All are hard workers," said Kinney in 1923, describing "the construction of a tramway . . . being built to use on a long pier out over the water for freight boats."[28] For young men, attending summer camp meant being exposed to the kinds of "manly" pursuits, such as building and fixing things, that many believed were a cure-all for the effects of modernity. On Adventure Island, boys operated a saw powered by an old car engine. They cleared brush, cut wood, built a dock, and painted cabins. Camp masters and hired local men did such things at Meenahga. They kept camp in operation, and their work was as much needed as it was appreciated.

Kinney's penchant for wood and metal work, and his own training as an industrial arts teacher, was grounded in the kind of manual training curriculum developed by Mabley's father, Calvin Milton Woodward. Woodward believed manual training went beyond improving hand-eye coordination. "I care little what tools are used, or how they are used, so long as proper habits (morals) are formed," he wrote in 1884, "and provided the windows of the mind are kept open toward the world of things and forces, physical as well as spiritual."[29]

8

Social Graces

Po-lite-ness let me tell you is a very gentle art.
It softens all asperity and heals a wounded heart.

—1928 *Pack and Paddle*

For campers and counselors alike, and especially for Alice Orr Clark and Kidy Mabley, it was important to maintain a graceful and dignified bearing—to the degree that they could—in as remote and rugged a place as Camp Meenahga. Their intention to do so was perhaps best manifested in the quality of the riding program at camp. Girls took English riding lessons from professional equestrians. Hans Berg was the first riding master, hired in 1917. He owned Berg's Riding Academy of Milwaukee. Besides working as Meenahga's riding master, Berg gave private lessons behind the Maple Tree Café in Fish Creek. Always impeccably dressed, Berg sat ramrod straight in his seat. From Milwaukee, Berg trailered fifteen to twenty American Saddlebred horses to Door County every summer, stabling them at George Beyer's barn near the Fish Creek entrance to Peninsula State Park and at Horseshoe Bay Farms in Egg Harbor.[1] Berg's horses had names such as Sungold, Fendago, Chocolate Lady, and Daisy. To enliven training on humid mornings, Berg often quoted Shakespeare, and Meenahga riders competed in equestrian games such as the paper chase. Berg and a camper rode ahead with bags of torn paper, leaving a trail as they cantered forward. After twenty minutes, sixteen camp riders started after them. "The paper led them through narrow trails, across country, and through the village until they finally caught a glimpse of the pursued. The chase was very pretty to watch," wrote Mousie Stix in *Pack and Paddle*, "and not only the campers, but many guests at Fish Creek, were interested spectators."[2]

Unfortunately, as much tragedy as triumph marks the history of horseback riding at Meenahga. In February 1924, a shocking telegram quoting a Milwaukee newspaper arrived at Lundberg's dry goods store. Hans Berg, fifty-seven, had killed himself. Reported the paper:

> While worry over financial affairs and a recently completed law suit was generally believed by friends to have been the cause of his action, a suggestion of mystery was thrown about the affair by statements from his wife, his physician, and the aged caretaker of his stables to the effect that some other matter was preying heavily on his mind.
>
> With his wife of ten months, Viola Speckin Berg, just thirty years his junior, in a state of collapse at her home, 717 Racine St., friends are trying to figure out what she meant by her hysterical exclamation a few moments after she returned to her home, from the scene of the tragedy: "That woman from St. Louis! He was worried! I hope she's gone."
>
> Mrs. Berg was the third wife of the riding master. She mentioned the name of the hotel where she believed the woman she referred to was stopping. She said she believed the woman is the owner of land at Fish Creek. . . .

> Walter Kerr, for nine years caretaker of the Berg stables, added the information that Mr. Berg had told him he feared a possible legal action from a black-haired girl from St. Louis, who two years ago spent the summer in Fish Creek.[3]

Dr. Schiapik, Berg's physician, revealed that Berg had confided to him a fear of legal entanglements from his acquaintance with a certain girl before he married his third wife. Schiapik believed Berg's fear mostly imaginary, but said Berg thought that "if the matter were made public it would cause trouble." The doctor added that Berg was also worried about a $10,000 damage suit awarded to a patron who had been injured in a fall. On the day Berg died, sixteen-year-old Tony Mecca, a stable boy, had witnessed Berg run suddenly from the office toward the hay room. Mecca heard a shot and ran to see what had happened. He described what he saw in the following manner: "Folded neatly across a bale of hay was his [Berg's] overcoat, and his derby hat was placed beside it with his gloves. He was dressed in his usual debonair and careful manner for which he was widely known, wearing a dark black broadcloth suit, a white shirt, and a black tie."[4]

Pack and Paddle shared the sad news this way: "It is with exceeding regret that we announce the death of Mr. Hans Berg, which occurred on Saturday, February 2, 1924. Mr. Berg was our riding master for six years and was most courteous at all times. He was kind and jovial and will be remembered with affection by all with whom he came in contact."[5]

Bernard Christopher Christensen of Chicago's Lakeshore Riding Academy accepted the role of riding master in 1925. Christensen added jumping and pairs riding and devised new games. In one race, riders carefully passed a raw egg between them, using only a spoon. Trail rides, which had always been popular, now included all-day treks to Baileys Harbor or Egg Harbor. "Vun, too, tree, vour; vun, too, tree, vour; don't hold him, don't hold him! Now you've got it! There! By golly, dat's de vay to ride hoss back!" instructed Christensen, who was from Denmark, while teaching the canter.[6]

INSPIRING ADVENTURES

When campers were not on horseback, they walked almost everywhere they went. Girls trekked to Shanty Bay or Fish Creek, thinking nothing of hiking several miles there and back. They walked to Eagle Tower. They followed trails with familiar names such as Hemlock and Trail Trampers Delight. They knew other paths by now-forgotten odd names such as Owl City, Kings, Sunrise, and Cornil's Bridlepath. Hikes, or what one camper called "a jolly good walk," often got started by a suggestion from counselors:

Often at meals a knock on the plate,
The counselor stands and commences to state,
"Good day for a hike, come on girls; let's go.
Much better to hike than attempt to row."
So off we go for a jolly good walk,
And as we tramp we talk, talk talk![7]

Without portable radios, hikers made their own music by singing. One favorite song went:

Watch us walk, hear us sing, listen to the echoes ring
As Meenahga comes swinging along.
Should it rain, should it shine, we will keep a steady line
As Meenahga comes swinging along.
So, it's hie, hie, hee, Meenahga Camp for me.

Shout out our colors loud and strong,
Where e'er we go, you will always know
When Meenahga comes swinging along.
Keep a-swinging when Meenahga comes swinging along.[8]

Eagle Trail was especially picturesque. Girls christened the shallow, water-cut caves along Eagle Trail "the palisades," above which the bluffs extended 150 feet into the sky. Below was the ceaseless whisper of sparkling blue waves. In 1920, Frances Ellen Tucker, from Madison, wrote of Eagle Trail in *Pack and Paddle*, "Oh that trail! Winding, turning, over slippery, dark pine needles, limpid purple shadows wave and beckon in the grottos and the deep hush of the woodland clutches softly at your heart . . . down upon the white rocks you drink the cooling, deep draughts from the heart of Cedar Springs."[9] That same year, New Yorker Agnes Matzinger reflected on a trek along an open, dusty road. When Matzinger and her companions reached Shore Road, they marched and sang:

Close beside the bay
Where a sail boat glides along
And the whitecaps play.
Trudging up the stony path,
Camp comes into view;
Friends and letters calling,
Happiness for you.[10]

A few years later, Janet Fish, equally mesmerized by Eagle Trail, remarked on its trees and the ghost plants around it in a *Pack and Paddle* essay. Scattered, sixty-foot white pines, spared from ax and plow, stood out. Eerily translucent ghost plants (Indian pipes) popped out of a leaf-strewn earth. Pinkish-white and uncommon in Peninsula State Park's moist woods, the flower species shares connections to the *miinagaawanzh,* the Ojibwe name for the blueberry plant.

> To tramp in the shimmering sunlight—white pines behind, blue sky o'er head, and out on the turquoise horizon an orange-winged sailboat—to walk through the leafy trails with the scent of dead pine, green with the moss-grown stones, dotted with waxy clusters of Indian pipes—with the breeze in your hair and joy in your heart—to answer the call of the open road—perhaps you call that hiking—I think it is a glimpse of heaven . . . and the overnight hikes! One who has never seen the moon kiss the proud pines from Sven's Tower has missed a great deal.[11]

Exercise and adventure inspired literature by campers. "One Monday, the girls and counselors decided it was too cold to go swimming," wrote camper "Jack" Matthews in *Pack and Paddle,* so instead they hiked to the Eagle Bluff Lighthouse. Perched atop a forty-foot bluff at Welcker's Point, Eagle Bluff Lighthouse had guided small vessels through the narrow Strawberry Island passage since 1868. Lighthouse keeper Peter Coughlin retired at the end of the 1926 maritime season when the Coast Guard automated the lamp with acetylene gas. Coughlin led girls up a winding staircase and outside to the tower balcony from which they could view the bay, a scene that moved one girl to write:

> It was a beautiful sight. One of the girls took a Kodak picture of it. We soon went back into the little room and the keeper took off the cloth which kept the dust from getting on the light. The light is a wonderful instrument. It is of French make and of such powerful glass that although only a small light is put inside, it is reflected and made so large that it can be seen for thirteen miles.[12]

Ascending Sven's Tower was a more thrilling adventure. Girls climbed Skyline Road, a route that took them by Agnes Kuechler's ramshackle cottage, to "spread their bedrolls" atop Sven's Tower. Mabley, in her fifties, often accompanied girls on their overnight trips. Her daughter Elaine liked to rough it. Mabley was no fan of heights, however, so she slept on the first landing while campers slept above her. At the top of the tower, "sleep certainly was out! The wind and the stars looking so close were exciting; watching the sunrise out of the mists below a rare experience."[13] Mousie Stix described one lofty campout in a 1926 poem titled "Sven's Tower":

A burnt orange full moon
Behind an inky pine,
A starless sky above
A straggly, bold shoreline.
Like a small child's writing,
Irregular but clear.
Hushed lapping of the waves
I can so faintly hear.
Lights of Menominee
Across the sleeping lake,
The plaintive, low, hoarse cries
The swooping seagulls make;
Cold whispering through my hair,
I feel with ecstasy,
Faint horizon stretching
Out to infinity.
Just for this night alone
All these belong to me.[14]

Every so often, campers left their tents after dark to get a look at a night sky lit up as if it were day. Elaine Mabley told of the "unwritten agreement" for nights when "glorious displays of the Aurora Borealis" cast sheets of shimmering light across the black Door County sky. "After 'lights out,'" wrote Mabley, "we could all go down to the pier, lie on our backs, and watch the show with no penalties attached. To city people, this was awe-inspiring and filled us with wonder."[15]

TEA AT THE COTTAGE

For all the good it did their campers, being awestruck by a sunset or cantering gracefully on horseback through a forest glen was not enough for Clark and Mabley. More was required of girls at Meenahga. Wholesome girls needed also to be courteous and presentable. Along with all the riding, tennis playing, hiking, and swimming, campers at Meenahga practiced etiquette and learned the art of conversation at formal teas and luncheons.

Clark hosted tea parties at the Cottage, the farmhouse around which were planted a rainbow of gladiolas and old-fashioned hollyhocks. Inside, steep steps led to small, second-floor bedrooms. Clark had workers remodel the back room for counselor meetings and a shed to use as an office. When members of the Evenson family visited one Sunday, they exclaimed that their former home had been "given over to happy girls."[16]

Over cups of tea, Clark and Mabley gave instruction that they thought would be more practical and important to girls' everyday adult lives than riding or swimming lessons. Both women believed that the ability to engage in witty and thoughtful conversation was a required skill for adult women, be it at home entertaining or in public cultivating support for worthwhile charitable causes. Meenahga tea parties were forms of mental instead of physical exercise, done to foster girls' skills in intelligent discourse and mannered restraint. Tea parties were also as entertaining as they were informative. Wrote one camper, "You can't imagine how much fun it was. First, it was a thrill to get the mysterious little note asking you to come; then it grew more exciting as you got dressed up spick and span at about quarter to four, and the last word in fun was to sit down in the Cottage and eat dainty little sandwiches, and sip tea while Mrs. Clark and Mrs. Mabley told funny stories about early camping days, their children, and themselves."[17]

Clark and Mabley had more to do than teach their campers how to sip tea, however. They also taught them how to sit and present themselves correctly. "We worked awfully hard on our postures," one girl remembered, hoping for a felt pine tree award that came with sitting up straight.[18] Two other friends wrote:

> Those poor little pine trees of green and white
> Are crying for better light.
> So please listen to our call,
> "Stand up straighter, one and all."[19]

Anna "Grizzie" Griswold Nichols summed up the Meenahga experience and its combination of urban sophistication and rural play. Clark and Mabley, wrote Nichols, "tried to teach us to be ladies, but they made sure we had fun."[20]

LUNCH AT ENGELMAR

On another of the islands just west of Camp Meenahga, a prosperous family had built a summer estate that campers often visited. Known first as Eagle Island and now called Horseshoe Island, it was home in the 1920s to E. F. Folda, a wealthy Nebraska banker, and his family. The thirty-eight-acre estate, called Engelmar, featured a six-thousand-square-foot lodge. Trails wound through a forest of cedar, birch, and balsam. During Meenahga's early years, the Foldas invited a dozen campers at a time to join them for lunch. Many campers were fond of the place, so much so that they dedicated the 1921 *Pack and Paddle* to Folda. Girls hiked from camp to the Anderson Dock in Ephraim. Folda's yacht, *Forrest,* and in later years, *Brigydon,* met guests. Captain Nels Jepson skippered the boat across Eagle Harbor. Folda, recognizable from a distance, stood waiting in white wool pants, white shoes, a navy sport coat, and a captain's hat.[21]

Once on the island, campers darted across a cobblestone terrace to chat happily with the Foldas' children, Bert and Marcelle. When they left the yacht, campers entered a bright and lofty hall with an immense fieldstone fireplace. Alma Letitia Woods Folda, Folda's wife, greeted them graciously. Household staff prepared a lunch of "marvelous sandwiches, cake, and ice cream, always more than enough for hungry girls," offering meringue pinch pie on a stone terrace and screened porch. It was Alma Folda's own recipe, printed in the 1931 first edition of Irma S. Rambauer's *Joy of Cooking.*[22]

Afterward, campers listened to Marsie, E. F. Folda's sister, describe her travels to Europe or the South Pacific. Folda told stories as well, "of times this region [Door County] was inhabited by Indians," or about "interesting objects, such as prehistoric pottery and petrified wood."[23] In the time they had left, girls explored the trails and the mysterious graves of early pioneers before returning to Ephraim.

Unfortunately, Folda's bank failed in 1936 after a series of setbacks, and the family fell into financial ruin. After the Foldas moved permanently to California, Horseshoe Island became a sailing destination. The Foldas sold what island buildings and treasures they could and eventually relinquished their life lease.[24]

ALL THE WORLD'S A STAGE

An additional way that Clark and Mabley encouraged their campers to have fun while also learning how to conduct themselves properly in public was to promote public performance, especially plays. Acting on stage was not so different from acting in a parlor. As such, the stage, Clark and Mabley assumed, was a place where polite children could learn to be interesting women.

Camp Meenahga had an outdoor amphitheater, built in 1916, that campers often made use of. In 1924, *Redbook* described Meenahga's outdoor amphitheater: "The girls enjoy a natural dramatic amphitheater in a field and grove where some of the best of the shorter plays are produced each season. Thus, in a camp which has been kept as woodsy as practicable, we found the arts and a sound and enterprising camp craft sustaining each other in a very satisfying manner."[25] Camp benefactors, people who leased park cabins, and tourists all paid to see performances.

Dance dramas such as *Apollo's Chariot* and *Pandora's Box* were popular. Onlookers sat hillside at the amphitheater, watching tableaux vivants set to simple music or poetry. Carol Mansfield Moore remembered "that one year I danced for a good ten minutes with no accompaniment except a six-line poem, 'The Fog.'"[26]

Music carried from the stage into many aspects of camp life. By the mid-1920s, campers had a Victrola, a talking machine that made playing music easy. "Oh, there's music in the air, tra la," quipped counselor Mary Carter Davis when girls moved the Victrola out to the porch.[27] Dancing naturally accompanied music. In 1926, a dance contest at which campers danced the enormously popular Charleston was the highlight of the evening.

Dindy Bay and Zaida Maguire were proclaimed the winners, and "the evening closed after numerous bottles of pop had been consumed, and we all trooped happily off to bed."[28] Sometime later, campers from Kentucky sparked an interest in clogging, a mountain folk dance in which footwear is tapped rhythmically against the floor. Another year, everyone was practicing the basic "swing out" step of the Lindy Hop.

Clark favored dance. She hired Elinor Rice, a student from Northwestern, to teach it at camp from 1927 to 1933. Rice left an impression on Meenahga cook and local girl Evelyn Bhirdo Franke, as Franke remembered that Rice "had coal black hair and lots of it, and she could dance."[29] Rice taught dance steps on the Lodge porch. At the end of Rice's first summer at Meenahga, campers playfully serenaded her:

> Of course, Elinor Rice thinks Northwestern's awfully nice—
> How we envy her raven black curls.
> She's stepped out a lot with her friends in a yacht,
> But she acts as though she's just one of the girls.[30]

BURNT CORK AND THE KU KLUX KLAN

Some performances given at Camp Meenahga would be seen as controversial and repugnant today. For many years, campers put on minstrel shows wearing blackface. The wearing of blackface was common in America during the first half of the twentieth century and would have been a familiar thing to girls from around the United States. At the time, however, its history, social influence, and painful ramifications were less understood—or ignored entirely. Wrote one camper:

> Who would ever have dreamed that a little burnt cork, graciously donated by Emma from the kitchen vinegar jug, could

> have transformed eight fair and only slightly sunburned maidens . . . into a group of black-faced comedians worthy of any Orpheum circuit. . . . The troupe came whisking in to a darky-town melody, took their places in a semicircle, and proceeded to crack the funniest jokes ever heard.[31]

Historians have largely overlooked the presence of African Americans in Door County. Campers at Meenahga did the same, as there are only scant mentions in *Pack and Paddle* of African Americans such as Bill and Adell Davis.

In 1922, girls performed *The Southern Syncopation,* a play featuring characters such as Dixie (a Kentucky belle), a Meenahga girl in blackface playing an African American child, and the Ku Klux Klan. A camper remembered that "the villain was very aggressive" in his attempt to court Dixie and "had to be forcibly subdued by the Ku Klux Klan."[32] Campers at other American summer camps acted out the same drama during the early twentieth century. D. W. Griffith's enormously popular *The Birth of a Nation,* a 1915 movie that romanticized white supremacist history, had emboldened the Ku Klux Klan and increased its visibility. Blackface performances at youth camps also reprised a kind of racial nostalgia as a response to an emerging civil rights movement.[33]

Pack and Paddle recorded additional instances of racism at camp. In 1941, counselors hosted a *Gone with the Wind* party. A horse-drawn cart brought girls to the Lodge, transformed into the Tara plantation depicted in the 1939 movie, where "Negro waitresses served their southern masters with apple pie à la mode and mint julep punch."[34] Later, in 1945, Meenahga staged an aria from George Gershwin's opera *Porgy and Bess* that featured a camper in blackface. A camper wrote, "The next act was one of the best of the show, when Dee Dee Griffith, dressed as a colored woman holding a baby, sang the spiritual 'Summertime.'"[35] Girls used burnt cork to imagine themselves as different, as part of an America with rigid racial boundaries and clear-cut racial roles. Given that boundaries and clear-cut roles were part and parcel to life at Camp Meenahga, this is somewhat understandable. It is unclear, however, to what degree campers identified with racial tensions, and it is quite possible, perhaps even probable, that many saw themselves in a racial light as part of a privileged and superior class.

NATIVE AMERICANS AND CAMP MEENAHGA

A different racial way of thinking put Meenahga campers in contact with various representations of Native Americans and their cultures. Part of being at Camp Meenahga, and nearly every summer camp in the United States during the twentieth century and into the present, involved and continues to involve a certain amount of "playing Indian." Appropriated and stylized versions of Native American place names, dress, stories, histories, and myths were part of Camp Meenahga as they were elsewhere in the United States.[36]

The 1917 *Pack and Paddle*, for instance, opens with a story of how Meenahga got its name. It is a story of "dark and rugged Indians" and "squaws" exiled after a wicked chief committed murder. The outcasts canoe with a new leader, Mahto Tatongo, to what campers knew as Camp Meenahga. A young warrior named Opeeche then stumbles into a thicket of ripe blueberries. After doing so, the Indians name themselves Meenahga. Years later, a young chief is unable to locate ripe fruit and curses the plant and the place. The blueberries disappear as a result. The frightened people flee, leaving only their tribal name and, more important, making room for Euro-American settlement.[37] In 1918, a mawkish poem written by a Meenahga girl fused trochaic tetrameter with a phrase from a popular ad, invoking both Longfellow and a Hamm's Brewery jingle. The poet asks rhetorically, "Would you follow on the pine trail / To the land of Sky Blue Waters?"[38]

In the early twentieth century, Indian place names and cultures were appropriated by camp owners and Americans in general to suggest that camps and rural getaways were part of a wilderness untouched by the effects of industrialization and modernity. As a result, the process perpetuated the American longing for a mythic past that never existed, and necessitated freezing Indian cultures in space and time, in the wilderness and the long ago.[39]

Notable as well is the lack of mention in *Pack and Paddle* of the totem pole funded in 1927 by the Ephraim Men's Club and the Door County Historical Society to "honor" the Potawatomi Nation that once lived in the region.[40] Charles Lesaar carved much of the original pole in 1927, and a replica was installed in 1970 after the original fell into disrepair. Potawatomi leader Simon Kahquados remains buried near it. The silence is understandable in some ways. Kahquados's burial took place on Memorial Day 1930, a month or so before Camp Meenahga opened for the season. As many as fifteen thousand people attended the ceremony. Kahquados was the last known chief of the Wisconsin Potawatomi and a timber cruiser by trade. Four years after Kahquados died, Congress passed the Wheeler-Howard Act, or the Indian Reorganization Act, which granted many Native Americans increased autonomy over their affairs in government, business, and education. It was the kind of legislative change that Kahquados had sought during many trips to Washington, DC, as a tribal spokesperson.

Like the poem in which Native Americans leave the land where Camp Meenahga was built because they can no longer feed themselves, the totem pole attributes Potawatomi relocation not to Euro-American settler encroachment and violence but to the natural order of things. One of the totem pole's decorative bands even shows Indians "leaving for places unknown." In truth, Door County Potawatomis were forced west of the Mississippi River, a fact that few, if any, Camp Meenahga girls were aware of.

9

Music, Writing, and Good Eating

> *There is no point in being successful and cooperative if one can't enjoy life at the same time.*
>
> —Mousie Stix and Maggie Woodbury, 1927 *Pack and Paddle*

Poems in *Pack and Paddle* and camp minstrel shows were part of the larger fabric of American culture in the 1920s. So were allusions to jazz. Written and played predominantly by African Americans, jazz fascinated chic, urban white Americans, especially in places like New York City. Jazz was played there in hundreds of speakeasies by big bands such as Duke Ellington's orchestra at the Cotton Club in Harlem. Langston Hughes later recalled the twenties as a time "when the negro was in vogue,"[1] and music historians claim that jazz's forceful rhythm, "bent" notes, and "swing" toward momentum, helped quiet disillusionment following the Great War.[2] At Meenahga, jazz was simply fun.

Girls fused the 1927 brassy hit "Crazy Words—Crazy Tune" with feelings of infatuation. They likely heard ukulele tenor Johnny "Honey Duke" Marvin's hit recording. Campers often sang to Alice Orr Clark's blond, curly-haired son, Benno, by then in his early twenties. "If he croons lovesick ones are sure to swoon," they sang to Benno. "Vo-doe-de-o!"[3]

THE CLUB: COMPLEXES AND FIXATIONS

At the start of the Jazz Age, the Clark and Mabley daughters were too old to be Meenahga campers. They were grown women but unmarried. Living in St. Louis as independent single women went against customs of the time, which meant that the girls had to stay with their mothers during the summer. The solution? The Club.

The Villa, the Club Rosa (shortened to the Club) was a building just north of the tennis courts. It had been part of Peninsula State Park's second golf course, a 1914 failed endeavor. Instructors who didn't bunk with campers, including the Mabley girls and Alice Clark, lived in the cozy cabin. The Club also functioned as a guest house for former campers longing for a short visit. Club women were single and just past their teens.[4] Not surprisingly, daughters Alice Clark and Frances, Hilda, and Elaine Mabley liked this arrangement, and their attachment to Meenahga remained strong. All were camp instructors before their marriages, and Alice Clark, after marrying, eventually became a camp director.

Club girls often planned elaborate camp festivities. At a Hollywood party, Club women dressed as movie stars Gloria Swanson, Rudolph Valentino, Alla Nazimova, and Mary Pickford. They also hosted events such as a lobster party, presumably with lobster on the menu, and a soup-and-nut party, serving soup as the first course and nuts for dessert. Additionally, camp rules were relaxed for Club girls. They routinely skipped morning drill and often arrived late to breakfast, all a "kittywampus."[5]

In 1922, women from the Club contributed a self-deprecating essay to *Pack and Paddle* in which they gave a nod to the theories of psychoanalysis being popularized at the time by Sigmund Freud:[6]

> In these days when psychoanalysis is the subject being discussed at all the most fashionable watering places and tea parties—where one's unconscious mind rules supreme—where upon one's complexes and fixations are blamed every fault and weakness—who could be anything but desirous to go into that still unchartered territory and draw forth what has all the time been there? Surely not the Club![7]

If girls in the Club needed psychoanalysis, it was to treat a complex that Club members shared in common: feeling unappreciated. Members of the Club felt especially unrecognized after making a witty remark that inevitably went over the heads of younger campers. Fixations were more numerous. The Club fixated on porcupines and mice seen under beds and inside trunks. They fixated on a local farm boy, Peter Fons, too. Every morning, Fons bellowed "Roll out!" as he delivered two buckets of water to the Club.[8]

LITERARY: PUNS APLENTY

Club members, like most campers and counselors, learned quickly to appreciate Camp Meenahga scenery. The grandeur and beauty of Peninsula State Park offered campers, among other things, all the artistic inspiration they could ever want. Startingly beautiful and wide open, the park presented campers with endless possibilities, including ancient cedars clinging to cliffsides, nearby farms, forgotten cabins, and all the boundlessness of Lake Michigan. The sound of its waves on the shore was a constant. On the water, camp canoes and sailboats maneuvered around large yachts and weather-beaten skiffs. The skiffs fished for lake trout and whitefish, some of which eventually ended up on dinner tables in the Lodge.

Not surprisingly, then, the Peninsula State Park landscape fired the literary imaginations of countless campers. "Literary" occurred on Sunday evenings. Girls not only wrote letters home, they also wrote essays, poems, and jokes. These were recited to others in front of the Lodge fireplace. At Literary, girls practiced writing, speaking, and listening skills, important both socially and, as times changed, in the working world. Literary works, included in each year's *Pack and Paddle*, told Meenahga's summer-to-summer story in the varied voices of the girls themselves. Many writers drew inspiration from what was familiar to them. In 1921, a writer cleverly used the name of a razor company to pun, "Oh Scissors, let's cut up! Would Gillette me?" Well-known nursery rhymes were fair game, too:

> Oh where, oh where has my middy gone,
> Oh, where, oh where can it be?
> I've lost my sock and my garter, too,
> Oh where, oh where can they be?[9]

Such things were a *Pack and Paddle* staple. "Did you ever hear Fish Creek?" a writer asked in 1924. Clever word play made local landmarks and camp activities part of the fun. "You tell 'em Ephraim, buy gum" and "You tell 'em Fish Creek, you're all abluff" were followed by:

> You tell 'em glasses, I can see through you.
> You tell 'em nose, you're a peeling organ.
> You tell 'em housekeeper, you've made a
> home run.
> You tell 'em flaps, you're on to the tent.
> You tell 'em sundae, you're saucy.

You tell 'em fingers, I'm counting on you.
You tell 'em flag, I've raised you.
You tell 'em pillow, I've got a case on you.[10]

If the intent was to get laughs, *Pack and Paddle* editors often pitched to their readers material that elicited smiles. Editors added poems about tent inspection that many campers found funny:

Inspectors, they are very cruel,
And stand upon their heads
To find a little cob-web
Or bulges in our beds.

Oh, dear inspector,
Give us ten today,
We've tried so hard to please you
In every sort of way.

We dusted every trunk,
And swept the dirty floor,
And who on this clean earth
Would dare to ask for more?

"I would," says she,
And spies a hated straw,
"Oh, don't take off for that,
It's one I never saw."

She glances at the table
And feels across the shelf,
"You can't take off for that,
'Cause I dusted it myself."

"Oh yeah," says she smiling,
"Oh yeah," says I real cross,
I wish I were a counselor,
And then I'd be the boss.

And now she exits slowly,
But she's up to her old tricks,
'Cause I feel it in my very bones
That we only got a six.[11]

Other Meenahga poems were unabashedly sentimental. In "The Answer," Marian Wickham, from St. Louis, described paddling "up the silvery path of the moonbeams" to find fairyland in "the land of dreams come true."[12]

Pack and Paddle prose could also be aphoristic. In an essay titled "Self Expression," Elena Margaret Fantoni, from Highland Park, Illinois, wrote, "The man who hugs his talents to himself, who shares not with another the expression of his God-given ability and dominion, is a miser in the cruelest sense of the word; not a romantic, pitiable figure, but a cheat, a robber, a murderer of his own and others' happiness."[13] Posy Oswald's "The Sentinel Birch" invoked favored truths as well:

The lone white birch in the group of trees.
I wonder if everyone notices and sees
That it's not afraid to stand alone
And the fact should be well known
That he who stands for what he thinks best
Will get much farther than the rest.[14]

Finally, *Pack and Paddle* editors gave credit to Clark and Mabley for the hard work and vision that made Meenahga possible.

Canoe outings and evening parties were commonplace at summer camps across the United States. Less ordinary was the encouragement, patience, and concern that Clark and Mabley showed Meenahga girls for more than three decades.[15]

GOOD EATING

In addition to art and music, camp life revolved around food as much as anything. Meenahga cooks served breakfast at seven thirty each morning, dinner at noon, and supper at six o'clock at night. Kitchen staff began their days at five thirty in the morning and ended them at eight o'clock in the evening. Campers were expected to arrive on time for meals, since Clark and Mabley saw punctuality as essential to good manners. When girls were late, they were often admonished for being "the last hair on a cow's tail."[16] Everyone ate their meals family-style at tables of ten.

Perhaps because Camp Meenahga was surrounded by farmland, campers were given, at breakfast and supper, all the pasteurized whole milk they could drink.[17] Milk came from a farm near Fish Creek managed by Harry Schuyler. Camp masters drove a rumbling 1931 Model A station wagon to fetch it.[18] In later years, Pleck's Ice Cream and Dairy Company provided milk, butter, and cream. Otto Voek's, in Baileys Harbor, sold meat and other groceries to Camp Meenahga.[19]

More than milk, meat, fish, or any other fare put before them, campers loved donuts. Five hundred delicious sour cream donuts with homemade applesauce were served Sunday mornings. Meenahga cooks let fresh cream sour naturally, giving the donuts a distinct flavor and zing. "Who makes them now with sour cream as we did then?" wondered Adeline "Tootsie" Peil, a Meenahga cook. "I still say those were the good old days, when life was simple and you had to use a lot more elbow grease to get things done."[20] One morning, a cook found a drowned mouse in the sour cream, so donuts went unserved—to everyone's dismay.

Eating too many donuts caused some campers to come down with the "donut blues." Barbara Becker Glass complained that donuts caused her to gain weight and that she "fairly rolled off the train going home."[21] Campers put the donut blues to an eponymously titled poem:

> Each Sunday morning
> When we awake,
> We think of our future
> Stomach ache.
>
> When we eat donuts
> Sugary and fine,
> It gives our figures
> A brand-new line.
>
> It isn't thin,
> It isn't right,
> It makes our shorts
> Feel awfully tight
>
> 110, 109
> Some think it's bad
> Some think it's fine
> We touch our toes
> Some fifty times . . .
>
> When I get in line
> And take off my shoes
> Donut blues.[22]

Kitchen staff saved the grease in which donuts were fried, purifying it with lye to make laundry soap. "It came in handy to wash the kitchen towels each day. Lye, in those days, could be bought for ten cents a can and an enormous amount of soap was made at a large savings to the camp," remembered Peil.[23] Cooks saved pancake scraps as well, letting them dry to be used as "bread" crumbs. Very little food went to waste.

KITCHEN STAFF

A well-staffed and well-stocked kitchen was needed to keep the camp fed. Mabley, who had managed a high school cafeteria in St. Louis, oversaw the kitchen and its staff. At first, Mabley and Clark hired cooks from St. Louis, such as Adell Davis.[24] Eventually, they started bringing in cooks from Door County. In 1927, Alice Reinhart Free became head cook at Camp Meenahga. Evelyn Bhirdo Franke became Free's assistant. "I was about fourteen when I started and I stayed there until I was twenty-one," remembered Franke. "I was the waitress at the head table and cleaned the Cottage. I earned ten dollars a week." Franke worked every day, sun up to sun down.[25]

Kitchen staff who lived within a few miles of Meenahga walked to and from work. Other kitchen staff camped north of the Lodge.[26] Kitchen staff rarely mingled with campers. Neither did they participate in activities. There was, however, at least in kitchen worker Irene Mae Pringle Pruitt's opinion, "no tension" between kitchen staff and campers.[27]

As there was no electricity at Camp Meenahga, food was cooked using two woodstoves. Every day, camp masters hauled and stacked split wood to the kitchen. Heat from the woodfires warmed water in stove reservoirs used for cooking and washing dishes. Workers washed dish towels on the back porch of the Lodge, using a bar of soap and a washboard.[28]

One or two local boys were also hired. Called chore boys, they moved cakes of ice from the ice house to the cooler, hauled meat and produce, and painted canoes dark green. Duncan Thorp worked as a Camp Meenahga chore boy for one summer when he was fifteen years old. He earned fifty dollars a month, which he referred to as "a small fortune then." Thorp was "desperate to earn enough money to buy a new suit for the start of high school in the fall—a suit with long pants, the epitome of sophistication, rather than knickers only worn by golfers and little boys." Thorp served in other roles by driving the old Ford to fetch mail in Fish Creek. Letters from parents sometimes included spending money or bank drafts for things such as sundaes, knickknacks, or riding lessons. At the time, campers could withdraw up to two dollars a week from their accounts. "The women [Clark and Mabley] carefully opened every envelope," wrote Thorp, "and shook out the contents. Any money, cash, or bank drafts were locked away and credited to the girls' accounts."[29]

One day, Thorp apprehended a sixteen-year-old named Roselyn stealing cigarettes from his tent. He ended up spending more time with her, breaking one of Clark's rules that he was not to associate with campers:

> We talked and agreed to sneak out to a public dance soon. Roz said I was to hold her letters out of the office to avoid the search and seizure process so she could get enough cash to bribe the counselor. In another week, we were spinning merrily down the road en route to a gin mill dance hall on the state highway. I don't remember much about the dancing except that Roz was surprisingly clumsy. We got back to the camp at about two thirty in the morning to find night lights on in the office and in Roz's tent—her counselor had taken her bribe and then reported her missing to the office. I was not punished but given a stern lecture on rules

of deportment by the proprietors. I was admonished never to socialize with the camp girls beyond a polite "good morning" or a "yes" or "no" reply to a question.[30]

CHICAGO BEEF AND AGED LAMB

Breakfast was usually predictable at Meenahga, but dinner and supper menus varied, sometimes offering the kind of choices found at the time in a fine restaurant. For dinner, "a roast, potatoes in some style or a starch substitute, a green vegetable, a raw vegetable, and an attractive dessert," could be expected.[31] Supper might be sandwiches, potato salad, and another type of salad.

Beef came from Chicago. Lamb and veal were butchered by custom order and hung in the camp's cold storage for two weeks or more. Franke recalled serving lamb "a lot. They loved lamb. They had a big cooler and they'd hang the whole lamb there because these women were used to their lamb aged. After it was done and fixed, it did taste good. We would put big pieces of it on big square pans in those big ovens."[32]

By the 1930s, John Kodanko had begun to provide Meenahga with potatoes, carrots, cabbage, and apples. He also collected food waste for his hogs.[33] The Kodankos leased land on Middle Road, and Kodanko's daughter Katherine worked in the Meenahga kitchen. In 1935, a camp master noted that John Kodanko was "really not mean but unusually shy." The camp master playfully teased Kodanko as well, singing:

There is a man whom you all know well,
O, Mr. Kodanko,
It's not himself but his goods that smell,
O, Mr. Kodanko,
His Dodge comes in with our fresh supplies—

They're put on the table to open our eyes
And carted away when they're covered with flies,
O, Mr. Kodanko![34]

JUST DESSERTS

Unlike much of the food that had to be delivered from elsewhere, pies were made from scratch at Meenahga. Campers sang, "Can she bake a cherry pie, Billy boy, Billy boy," until cooks came out of the kitchen and into the dining room to take a bow. One cook teased, "You'll get more pies if you don't sing."[35] If pie were not enough, ice cream cones were available for a nickel at the Maple Tree Café in Fish Creek. Wilson's in Ephraim was famous for its desserts, as was Hanson's Ice Cream Parlor. Campers loved sundaes and banana splits (advertised by O. C. Wilson as a specialty in the 1918 *Pack and Paddle*). By the late 1930s, the girls at Meenahga could not get enough "velvets," something new from Wilson's. "A velvet was super thick," wrote Elizabeth Lanier DeRamus. "It was chocolate ice cream and marshmallow sauce, and probably chocolate sauce, no other liquids, all whipped up together. Maybe there was some vanilla ice cream. It was so good!"[36] Devil's food and red velvet cakes were also camp favorites. On the last day of camp each summer, Meenahga campers treated their parents to chocolate devils, described as "a chocolate devil's food cupcake with the center scooped out, replaced with a dollop of ice cream and covered with chocolate syrup."[37]

Of course, Clark and Mabley would have had their campers stay away from sugar. More than one camp brochure informed parents that "the girls are supplied with an abundance of sweets in various forms and do not need more than we give them. Not only does a box of candy upset them physically, but it creates irritability hard to believe." In a different brochure, written over a decade earlier, Clark and Mabley wrote, "Boxes of candy and other edibles sent to our girls are strongly advised against and should this practice continue we will make such disposition of the contents as we deem necessary."[38]

Campers knew they were well-warned to stay away from sugar. A poem in *Pack and Paddle* titled "Dieting" sums up many campers' approach to treats and sweets during their summers in Door County:

> One thing I have decided,
> Although I often try it,
> Of all the places in the world
> Camp's *not* the place to diet.
> It was but a few days ago
> I tried this silly thing;
> I kept it up pretty well—
> Yes, till ice cream came in!
> "Do you think it will really matter
> If I eat a bite—or two?
> Or don't you think I could get fatter?
> Please tell me if you do!"[39]

After meals and dessert, campers often matched piano chords with vocal harmonies. Cole Porter's "Night and Day" was a favorite song. Added to it was the clinking of plates and silverware as the dishes were cleared.

Campers sit in the back of the camp's 1931 Model A station wagon, often referred to as the "Camp Meenahga Woody." COURTESY OF BARBARA BECKER GLASS

Campers had to clean their tents to pass tent inspection. In this photo from the 1941 *Pack and Paddle*, a camper cleans her tent while others relax. COURTESY OF THE WISCONSIN DEPARTMENT OF NATURAL RESOURCES

Campers played tennis on grass and, later, clay courts. Girls are shaking hands after a match in this photo. COURTESY OF SIGNE GUNDERSEN SCHROEDER

A postcard showing the entrance to the Peninsula State Park golf course. COURTESY OF THE WISCONSIN DEPARTMENT OF NATURAL RESOURCES

For those who could afford it, horseback riding was a major part of their experience at Camp Meenahga. Girls are shown here on horseback preparing for a ride. COURTESY OF MINERVA CANAVAN

The annual August derby at Camp Meenahga was an event that people from around Door County attended. In this photo, onlookers watch from a hillside as campers line up in formation. COURTESY OF GIBRALTAR HISTORICAL SOCIETY

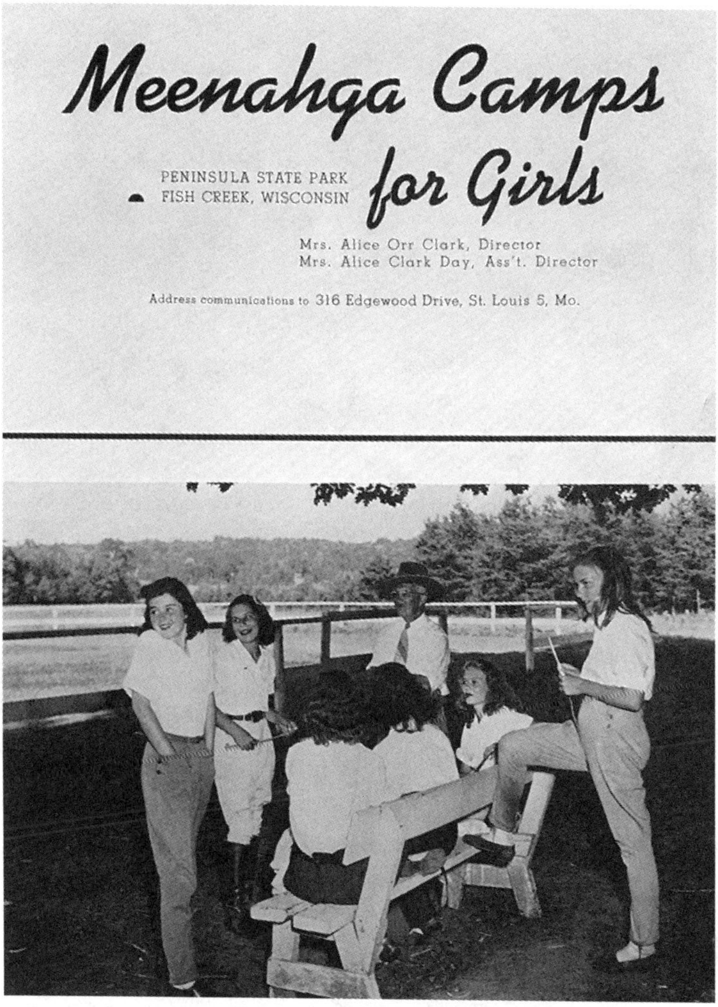

The most effective way for Clark and Mabley to market their camp was with a brochure. The cover of the brochure from 1939 is shown here. COURTESY OF THE WISCONSIN DEPARTMENT OF NATURAL RESOURCES

Three campers practice archery with longbows. COURTESY OF SIGNE GUNDERSEN SCHROEDER

The Villa, the Club Rosa. The Clark and Mabley daughters, as well as many others, spent time at the Club. COURTESY OF ADELINE PEIL AND LYNN MATKE

Adeline "Tootsie" Peil grew up in Door County and worked in the kitchen at Camp Meenahga for a number of years. COURTESY OF ADELINE PEIL AND LYNN MATKE

Mike Orwig was a beloved sailing instructor at Camp Meenahga. His loss was felt by all at Camp Meenahga when Orwig died during World War II. COURTESY OF SIGNE GUNDERSEN SCHROEDER

Wilson's in Ephraim was and remains a popular spot to get ice cream in Door County. Camp Meenahga girls are seen in this photo taken at Wilson's sometime in the 1940s. COURTESY OF GRACE LANIER BREWER

(*right*) Sailing was an enormously popular pastime at Camp Meenahga. Campers race their sailboats in this photo from *Pack and Paddle*. COURTESY OF THE WISCONSIN DEPARTMENT OF NATURAL RESOURCES

(*below*) Campers canoed around Green Bay day and night. Three campers canoe across Green Bay in this photo from the 1930s. COURTESY OF GRACE LANIER BREWER

(*left*) The pier at Camp Meenahga extended far into Lake Michigan. Beyond it is the diving raft with the sun shining on it. COURTESY OF VIRGINIA THEIS COLEMAN

(*below*) Campers often sunbathed in the afternoons. Girls are sunbathing on the pier in this photo from the 1940s. COURTESY OF VIRGINIA THEIS COLEMAN

The Purples in 1941. COURTESY OF SIGNE GUNDERSEN SCHROEDER

The Yellows in 1941. COURTESY OF SIGNE GUNDERSEN SCHROEDER

For more than thirty years, campers gathered at the Lookout to pose for photos like this one. COURTESY OF VIRGINIA THEIS COLEMAN

Campers, counselors, and staff watched sunsets from the Lookout for decades. In this photo, Janice Chamberlaine Pierce and others watch the sun sink below Green Bay. COURTESY OF JANICE CHAMBERLAINE PIERCE

10

The Bitter with the Sweet

The wind's a ghost astride a horse,
A phantom hunter . . .
Sometimes he is a laughing child,
Plays tag with falling leaves and vines;
Alas, at night, poor boy, he'll come
And cry his heart out in the pines.

—Nancy Stern, 1929 *Pack and Paddle*

Sentinel. Sanctuary. The Lookout angled against the land, balanced on a circle of sturdy stones. It stood twenty feet or so higher than Lake Michigan on a low ridge of an ancient shoreline. Alice Orr Clark could see the Lookout from her cottage and often walked across Shore Road to sit upon the gazebo's round bench.

The Lookout provided a place for the kind of restful escape from worry that Clark sometimes needed. She was not alone in that regard. By the end of 1929, the Lookout was just the kind of place many Americans needed escaping to. In October 1929, just two days after Clark's fifty-fourth birthday, a stock market plunge had shaken the American economy. Four million Americans were looking for work, and most were unable to find it. Within three years, fifteen million Americans (more than 20 percent of the US population) would be unemployed.[1]

At Camp Meenahga, the way ahead looked uncertain as well. By October 1930, Kidy Mabley, at age sixty-one, had begun to plan her exit from camp life. She looked forward to retiring after the 1931 season, leaving Clark as sole owner and manager of the camp, reorganized into a corporation called Meenahga Camps, Inc.

With or without Mabley, Meenahga had a bright future. Clark had no plans to follow her partner into retirement. Nor could she. Clark, after saving for years, had managed to purchase a home in St. Louis, but she otherwise had no real savings. She needed to keep Meenahga going to support herself financially.

MEENAHGA MERRYMAKING

In 1930, the editors of *Pack and Paddle* wrote, "'Happy Days Are Here Again' are five little words which exactly express the way everybody felt on arriving at camp." Despite the economic downturn, the 1930 summer was a pleasant one at Meenahga, as the *Pack and Paddle* reference to a popular song indicated.[2] Indiana camper Nina Brown was even inspired to pen original lyrics to the same tune:

> Camping days are here again,
> The girls we love are here again,
> We have made our friendships true again,
> Camping days are here again . . .
>
> Camping days are here again,
> Our days of joy begin again,
> We're back on old Green Bay again,
> Camping days are here again.[3]

Sometimes Clark and the counselors organized a carnival or stunt night. Costumes and decorations were thought up and made on the spot. Walpurgis Night, inspired by German and Scandinavian traditions, was another favorite. It began when Wita, a swimming instructor, woke campers from their beds. She whispered, "Get up, the fairies are coming." Campers then met counselors, dressed as characters, for a night of adventure. An elf led wide-eyed girls down a dark, lonely trail. Then, suddenly, a black cat sprang out of the woods and streaked across the path. Campers met a witch, dancing fairies, and King Neptune at the pier. He slipped away into the watery deep just as the Lady of the Lake glided into view.

Clark's niece Katherine Orr once played the part of the Lady of the Lake. She stood barefoot in the middle of a canoe, wearing a flowing white gown as the canoe drifted across the water. Kerosene lanterns cast dreamy shadows. The wind swirled around Katherine's garment, lifting gauzy veils of fabric. "She was the Lady," recalled Orr's daughter. "She had long blond hair and it was all very exciting. . . . And it was so funny! Everyone would come to watch."[4]

After the Lady of the Lake disappeared, campers followed the elf toward the Lodge, stopping at the pumphouse. A strange creature gave warning to be grateful for all things around them. Campers then had refreshments in the Lodge before returning to their tents.[5]

A LOOMING CRISIS

Clark maintained a cheerful attitude and façade into the summer of 1931. She had reasons for worry, however. Not only was it her partner's last summer on the job, but C. L. "Neal" Harrington, superintendent of forests and parks in Wisconsin from 1923 to 1958, had begun to take a close look at Meenahga's lease, up for renewal that year.

A few years earlier, in a letter to Albert E. Doolittle, Harrington had cautioned against camp upgrades and suggested reducing the annual camp improvement fee (rent) from $600 to $500, a move prompted by a downward turn in the economy. Nevertheless, by 1931, Harrington had learned that Meenahga needed expensive septic repairs that his agency could not afford.[6] He would need to get more money from Clark and Mabley under the terms of their next lease, money Clark and Mabley neither had nor felt they owed Harrington. Sensing administrative disquiet, Clark and Mabley had visited people throughout Door County in 1930, drumming up support in the event they needed to initiate a letter-writing campaign to save Camp Meenahga. Clark and Mabley knew Meenahga brought dollars to Door County, and they anticipated support from its residents.[7] To get ahead of Harrington, Clark provided a detailed list of camp expenditures since 1916. The total was $31,865, or nearly $500,000 by its modern equivalency.[8]

That America had entered the Great Depression just as the camp's third five-year lease expired was unfortunate for Meenahga's proprietors. In January 1931, Clark wrote to Arthur Doe, formerly a camp master at Meenahga and now an attorney at Quarles, Spence & Quarles in Milwaukee. "If we are put out, it absolutely breaks us," Clark wrote to Doe. "Our investment and our years of work will go to nothing. There is nothing we can sell. In other words, we could realize nothing but failure." Clark told Doe that Meenahga rent had funded the extension of Shore Road in Peninsula State Park. In a less material sense, she also explained that Meenahga built up "fine citizens and thinking women." In the end, she asked "for a fair and square deal."[9]

Clark and Mabley were not the only ones wanting to be treated with financial fairness in 1931. Many Americans with savings accounts hoped for the same. Clark and Mabley kept a

Meenahga savings account at the Door County State Bank of Sturgeon Bay. In early September 1931, the total account balance was $2,247.81, with $1,162.68 designated for facility improvements, such as repairs to the Lodge roof, and to pay rent. The remaining $1,085.13 represented profits from the 1931 season. Unfortunately, in late September 1931, the Sturgeon Bay bank failed, taking Clark and Mabley's money with it. All told, the bank lost more than $800,000.[10] On October 16, 1931, the State Banking Department of Wisconsin published notice in the *Door County Advocate* directing creditors to provide legal proof of claims against the delinquent bank by January 2, 1932.[11] Eight years passed before the state banking commissioner awarded Clark and Mabley any of their lost money. In the end, the business partners received $640.56, far less than what had been lost.[12]

After Mabley retired at the end of the 1931 season, Clark struggled to pay wages due to local laborers. Some men waited for nearly a year to be paid. The Noble Refining Company, which had sold cement to the camp, was not so tolerant. Claimed the company: "We wrote Mrs. Clark on November 4th . . . but she has not seen fit to respond."[13] Eventually, the company got the $200 it was owed, and Clark and Mabley were on the hook for the bank's protest fee of $2.12.

TO THE PENNY

A flurry of letters written in 1932 and exchanged between Wisconsin Conservation Commission personnel and Arthur Doe provide a window into Meenahga's difficult circumstances. The Commission demanded that Clark and Mabley verify receipts to the penny.[14] Months passed while Doe negotiated terms demanded by the Commission in the new five-year lease. In the new lease, the Commission requested three payments from Meenahga. The first was for rent, $500 the first two years, increasing to $600 the last three years. The second was a $100 annual fee for facility improvements and repairs. The third was a sum of $1,162.70 (two cents higher than the $1,162.68 Clark and Mabley had lost in the bank failure) for recent repairs and back rent, which Clark had thus far been unable to pay. The third sum was to be paid in five equal annual installments of $232.54. Payment was due by October 1 of each year.[15]

Doe thought the Commission's demands extreme. "The necessity of paying in excess of $800 in 1932 and 1933, and in excess of $900 for the remaining three years constitutes a burden out of proportion, considering the trends of the times," he wrote to the Commission in a letter dated January 4, 1932. He closed by asking the "indulgence of your honorable body" to consider the possibility of a "lease being granted which, even if it did not constitute a reduction in the rent under the old lease, would at least not involve an increase."[16] By March, with the Commission refusing to bend, Doe wrote, "I shall be compelled to advise the ladies to discontinue the camp."[17] Clark, however, chose to persevere and opened camp for the 1932 season. By September, she had signed the lease.

By fall, letters from Clark to Harrington included restrained phrases seething with unsettled emotions. Clark prepared to depart Meenahga for St. Louis but first wrote Harrington, reporting that she had paid various bills, including labor and materials for reroofing the Cottage. "You may not see this as I do, but the very fact that I have held my business together and am still an established camp with bright prospects for next season, seems to me a rather good accomplishment, in spite of the fact that I cannot touch the rent."[18]

Harrington responded to Clark by post, but when Clark did not reply, Harrington pressed Doolittle. "I wish you would let me know whether Mrs. Clark is still up there," wrote Harrington. Doolittle waited a week to respond, informing his boss

Harrington that Clark had departed Door County three weeks prior, side-stepping involvement by noting where she could be reached.[19]

Back in Missouri, having managed to keep Meenahga afloat for another summer, Clark gathered her thoughts and put pen to paper. "Your letter of September 14 came to hand just as I was preparing to leave for St. Louis," she wrote Harrington, "and most of the material to which I had to refer had gone on ahead of me." The letter, dated October 10, 1932, continued with financial details. Clark then wrote:

> I want to ask you this. We are supposed to use a sum equivalent to $1,162.68 within the next five years in improvements. Where is the money going to come from to pay those checks which were not honored last year? I imagine that I will be privileged to include the sums I have to pay these workmen on the 1931 account in this $1,162.68. . . . I will have another bill to send you soon for repairs on the Cottage. The supporting braces have rotted away—those had to be replaced to keep the Cottage from falling down.[20]

Money funding the facility improvement account came from the past summer's camp fees. In her letter, Clark explained that the balance was closer to $1,400 rather than $1,162.68 because of the Cottage repairs, writing, "I trust that I have elucidated this matter."[21]

The Commission permitted the outstanding unpaid wages from 1931 to be drawn from the improvement fund, as Clark requested. The new annual rent of $500, however, remained past due; sanitation facilities were below code; and detailed, mandatory financial reports were missing.[22] In response, Clark reminded the Commission that "no salaries to the directors have been paid for the past year" and that camp was started in 1932 on an advance tuition payment by one of the parents. "I have succeeded in holding [Meenahga] together and paying all the current expenses," she wrote, "but there is absolutely nothing left for the rent."[23]

A WELCOME DIVERSION

Banks continued to fail throughout the early 1930s, and by 1933, nearly half the banks in the United States had gone under. Financial calamity was everywhere, the backdrop against which even the happiest of events took place. Clark and her family, for example, set worry aside for a day on July 15, 1933, when Alice Clark married Laurence Sturgis Day. Max Friedman hosted the ceremony on Peninsula Players Road in the garden of his Fish Creek estate. So that she could look after her daughter's wedding, Clark asked her niece Katherine Orr to step in as assistant director.[24]

Later, in October, distressing news again reached Clark. Bernard Christopher Christensen, Meenahga's riding master, had passed away. Clark hired Chicagoan Thade "Ted" Cornils to take Christensen's place.[25] Cornils introduced formation riding to Meenahga campers. Like Christensen, Cornils also scheduled all-day rides. He added overnight trips on horseback, and Moonlight Bay near Baileys Harbor was a favorite destination.[26]

Cornils used his own horses, as Christensen and Berg had. He trailered twelve American Saddlebreds to Door County for the summer. Cornils owned 120 acres of land near the intersection of County A and Highway 42, which he had purchased years before while vacationing in Door County and where he established the Circle C Ranch. When Clark hired him as riding master, Cornils began spending summers in Door County, building up a family riding business apart from Meenahga that lasted into the 1970s.[27]

QUIET ALLIES

As time went on, Clark's relationship with Harrington remained contentious. In March 1934, when needed roof repairs to the Lodge were estimated at $400, Clark wrote, "It is utterly impossible for me to have this done at the present time. I have managed to hold the business together and pay small salaries, but there is nothing left over." She went on to suggest that "as long as this [Meenahga] is state property," the situation should be placed before the Civil Works Administration—a New Deal work program that created jobs for the unemployed—because "the farmers are more or less benefited by the New Deal, and I think my need is as great as any farmer's."[28] In April, the Leathem D. Smith Dock Company posted a summons in garnishment against Meenahga Camps, Inc., in the *Door County Advocate*, for the amount of $18.20.[29]

Unbeknownst to Clark, she had an ally on the Wisconsin Conservation Commission board. Haskell "Hack" Noyes, chairman of the committee, had previously argued her case to his colleagues. Noyes started his career as the head basketball coach at the University of Wisconsin–Madison before holding the same position at Yale University. He then became a prominent Milwaukee businessman and lifelong conservationist. In 1932, Noyes wrote to Commission director Paul Kelleter. "They [Clark and Mabley] have been very desirable tenants," Hoyes pointed out. "I believe we should do our part in enabling them to carry on."[30] Less than two weeks later, Noyes wrote to Kelleter again, "My own feeling in the matter was expressed in my letter to you, and I personally feel it will be a mistake to insist upon terms which will cause the closing of this camp. . . .

However, if this is your final judgment in the matter, I shall make no further recommendations."[31] Several years later, as the Commission was still seeking money from Camp Meenahga for unpaid rent and facility repairs, Noyes's daughter enrolled at camp. He sent a three-page, single-spaced typed letter to new Commission director Harley MacKenzie, carefully reviewing past discussions. "It seems to me that Mrs. Clark has made a very remarkable showing the past five years under all the circumstances, and it does not seem to me ... that she should be treated harshly by any department of the state." Noyes then shared his impression that the bank would not likely give more than 20 percent to depositors who had lost money: "When you consider not only what the federal government but the states themselves have done in declaring moratoriums on interest and rents and canceling debts and reducing interest charges, it does seem to me that the State of Wisconsin should not be too tough on a desirable tenant, and that instead of increasing the rent as was done in 1932, that actually a reduction would have been in order."[32]

Doolittle was working just as hard as Clark to settle Meenahga's financial disputes with the state. He crafted detailed camp accounting records for years 1931 through 1935 after they were demanded by the Commission.[33] In 1936, with rent still in arrears, Doolittle wrote Harrington, "I admire her [Clark's] stand in trying to hold on ... it is a case where she is doing the best she can." Harrington had pressed Doolittle to be more severe in his treatment of Clark, but Doolittle refused. Instead, he wrote, "For me to suggest any thing puts me in a bad way.... She [Clark] has been and certainly is a lady, and has run a clean and educational camp. The state in a way has not really lost dollars and cents, as she has put all real money spent there on improvements herself.... You will have to figure this out with the director's help, I think."[34]

SET A COURSE FOR SAILING

Meanwhile, Clark was learning to set a new course, to run the rigging by herself. Short newspapers replaced Meenahga's fifty-page *Pack and Paddle* yearbooks between 1931 and 1938, a hint at how Clark managed Meenahga during a lean financial time. In the same vein, beginning in 1935, Meenahga began requiring a reference from would-be campers that confirmed the good financial standing of an aspiring camper's family.

In 1935, Clark hired Mercer "Mike" Orwig as sailing instructor. Orwig was a master mariner from St. Louis. He brought his own boat, an eighteen-foot wooden sloop in a class of sailboats known as Seagulls. Seagulls were popular—especially at the Ephraim Yacht Club—because they handled well on Lake Michigan. Orwig called his boat *Kelpie*. A Scotsman, Orwig also brought bagpipes and a collie dog to camp. Girls paid extra for sailing lessons and signed up weeks in advance. Orwig offered free instruction for those without funds.

The girls took notice of Orwig's Scottish accent. "We differ from other camps," Mary Ellen Crane revealed in *Pack and Paddle*, "in that we have sailing with a Scotch accent. . . . We weather the gales of Green Bay while Mike sings."[35] Another camper told of Orwig's rope-grommet awards for excellence in sailing, as well as stories of learning the bowline, clove hitch, and square knots. "Peanuts McDonald," wrote a camper, "was one of the few who mastered the enigmatic triple-mast knot."[36] Campers wittily described the challenge of learning all the knots and nautical talk in a poem titled "I'll Never Learn":

Whenever I go sailing upon the *Kelpie* fair
I try to learn the names of all the ropes and gadgets there.

"Watch the boom crutch when it falls," Mike cries. "Now
there she goes!"
And before I realize what it is, it's fallen on my toes.[37]

Sailing was incredibly popular. A few campers brought their own sloops, one-masted sailboats with a fore-and-aft mainsail and a jib. One year, there were three identical sloops in Door County connected to Meenahga: *Kelpie, Wind Bird,* and *Cutty Sable.* Boats were moored at the Fish Creek docks.

Judy Clark Stephens described a 1939 sailing trip to Horseshoe Island in a letter to her Aunt Polly. Mike Orwig led a group of four girls on an all-day sail, leaving camp at ten o'clock in the morning to arrive at the island at noon. "We were about starved by then so we ate our lunch on the beach," Stevens remembered. The girls investigated the abandoned buildings, "all dark and cobwebby. . . . After we had looked the whole house over, we walked all the way around the island on the beach. By then we were pretty hot so we all put on our bathing suits and went in swimming."[38]

WIND IN HER SAILS

In September 1936, Harrington again pressed Clark for back rent, perhaps pressured himself by Harley MacKenzie. "When we conversed about this matter not long ago in the park," Harrington wrote to Clark, "I thought that I had made it perfectly clear" that rent payment was "the most important item" from the perspective of the Commission. Harrington complained further that "irrespective of all other circumstances, the fact remains that the terms of the contract" were not being carried out. He acknowledged his dispatch as "a harsh letter."[39] Still, Harrington recommended to MacKenzie that Meenahga's lease be renewed. Ultimately, he was moved to note that "there is no question that the camp has been operated in a highly creditable manner."[40]

Hack Noyes, meanwhile, arranged an inspection of camp with Commission representative L. M. Hobbins in late fall 1936. "I appreciate very much your taking the day off with me and I hope that the trip had no bad effects on your condition," Noyes wrote to Hobbins. He recommended that annual expenditures for improvements not be stated specifically in the lease but be approved by the Wisconsin superintendent of forests and parks, who was Harrington at the time. Noyes advocated that Meenahga's "old indebtedness should be either eliminated entirely or else cut in half with the understanding that Mrs. Clark will assign to the Commission her interest in any payments which she may receive from the bank in Sturgeon Bay in the way of dividends on her former account."[41]

In the end, Camp Meenahga weathered the financial storm. On March 1, 1937, Clark signed Meenahga's fifth five-year lease. "May I express again," she wrote to Harrington, "my appreciation of your interest and understanding. I trust that I shall see you at camp this summer."[42]

11

Games, Capers, and Characters

> *In our Meenahga world we learned that by looking for good, we found it.*
>
> —Polly Messinger and Maga Cole, 1942 *Pack and Paddle*

Adeline "Tootsie" Peil entered the Lodge at Camp Meenahga in 1937 to interview for the job of head cook. Peil grew up on a farm in Baileys Harbor and left high school in her early teens to work as a cook. Each week, Peil baked up to twenty loaves of bread and made dishes such as roasted chicken with potatoes and sour cream gravy. As she got older, Peil went to Milwaukee each winter where she made a better living in domestic service. She returned to Door County in the summers. During her interview with Alice Orr Clark, bats swooped high above her in the rafters. Peil observed that Clark did not give the bats much notice. Instead, Clark droned on softly about braised vegetables. "As frightened as I was of bats," Peil wrote later, "I really had to think twice about accepting the position."[1] Peil was thirty years old when she accepted the position of head cook, and she stayed at Meenahga through the 1941 season. Clark always gave her glowing references when Peil left each fall to find work elsewhere. "She managed the kitchen, and the four maids under her," Clark wrote of Peil, "with kindness, firmness, and tact. She is a splendid cook and economical. Her kitchen was always clean and she herself was the pink of neatness."[2]

MEENAHGA'S TOUR DE FORCE: THE DERBY

The summer of 1937 was the first at Camp Meenahga under the new lease Clark had signed in March. That summer, too, Thade "Ted" Cornils started stabling his horses in the former Beyers' barn near Peninsula's Fish Creek entrance. Two years earlier, the Civilian Conservation Corps (CCC) had remodeled it to use as a garage.[3] The CCC worked at Peninsula State Park from 1935 to 1937. Among other projects, CCC boys built the beach house, the toboggan run and ski jump, the stone wall at Sven's Bluff, and the stone wall leading up Game Farm Hill to Eagle Tower. As many as one hundred men lived in tents and later barracks at Camp Peninsular, located behind present-day Gibraltar School. Although the CCC was very popular nationwide, the CCC camp in Door County proved controversial. Several prominent citizens worried about safety. Hack Noyes wrote the Wisconsin Conservation Commission asking for assurances that his daughter, who attended Camp Meenahga, would not experience any unpleasantness "or worse due to the laxity of discipline in the CCC camp or through any lack of good manners toward girls or women in general."[4]

Albert E. Doolittle also protested the CCC. He stated that National Park Service (NPS) leaders, who had some jurisdiction in CCC affairs, had ignored his recommendations. Soon, sparks flew between Doolittle and his long-time adversary, Hjalmar Holand, who served on the Door County Parks board seeking CCC assistance. Doolittle won out in the end when an NPS inspector recommended that Camp Peninsular disband, which it did on June 30, 1937.[5]

The unexpected availability of the Beyers' former barn, now a garage, was a lucky break for Cornils, who wanted horses closer to Meenahga rather than at his stable on Highway 42. He soon employed Leo Grassman to lead Cornils's American Saddlebreds to camp each day. In the evenings, Fish Creek boys such as Itsie Krause walked the horses to the small beach just east of park headquarters, where they were washed and brushed. Each boy rode one horse and led two or three others. "That was a highlight," remembered Krause, "and so much fun."[6]

The August derby was another memorable experience, the pinnacle of summer for some. Meenahga campers, their families, community members, and park rangers gathered on the hill above the riding ring. The ring stood a bit southeast of the Lodge, encircled by a bright white Kentucky fence. On derby day, parked cars circled the riding field "filled with residents of Cottage Row, friends from Ephraim and Fish Creek, and queer, bird-of-passage tourists from everywhere!" After each demonstration, spectators sounded horns in assorted tones.[7]

Spectators watched Meenahga equestrians "horsed up in snow white breeches and painfully shiny boots," wrote Josephine Pridmore from Wilmette, Illinois, in *Pack and Paddle*. She and others who chose not to ride or could not afford extra fees for lessons watched from "the crowded hill above the ring."[8] Sally Simmons, from St. Louis, thought the derby both interesting and beautiful when it began with a short military drill: "This was followed by a lively ribbon chase. A ball game resembling polo was played next with a great deal of excitement."[9]

A flag-raising ceremony opened the derby. Next, a sputtering tractor pulled a hayrack carrying campers. The tractor led a parade of dignitaries, including Clark, who drove a harness buggy. Mike Orwig, playing bagpipes, followed behind. Suddenly, tandem riders trotted into the ring. Applause from onlookers mingled with the whinnying of horses. Riders halted in quiet formation, signaling the entrance of the riding master. Cornils, astride Butcher Boy, entered the freshly oiled ring, and the competition began. Prizes included riding crops and pins, engraved "Clark-Mabley" and "Harwood" cups, ribbons, and the Cornils Scholarship, a season of free lessons to the most improved rider.

WATER SPORTS

Meenahga hosted a water carnival in August as well. Diving and swimming tricks entertained guests. The carnival ended on a lighthearted note when campers in silly getups pranced along the dock. During the 1940s, boys from the camp on Adventure Island joined the carnival.[10]

Camp directors added water ballet (synchronized swimming) to the water carnival in the late 1930s. Milwaukee native Katherine Whitney Curtis, who later retired to Washington Island in Door County, brought the sport, made popular by American swimmer and actress Esther Williams, to Meenahga. A Meenahga troupe formed bobbing chains, coordinating leg and arm strokes. For the grand finale, girls swam into a tight circle that gracefully expanded, forming the letter *M*. All wore matching one-piece suits and white bathing caps with chin straps.

Overnight canoe trips continued through the years and were a highlight for Kentuckian Grace Lanier Brewer. In 1938, Brewer and friends Edith Leopold, Patsy Mayer, Caroline Jones, and Charlotte Widen conspired to paddle to Gills Rock, more than twenty miles from Camp Meenahga. "It had never been done before, and we had a young counselor that was not wise to our change in plans," remembered Brewer. The girls made it by abandoning the shoreline and paddling across the harbors. They camped on shore. "That night we suffered torment with rain and bugs galore. We thought we were in Hades. But oh! It was still

Death's Door! . . . The next day the lake had become rough with white caps and we knew we weren't going home," wrote Brewer. A counselor somehow telephoned Clark that the group needed rescuing, and plans were made to fetch the wayward canoeists. Camp masters hauled canoes by truck. Help, however, could not arrive until the end of the day. Added Brewer: "We decided to continue our adventure and took the ferry out to Washington Island. I know we had a good time. I think Mrs. Clark was upset with us and the counselor, though."[11]

Campers in 1938 had a rare opportunity to play on the waters of Lake Michigan in another way. An invitation to board Herman Falk's yacht *Seaforth* elicited "wild gesticulations and delighted screams," on August 12, 1938. "Moored in Shanty Bay," reported *Pack and Paddle,* "the *Seafort* presented a glorious spectacle. She lay anchored under the warm sun; her one-hundred-and-sixty-foot hull shone spotless clean and white."[12] Falk was a Milwaukee industrialist. After his brewing business burned twice, he turned to mechanics, first fixing wagon axles and later working with electric street railways. By 1944, he was manufacturing gears for battleships that could ferry and land troops to places where there were no harbors. Falk Corporation was one of a dozen Milwaukee companies that dominated the metal fabrication industry in the mid-1900s.[13]

Falk welcomed girls aboard and permitted them to inspect the ship. Then, Falk set sail for Chambers Island, about seven miles southwest. Some girls explored the island, others fished. Jackie Sherman caught a four-pound perch and presented it to Falk. On the return voyage, Martha Howard won honors for steering the boat in the straightest line, while Katty Jones captured the booby prize for the same task. Only "one casualty occurred that caused bedlam aboard the ship. Someone stole the egg from the crow's nest! Is your face red, Martha Apple?" asked *Pack and Paddle,* as "The crew still suspects you."[14]

ADVENTURE ISLAND'S BULGARIAN BRIDE

The summer of 1938 was not without tragedy. Near the end of the season, Alexander Macreff, a cook at Adventure Island Camp for Boys, found his wife of only three months unconscious in the couple's cabin. Anka Macreff, from Bulgaria, had spent most of the summer with relatives in Iron Mountain, Michigan, and had arrived in Door County just days earlier.

According to Macreff, Anka "complained that morning of needing further rest" after preparing breakfast. Marcreff returned at noon and found his wife lying on the bed. Two empty bottles of rubbing alcohol and a small bottle of hair tonic were nearby. By one account, "A boat was dispatched to the mainland and by two thirty in the afternoon Dr. Grota was on the scene." Grota left medicine to administer, should Anka regain consciousness. Meanwhile, two camp staff "spent ten hours rendering artificial respiration" to no avail. By nightfall, Anka had passed away.[15]

The next day, Sheriff Walter Otson chartered a boat with fisherman Henry Pelletier to retrieve the body. Officer Arthur Groski accompanied them. County coroner Elmer Christenson soon called an inquest by jury. Witness Skipper Kinney identified Macreff as a "close friend for a number of years." He testified that the couple had seemed "unusually happy" Friday morning, when he saw them together before he left the island to run errands in Sturgeon Bay. Anka had said "Good morning, Skipper" and seemed pleased when Kinney complimented her English.[16]

Macreff, however, sworn in after Kinney, told the six-man jury that his wife was despondent over difficulty learning the English language and adjusting to American customs. He had met her through his parents, who still lived in Bulgaria, where

Macreff had traveled to marry Anka. Macreff had immigrated to the United States as a boy and studied languages at the University of Illinois, Champaign–Urbana, earning BA and MA degrees. His wife was a registered nurse and a specialist in obstetrical cases.

The jury ruled Anka Macreff's death a suicide.[17]

12

Foreboding Winds, Dead Calm

I think the moon's a prisoner,
And in a palace kept—
A gloomy prison owned by Night;
The stars are tears she's wept.
—NANCY STERN, 1929 *PACK AND PADDLE*

February 1940 was a day longer than usual on the calendar because of the leap year. Kidy Mabley could have gone without it. Twenty-eight long and painful days were enough for her. Mabley's oldest daughter, Fanny, died at the Jewish Hospital of St. Louis from non-tubercular Addison's disease in February 1940. It was the second major incident members of the Meenahga family had endured that month. A few weeks earlier, Adeline "Tootsie" Peil's brother Roland Peil and his friend George Reinhardt had survived a horrible accident. They were driving over Lake Michigan toward Camp Meenahga in a truck loaded with ice blocks cut from Green Bay. Meenahga had no refrigeration, so workers cut ice from the bay each winter to store in a huge ice house. Camp masters used large tongs to lift and haul the frozen blocks into the kitchen ice boxes.[1]

On February 2, Peil's truck broke through thin ice and sank in twenty-five feet of water. As far as Clark was concerned, the forty- to sixty-cents-an-hour wage she paid for such work could hardly have been worth the trouble. The *Door County Advocate* told the story:

> Smashing one of the cab windows, Roland Peil, the driver, crawled out to safety and dragged his companion, George Reinhardt, with him just before the truck disappeared below the surface.
>
> Coast guards from the Canal and Baileys Harbor stations were called to rescue the truck. With Roy Brown of the Canal in charge, the crew worked from one o'clock Tuesday morning until dark and then from nine o'clock Wednesday until 4:15 in the afternoon before being successful.
>
> Except for the broken window, a dented fender, and a good soaking, the machine was little worse off for its dunking.[2]

Peil and Reinhardt kept at their work, come what may. Clark, and soon the United States, was determined to do the same.

WE CAN HOPE

Camp Meenahga opened for the 1940 season as Adolf Hitler's German army was completing a successful blitzkrieg campaign in France and much of Western Europe. News spread quickly when German forces occupied Paris on June 14. Meenahga girls had not been completely deaf to the conflict in Europe. "I remember specifically [the staff] talking about the Nazi encroachment and the fall of Austria in 1938," recalled Elizabeth Lanier DeRamus.[3] Regardless, life at Peninsula State Park and Camp Meenahga went on as usual.

For one thing, campers continued to sail. In July, Mabley's granddaughter Judy Clark Stephens wrote to her Aunt Polly,

"Last Saturday, another girl and I, with Mike [Orwig], sailed in the big race of the year, the Ephraim Regatta. It was loads of fun. The first time around it was fairly windy but the second time it was a dead calm. We came in sixth in the whole race which wasn't so very good. In the afternoon, Mike sailed in the championship race."[4] The following year, Orwig wrote in *Pack and Paddle,* "Sailing at Meenahga in 1941! What a variety of scenes and situations are recalled when we think of it. Breezy days and crisp white caps that sent spray flying back from the boat's bluff bows, drenching those who were sitting forward in the cockpit. Reefed sails dipping close to the leaping waves." Orwig reflected later in the summer that "with the world so terribly troubled, none of us can look clearly into the future, but we can hope. I have a hope and a wish. I hope that many of us, if not all, may be able to cast off from mooring in Fish Creek, and enjoy again such sailing moments as we've had this fine summer."[5]

Sailing was not Meenahga's only amusement that year. Girls "rolled about under the bell" three times a week when Chicago counselor Joan Greenberger introduced tumbling. Headstands, cartwheels, and balance tricks were part of an August exhibition. Even with so much going on, however, it was hard to be "on the beam" all the time. Pals Marianne "Peanuts" McDonald and Janice Chamberlaine wrote "Our Dip and Breakfast Trouble" to the playground tune "Cooties and Bedbugs" for the 1941 *Pack and Paddle*. A "counselor will get sore if one confessed feeling a mess," they lamented, "or didn't have enough zip for the early morning dip."[6] McDonald and her sister, Camille, who also attended Meenahga, grew up on Chicago's Lake Shore Drive. Peanuts returned to Meenahga for several years as a counselor. She later moved to England. In 1954, her friend Chamberlaine married Scott Pierce, brother of former First Lady Barbara Pierce Bush.[7]

WORLD WAR II AND CAMP MEENAHGA

On December 7, 1941, Japanese naval and air forces attacked the United States at Pearl Harbor in Hawaii. The next day, Congress declared war on Japan, and on December 11, it did the same against Germany. America was once again involved in a world war.

Just as they had during the Great War, Meenahga girls took up their part in the fight. Campers knitted afghans for the Red Cross and purchased war savings stamps each week, while striving to be "as good as good can be. That's the way to help our Uncle Sam. We can take care of sister and brother while Mother's at Red Cross. That's the way to help our Uncle Sam. Be truthful, loyal, and pure. That's the way to help Uncle Sam."[8]

The war came to Door County as well. "Occasionally," remembered Laurence Day,

> we would see German prisoners of war being transported on open, flat-bed army trucks, sitting silently facing each other, moving over Highway 42. The prisoners' camps were hidden quietly off somewhere on farms and there was no fraternizing allowed and no indication where they were located exactly. At least I didn't know. I think they may have used them for cherry-picking. Some people of German descent [living in Door County] tried to make contact with them, but that was quite frowned upon. They were our hated enemy then.[9]

During the summer of 1941, there was one camper at Meenahga who had already experienced the terror of World War II firsthand. Kathy Hinch had arrived in the United States via England, which had been at war with Germany since 1939.

Hinch wrote an essay titled "Air Raid" for *Pack and Paddle*. She described practicing air raid drills at her English boarding school. Hinch later evacuated to Wisconsin, where her aunt lived. Meanwhile, her missing parents became prisoners of war in Singapore.[10]

A MUTED REALITY

Beyond the sighting of German prisoners of war, residents of Camp Meenahga saw few reminders of the war in Europe and the Pacific. Campers continued to enjoy an idyllic life at Meenahga. Girls still canoed, often to Ephraim where they mailed postcards and purchased supplies after stopping for ice cream at Hanson's or Wilson's. Dinner was still served in the afternoon and songs still sung in the evening.

On one typical night in the 1940s, one camper wrote, after "a delicious . . . [meal] . . . of hamburgers, onions, and all the trimmings . . . Betty Remick dreamily sat at the piano and sang the bluesy 'Can't Stop Loving that Man of Mine.'"[11] Music remained just as popular and as much a part of camp life as ever. Girls spent "countless nights out on the porch," according to one camper, having "what is commonly termed a jam session with Jackie's 'Vic' going full tilt and stacks of records lying here and there. Over in one corner would be Bunch and the Duchess doing these fancy Louisville steps, while St. Louis would be going to town on the other side of the room, with Martha and Payne shinning."[12] Perry Como's "Girl of My Dreams" was likely one of those vinyl records, for a version of the tune, set to original lyrics, had appeared in *Pack and Paddle* in 1930:

> Camp of our dreams, we love you,
> Honest we do—you're our ideal.

Could we spend one summer more
On Green Bay shore,
Then life would be complete!

When we are about
Life is but a dream,
But we'll all come back again,
And after all's said and done,
There's only one
Camp of our dreams, it's you![13]

NO MATTER WHAT

Edith Leopold accepted an invitation from Clark to be a counselor at Camp Meenahga in 1940. Raised in Burlington, Iowa, Leopold eventually graduated from the University of Wisconsin–Madison, where her uncle, Aldo Leopold, had by 1940 become a renowned conservationist. Leopold planned to return to Meenahga for the 1941 summer but changed her mind. Instead, she became a first lieutenant in the US Women's Army Auxiliary Corps (WAAC) only months before the attacks at Pearl Harbor.

Other counselors did return to camp during the war. "I had not planned on coming back," remembered Grace Lanier Brewer. "I had already scheduled a visit to the local naval academy. . . . Mrs. Clark phoned and begged me to return for another season. She had staff shortages because the swimming counselor had been sick. I canceled my plans and returned to teach swimming in the summer of 1942. Mrs. Clark was a woman that any of her girls would help, no matter what."[14] Before long, however, Brewer's sense of duty to the United States won out. She joined the staff of the army hospital at Camp Campbell, Kentucky.

Many other Meenahga campers and counselors answered the call of duty. Wita Jones had "a very interesting job with the Red Cross in Birmingham, Alabama."[15] Brothers, sons, and camp masters enlisted, too. Benno Clark served in the Navy following his November 1942 marriage to Marjorie Bach. Mike Orwig joined the US Coast Guard as a boatswain's mate second class. While he was on duty, Orwig's thoughts turned to Door County and better times. He wrote the following letter, which Clark shared with all:

> August 25, 1942
>
> Dear Campers, Counselors, and "Commanding Officers" of Meenahga:
>
> This is your old Skipper "sounding off" to tell you how much he wishes he could be with you tonight. . . . As I write this, I have just come in from sea, and am glad to stand on firm ground for a few hours. The ocean was really wild on this trip. Green Bay was never like it, thank goodness. When the job that keeps me and so many of us from the places we'd like to be is victoriously ended, I want to smell the Wisconsin woods again and dip into fresh old Green Bay. Someone else can have the Atlantic Ocean, and I'll take Green Bay and its surrounding rocks and pines. I hope that the *Kelpie* has behaved herself, and that you have all had a good sailing season. . . . Let me wish my favorite sailor wish for you all: "Fair winds and fast passages for you throughout the coming year and always."[16]

Mike Orwig never saw Camp Meenahga or Green Bay again. During the second year of his tour, he returned to the United States to receive treatment for stomach problems, but he never recovered. Girls remembered how he dressed in a Scottish kilt to play the bagpipes at riding derbies and serenaded campers at dusk, ghost notes that wound through evergreen branches before drifting out over the bay.

MY HAPPINESS

In Door County and around the United States, local girls filled in for fathers, brothers, cousins, and friends fighting overseas. Sturgeon Bay and Manitowoc shipbuilders hired women to assemble submarines. Kewaunee shipbuilders recruited workers to make landing craft.[17] Clark continued to recruit camp masters from colleges and universities, though many now prepared young men for service during a twelve-week summer session. As such, there were few male upperclassmen or civilian students to hire. Clark wrote Albert E. Doolittle on April 20, 1942, expressing her concern at the situation: "It doesn't look as though we will be able to get any chore man for the job at hand, so we are trying to get three college boys to do as they did last year to take care of the life saving and keep the place in order."[18] Replied Doolittle: "Help is hard to find as every one that wants to work can go to one of the shipyards. We are going to be shy of men in the park and maybe, before the summer is over, they might have regulations and classifications for all. If so, I look for a drastic change for the men who are capable of doing defense work."[19]

Eventually, Clark managed to find help during the war. The young men she hired came from Missouri, Tennessee, and Indiana. Finding college girls to work as counselors was easier. Minerva Carr Canavan registered as a camper, but Clark, needing staff, asked her to help as a counselor. If Canavan agreed to do so, Clark would waive the camp fees but could not pay her wages. Canavan wrote that "I received no pay, didn't expect any, and in eight weeks I had one day off."[20] Clark also struggled to fill kitchen positions. During World War II, shipyard earnings were higher than the weekly pay Meenahga offered. Clark's solution to Meenahga's labor shortage was to recruit a few girls from St. Louis. Irene Mae Pringle Pruitt was fifteen years old in 1945, the year she took a bus from St. Louis to Sturgeon Bay. She joined local girls Marcella Gauger Desotelle, Joan LeClair, JoAnne Henry, and Carolyn Swenson. They "prepped vegetables and did the dishes" at Meenahga.[21] All needed money "mostly for school clothes. We had to buy our own. And some went toward buying our school books."[22] Irene saved some of her earnings to buy a wristwatch. "It cost me thirty dollars," she remembered. "I lined up a block-and-a-half to purchase it."[23]

Like counselors and campers, kitchen girls formed lasting friendships. Sometimes after work, they strolled into Fish Creek to enjoy an ice cream cone.[24] Some days they picnicked in Peninsula State Park or went sightseeing, driven through neighboring villages in Clark's car by a camp master. Back at camp, remembered Desotelle, "we could hear 'My Happiness' on the jukebox over the water. We would hear it at night, and fall asleep to it."[25]

MR. D RETIRES

An additional and unprecedented challenge of a different sort, one that had nothing to do with the onset of war, arrived during the early 1940s. Doolittle, the first and longtime superintendent of Peninsula State Park and a tireless supporter of Camp Meenahga, was not well. In April 1942, he had been hospitalized in Madison. Clark opened a letter to him, "I hope by now you are all settled in Fish Creek again and feeling your old self."[26] Doolittle responded, "I am still under the weather and can only walk short distances and very slowly at that. . . . As always, I will be so glad to help you in any way that I can. But that will have to be in an advisory way for I am only a cheerful old has-been and not much good anymore."[27]

Doolittle had ably created the blueprint for Peninsula State Park—the roads and trails, the campgrounds, the planting of tens of thousands of trees. His vision became his legacy. By 1942, Doolittle's steely will, which for decades had served him well, had turned cantankerous. To complicate matters, the lines between his state job and the cottages he personally owned and rented near the park entrance had become fuzzy. The fall before, Doolittle had been prompted to defend himself to C. L. Harrington, who then wrote to Harley MacKenzie about the matter. Doolittle did indeed mention his private cabins to park visitors who asked about overnight lodging, but he also recommended other Fish Creek accommodations to travelers.[28]

Around this time as well, Doolittle issued an ultimatum to Bob Newberry, a long-time and popular park ranger. Newberry could either correct past mistakes or be fired. Doolittle's written reprimand claimed Newberry had not turned camping fees over to Peninsula's young assistant manager, Ralf Halvorsen, as instructed. Doolittle said Newberry referred to Halvorsen by abusive names and had refused to meet on professional terms to settle the matter. "I am not forgetting, nor never will, your good qualities and the fact that you have so faithfully worked, early and late," wrote Doolittle to Newberry. Doolittle added, "Bob, it's up to you. Never too late after reading this and pondering over the situation. It is your next move."[29]

It turned out that Newberry's next move was to ask campers to support his plan to expose Doolittle's alleged use of state labor and materials for his private cabin business.[30] Doolittle countered by conducting an investigation. He sought sworn testimonies from park employees, then recorded their statements in an official capacity as a notary public. Statements went to character. According to testimony recorded by Doolittle, employee Roy

Grovogel described a time when Doolittle sent Newberry to find the whereabouts of Peninsula's sawmill crew.[31] It was storming. The group had sheltered in a cabin lawfully leased by Peninsula State Park worker Herman Krause. Newberry entered the cabin and picked a fight with Oscar Flock, who was lying on a bed. Newberry reportedly pulled out a knife and told Flock he "would cut his . . . heart out." Another man grabbed the weapon away. In the testimony recorded by Doolittle, Grovogel said that "he would doubly feel that treacherous acts were liable to happen to anyone that might have offended his dictatorship [referring to Newberry] as a straw-boss, especially if he had a drink of liquor."[32]

In the end, Doolittle's feud with Newberry was more of an ill-timed nuisance than any kind of tipping point. By this time, Doolittle's health was in serious decline. The Wisconsin Conservation Commission voted to put him at half pay. Doolittle was devastated. The schedule did not matter, wrote E. J. Vanderwall, director of the Commission, to Doolittle in February 1943, in an attempt to soften the blow. Vanderwall told Doolittle that he could work "half day, half week, every other day, every other week, part of a month, every other month, or even part of a year" and that the work could be inside or outside. He gently chided Doolittle about a recent fall on the ice when he had not followed the doctor's orders and for placing calls to Madison about matters that were "a closed issue and water over the dam." "You're like an old fire horse," wrote Vanderwall. "Each time the alarm bell rings, you feel that it is necessary to jump and run. How difficult it must be to suddenly become inactive and dismiss thoughts that have long been uppermost. You have worried about the affairs of Peninsula State Park long enough and from now on let someone else do the worrying . . . the entire program will go forward in an orderly way long after you and I are gone."[33]

Clark officially learned that Doolittle was out in March 1943, when Harrington wrote to her, answering a question she had asked about replacing the well at Meenahga. "I am inclined to feel that when this job is undertaken," Harrington wrote, "we will find that we will have to share the expense involved." He then told Clark that effective January 1, 1943, the Commission had voted to place Doolittle on the retirement list at half pay. Paul Lawrence, the park manager at Wyalusing State Park in Wisconsin, would be taking over.[34]

Doolittle passed away on March 22, 1944, at age seventy-four, shortly after his and Lettie's fiftieth wedding anniversary. He had been so upset at being ousted that he transferred his mother-in-law's grave from Blossomburg Cemetery elsewhere. Lettie lived several more years, residing in one of her cottages. In time, the Doolittles were laid to rest in Sturgeon Bay, but several Doolittle children and spouses later chose to be interred at Blossomburg Cemetery.

Upon Doolittle's death, the Commission issued a proclamation citing his untiring devotion to creating recreational features in Door County state parks, his great energy, and his forthright decisions and actions. Grand signatures nearly obscure one that is small and tightly looped into "Aldo Leopold."

TAINTED WELLS AND PORCELAIN THRONES

Clark maintained a professional and cordial relationship with Paul Lawrence. She sympathized when his wife was hospitalized soon after arriving at Peninsula State Park but otherwise kept her distance. Lawrence oversaw fixing the well at Meenahga and initiated a process to replace its toilets. During Lawrence's term, Clark signed another (Meenahga's sixth) five-year lease, the signing of which had been delayed a year by Doolittle's departure. This new lease stated the Commission's plan to discontinue the leasing of state park land for commercial enterprises. The names of Clark's sisters, Mary and Belle, and her daughter, Alice, appeared on the lease.

Lawrence's tenure ended up being very brief. Bill Beckstrom replaced him in 1944 after a successful career at Point Beach State Forest in Manitowoc County, Wisconsin. One of Beckstrom's first tasks in his new job was to make sure Camp Meenahga had working toilets, a job Lawrence had started. When Clark and her staff arrived for the 1944 summer season, they found that only six of twelve toilets functioned for a camp of a 108 people. Clark immediately wrote Harrington to complain, which caused Beckstrom to play defense. He wrote Harrington too, stating in detail that Clark had not tried to contact him about the broken toilets. Beckstrom admitted, however, that "the toilets and tank are not of the best and some have defective valves." The state had installed cast-off toilets from Devil's Lake State Park in Baraboo that were "quite old." Parts were therefore difficult to obtain. In the end, Harrington shouldered the blame, writing, "The item of the new toilets falls on us as it's not their fault that we didn't know what we were talking about in the first installation." The toilets were replaced but not until 1945.[35]

A PIVOTAL YEAR

More than two years into America's involvement in World War II, in 1944, a traditional Literary program at Camp Meenahga was given over to the dedication of a new flag made by Alice Clark Day. The flag had on it a star for every former Meenahga camper, camp master, and nurse in the armed forces.

After reciting the Pledge of Allegiance, Jeanette and Ruth Dennis, with brothers in the US Navy, carried in the flag.

Campers and counselors with close relatives in the service formed a *V* behind them. Alabama counselor Bubs Owens directed a Meenahga chorus, which sang "Song of Peace" from "Finlandia," by Finnish composer and violinist Jean Sibelius. K. K. Lee shared "O World," by George Santayana, reciting in part:

> O World, thou choosest not the better part!
> It is not wisdom to be one wise,
> And on the inward vision close the eyes,
> But it is wisdom to believe the heart.

Girls raised the flag and closed the ceremony with a singing of "America the Beautiful."[36]

Adolpha M. Meyer, a counselor from Missouri who spent the 1940 summer season at Meenahga, was among those honored. Meyer served as a second lieutenant in the US Army Nurse Corps, at much lower pay than her male counterparts. In 1942, she and other nurses were suddenly imprisoned at a civilian concentration camp at Santo Tomas University in Manila. They nursed about four thousand civilian prisoners, including survivors of the infamously brutal Bataan Death March. The nurses became known as the "Angels of Bataan," and Adolpha and her comrades remained in the Philippines until 1945.[37]

Back in Door County, Bill Beckstrom continued to be flummoxed by Clark's many requests for materials and services, such as mowing. Nor did things get easier for Beckstrom when the camp closed in October. That month, someone broke into the Lodge and destroyed the lock on the bread box and cut the screen on a cupboard. Nothing was missing, but Clark wrote Beckstrom to tell him, "I know that you will look in at the camp whenever you pass by, and I would appreciate your notifying me, and also the sheriff, if anything is amiss."[38]

TWO WONDERFUL THINGS

By 1945, Allied victory was drawing near. Months of tense anticipation stretched between Germany's surrender in May and Japan's defeat in August. "The war is a strenuous tiresome thing," wrote Lois Write and Lee Karchar in *Pack and Paddle*. "Death and tears [are] what it brings."[39] Camp fun hastened time. A clever announcement heightened anticipation for the annual counselor's party. Early on the day of the party, Clark pretended to read from the *Chicago Sun* and announced the opening of a new night club called Ce soir. When campers arrived at the Lodge, or Ce soir, they saw candlelit tables, crepe paper, and flower borders. Counselors had cleared space for a dance floor. Dressed in night gowns, counselors serenaded younger girls with popular songs such as "Someone to Watch Over Me." "Smoke Dreams" was a jazz standard sung at the event.[40]

Essays about impending triumph in the Pacific appeared in *Pack and Paddle*. Germany's surrender on May 7 inspired Kentuckian Harriet Chambers to write:

> It's come! At last the thing that every family has prayed for, and it's come! The war in Europe is over for sure, our men are on their way home and now there is rumor that peace is being established in the Pacific. If this is true, just think what this will be to us all. There will be no uncertainty for our fathers, brothers, husbands, or friends for they will be home within reach. The losses are great and there will be many once happy homes shattered. We can all thank God that our native land hasn't been shattered, so we can carry on, though we will always miss and remember these men who gave their lives. It will make us fight even harder to ward off the next war.[41]

Years later, counselor Anna "Grizzie" Griswold Nichols described 1945 this way: "Two wonderful things happened. They built a real bathhouse with flush toilets and hot and cold running water in the sinks and showers. . . . The other wonderful thing was that World War II ended."[42]

Peace came to the Pacific when Japan surrendered on August 15, 1945, after the United States dropped an atomic bomb on the Japanese city of Hiroshima on August 6 and another on Nagasaki three days later. Both Camp Meenahga and Adventure Island Camp for Boys heard about the bombs from US Army Air Force pilots. That summer, Claude Robinson, from Highland Park, Illinois, was Adventure Island's director. His wife Nancy's brother, Captain Theodore "Dutch" Van Kirk, had been granted a three-week leave from the US Army Air Force after a recent mission and had come to Door County to spend time with his family. Laurence Day was enrolled at Adventure Island Camp for Boys at the time. "We knew of the bomb being dropped," he remembered, "but had no idea what it was or meant." Nor did Day know immediately about Van Kirk's connection to the bomb. Dutch, age twenty-four, was navigator on the *Enola Gay*, the B-29 Superfortress bomber that dropped the bomb "Little Boy" on Hiroshima.[43]

Another war hero visited Camp Meenahga as well. Colonel James Howard, brother of former camper Martha Howard, visited about a week before V-J Day. Howard's flying prowess was already legendary. He'd single-handedly flown his P-51 Mustang into a swarm of thirty Luftwaffe fighters attacking American B-17s. A few years earlier, he'd joined the famous Flying Tigers in Burma. A native of St. Louis, Howard was six feet two inches of lanky muscles and broad shoulders. In time, he rose to the rank of brigadier general.[44]

On this visit, reported *Pack and Paddle* editors Marianne "Peanuts" McDonald and Jo Ann Straube, Howard spoke during lunch, "telling of the new discovery, the atomic bomb. He told us of the great damage it did in Japan and that he felt that soon the war would be over." On Sunday, August 12, Nancy Hamel mistakenly announced the war was over during Literary. "Shouts and screams of joy filled the air and many girls had a hard time singing 'The Star-Spangled Banner' amidst their tears of joy." After saying goodnight to Clark and Alice Clark Day, girls hurried off to bed only to awaken and learn that the news was a false alarm. For the next two days, "every camper at one time or another hurried into the Lodge to listen to the radio." Finally, five minutes after the dinner bell rang on Wednesday, came the report that Japan had surrendered. With joy and wonder, girls sang every patriotic song they could think of all during the meal and just as loudly as possible.[45]

13

Suddenly, Goodbye

> *I like to think that those who came here years ago and loved it as we do now come back in wind to stand guard during the longer summer nights.*
>
> —GRACE LANIER, 1938 *PACK AND PADDLE NEWS*

Another year came and went. Then, two weeks before camp opened in 1947, Alice Orr Clark received word that her cherished friend Elizabeth Crunden had passed away in St. Louis, one day shy of her eighty-second birthday. Gone now were many of the people who had been so instrumental in making Camp Meenahga a reality in 1916. Kidy Mabley had retired, and Albert E. Doolittle and Elizabeth Crunden had passed away.

Clark kept on course and did as she had for more than thirty years: she looked to the future. After Meenahga closed for the season in 1947, she wrote Harrington:

> We have one more year to run on this lease. We would like very much to have your assurance that we will have another five years or more lease before we make the repairs and improvements we feel are necessary. Naturally we do not wish to spend the amount we would have to spend if our lease is

> not renewed. We should also like your suggestions on the water supply and the purification of [the] same. The camp looks very lovely and we were proud of it this summer.[1]

Clark included in the letter a rent check for $600. Harrington acknowledged receipt of it in a letter dated November 18, 1947, adding:

> I note from your letter that you have one more season to operate in [Peninsula State Park]. We have not given any consideration as yet to just what will be done following the termination of the present contract. This is a subject, however, that I am sure we will have to take up for active consideration here before long.
>
> I have been wondering whether you have been making any moves to re-establish the camp at some other location. I have not looked over the present contract for some time, but my recollection is that it contains a stipulation that at the end of this particular period the camp was to be discontinued in the park, and of course the thought occurs as to whether or not you have been making any moves to bring this into effect. This would have a very important bearing on any improvements you might have in mind, including improvements to the domestic water supply.[2]

Quietly, Harrington had begun to search for possible new tenants, including the Girl Scouts of the USA. The Girl Scouts toured Meenahga before deciding to go elsewhere. As carefully as he could, Harrington was making his intentions known to Clark, who kept them, perhaps out of love for her campers, counselors, and Meenahga, to herself.

MEENAHGA'S FINAL YEAR

The 1948 season followed in turn. As girls like them had for more than thirty summers, campers paddled canoes singing the good old songs—songs imbued with memories—until the sun set and the melodies died away. Girls ambled along trails, stepping nimbly between patches of sunlight filtered by leaning birches and pines, letting their feet sink into the cool, damp earth.[3] In August, campers gathered Michaelmas daisies for the final banquet, cheered the Purple and Yellow teams, and sang songs such as:

> The time is growing very near
> When we must say goodbye.
> Another season finds its end
> But memories will not die.
> We owe you much, Meenahga,
> For all that you have done,
> For friends we've made
> And friendships gained,
> Meenahga, fare-thee-well.[4]

THE FINAL BANQUET

At the end of each season at Camp Meenahga, everyone gathered in the Lodge, including parents and special guests such as the Doolittles and Crundens, to enjoy a special banquet. In Meenahga's early years, Clark and Mabley dressed in long evening gowns and presided over the formal affair. Clark announced awards while Mabley lightened the mood with good humor as toastmistress. Each girl's seat at a table was marked with a personalized place card.[5]

Bowls with dainty purple asters and evergreen sprigs adorned the tables. The fireplace was banked with goldenrod and "the glorious purple and yellow bouquets of wildflowers, our camp colors, which we picked for decoration at our closing banquet. No one forbade us to pick wildflowers then," wrote Elaine Mabley, "only later not the blue gentian."[6] A beautiful arrangement of moss and wildflowers shaped in the letter *M* adorned the center table.

Chocolate devils were served at the end of a full-course meal. Clever counselors acted as toastmistresses after Mabley retired. Amusing themes shaped each banquet, inspired by the persona of the toastmistress. Counselors organized banquets around themes, such as father time, a chef with a cookbook, and the good ship *Meenahga,* the latter inspired by a Shirley Temple movie.

Banquets included telegrams from well-wishers and words of praise from the captains of the Yellows and the Purples. Counselors sang songs to the campers, and vice versa, with everyone extolled in a teasingly fun way. Campers sang this song to counselor Anna "Grizzie" Griswold Nichols:

> Oh, who's the cheerful southern gal
> Who always says, "How do"?
> Grizzie's Spanish dance was cute
> And boy, she can canoe.[7]

A delicate tinkling of a spoon against a glass hushed the crowd when Clark stood to announce the awards and name that year's Camp Spirit Girl. There was a breathless pause. When Clark revealed the name, "it was with an unforgettable mixture of tears and gladness in our hearts that we cheered."[8] Being so named was Meenahga's highest honor, bestowed upon the person who most expressed kindness, truth, and service. The names of camp spirit girls were etched on a silver cup.

Awards represented camp values.[9] Knowing right from wrong was not enough. A Meenahga girl had to embody sincerity, compassion, and tolerance.[10] Meenahga spirit meant playing to win, but playing fairly, for one's team, not one's self. Spirit, one camper wrote, is empathetic and seeks the virtues, not the faults, of fellow campers. It means playing the game to win, not for oneself, but for her side and, if defeated, knowing she played fairly and did her best. "And if, perchance, the spirit of mischief becomes too strong within her, she takes her punishment with a smiling face and acknowledgment of its fairness. She does nothing that may bring trouble or pain to anyone else."[11]

In 1940, swimming counselor Katherine "Sibbie" Sibley said as toastmistress to the crowd, "I am wishing for you, the present campers, many more seasons of happiness and inspiration here at Meenahga, so that you in turn may spread its [Meenahga's] spirit of loving fellowship—'camp spirit'—into the troubled world you may find away from here."[12] At the 1941 banquet, months before the United States entered World War II, Clark's son, Benno, declared that the purpose of Meenahga was "to instill in each and every one of you young women and girls the kind of stuff it takes to go out and do a real constructive job and in so doing to make it easier for you . . . to do it."[13]

When the banquet ended, the night was not quite over: "Remember," recalled one camper, "the prowling around after the banquet, with everyone loathe to go to bed before two o'clock in the morning? The Northern Lights helped us celebrate that night, too. We also heard rumors to the effect that there were lights down at the cemetery which had nothing to do with the north!"[14]

TIME TO CLOSE

Campers in 1948 probably had no idea they would be the last to leave Meenahga at the end of the season. The following

December, the Wisconsin Conservation Commission board prepared to offer a two-year extension on Clark's lease with the possibility of offering a lease that would extend through Clark's lifetime. The board was aware of roof repairs and other costly needs.[15] Whether the state made such an offer and whether Clark responded to it is unknown, as there are no corresponding files in the records.

If Clark realized that 1948 was Meenahga's last summer, she kept it a secret. Later that fall or perhaps early winter, she wrote from her St. Louis home at 316 Edgewood Drive:

> Dear Meenahga Girls All, from 1916 through 1948:
>
> There is always a beginning and by that same token there must be an ending. So, after thirty-three years of running Meenahga, many of them with my dear friend Mrs. F. W. Mabley as my partner, I feel that it is time to close and have our camp a very happy memory.
>
> I hope all the girls and counselors who have passed through its paths and forests will look back and feel, as do I, that Camp Meenahga has given them a wealth of joy, growth, and progress. I am sure that no one woman has gleaned as much solid satisfaction and happiness as I have. Each girl in the many years has given me more than she knows.
>
> Thanks to you all from the very first Meenahga-ite in 1916 to the very last one in 1948. My love and undying interest follows each one. My daughter, Alice Day, joins me in all that I say, and adds that she, too, will miss you and camp. Do keep in touch with us always.
>
> Yours in happy days,
> Alice Orr Clark[16]

Said Alice Clark Day of the closing, "Our lease with the State of Wisconsin had expired and my mother was getting along in years (an expression she never cared for), and so it was decided to close our beloved camp, our summer home for thirty-three years."[17] Clark McAdams Clifford, who had been a camp master at Meenahga in 1927, was then serving as an aide to President Truman. When he learned that Camp Meenahga would not open in the summer of 1949, he wrote a letter addressed to Clark, whom he referred to as "My dear Queen." Clifford wrote as well, "Sometime before we all have to depart this vale of tears, there should be a grand final banquet at which time we could all visit together and note with awe how time does wreck. My best to you Alice, and to you always."[18]

The grand adventure was over.

THE BIG SALE

Guido Rahr Sr. convinced his fellow Commission board members to allow Clark and Day to occupy camp in 1949 so that movable properties could be sold, and again in 1950, to make final arrangements. During the summer of 1949, Clark and Kidy Mabley hosted a Mabley-Clark reunion at Meenahga.[19]

To sell camp goods, Meenahga advertised a "big sale." Cots, mattresses, cabins and canoes, kitchen utensils, and all the rest were sold. The china embossed with the letter *M* was sold for practically nothing. A former camper bought the ship's bell that Doolittle had given to the camp. The sturdy white wicker furniture in the Lodge, sat upon by countless girls and witness to their giggles and tears, sold for a few dollars.[20]

In 1950, Clark and Day spent a bittersweet fortnight at the Cottage, settling the last of their Meenahga affairs. Day's husband and son, Laurence Sturgis Day and Laurence Clark Day, accompanied the women. That autumn, Laurence Sturgis Day fell from a ladder in St. Louis. He died from complications on December 17. Five years after camp closed, on May 14, 1953, Clark suffered a cerebral hemorrhage and passed away. She was seventy-seven. Mabley died three years later at the age of eighty-six.

MAPPING MEENAHGA TODAY

It seemed it would go on forever—the splash of canoe paddles, the nickering love talk of pampered American Saddlebreds, the thwacks of rackets against tennis balls. Even now, if one frees the imagination and walks the sylvan groves of old Camp Meenahga, little lake breezes sound like girlish whispers and dancing tree shadows melt into silhouettes. There, the triangle of a tent. There, the swishing curve of a horse's tail. And close by, the shape of a woman.

"Suddenly," wrote Lily Anne Peck in *Pack and Paddle*, "you want to see everything again" and look at everything you learned to love. "You run down the path, and see the beautiful lake with white caps topping its blue crests." The horizon looks far away. You turn, climbing up the hill where you see the little Cottage. You hurry past Tin Can Alley, Fifth Avenue, and "even . . . past Greenwich Village. When you get to the hill, there are two views waiting for you, the dear old riding ring . . . and on the left the archery field and amphitheater."[21] All was moved or razed decades ago. Forest, including patches of pine plantations, now covers it. Memories of fusty canvas smells and happy, hurried footsteps fill the empty spaces.

Camp Meenahga faced west, taking full advantage of glorious, ever-changing sunsets. "Chambers Island and the Strawberry Islands were clearly seen from our dock, our Lookout, our porch," remembered Alice Clark Day.[22] The dock is long gone. Bulky gray limestone steps, leading down to the water, lay lopsided, like uneven piano keys. The much-loved Lookout is a curving, crumbling arc of stones.

Remnants of other camp structures are just as tumbledown and elusive. Foundations are hidden beneath tangles of honeysuckle, smothered with thick, green moss. Aspens, maples, and cedar trees, grown up since 1948, sprout from stone fences and concrete slabs. Traces of camp continue to disappear.

Adeline "Tootsie" Peil wrote of the changes she saw. She wrote Alice Clark Day in 1976:

> My daughter and I drove up to [Peninsula State Park]—and finally came across the cement steps leading to the camp kitchen. No trace of where the Cottage once stood. It brought tears to my eyes, and I felt saddened at the loss of something that was dear to my heart. Truly the buildings should have remained for historical purposes. I can still visualize the old wallpaper on the Cottage wall . . . Julie (William) Peil, my sister-in-law, and I often reminisce [about] the good [old] camp days. Each summer was special."[23]

PERIWINKLE AND STONE FENCES

First, look for a thick mat of periwinkle. Presumptuous and pushy, this garden escape, when found in the woods, indicates the site of a former farm or cottage. It persists for decades, intent to preserve memory. At Meenahga, dark green, waxy leaves grow low to the ground east of where the Cottage once stood. In May, look for purple blooms.

Near the periwinkle, buried under brambles and weedy shrubs, the Cottage foundation lies in a heap. In this same area stood the nurse's tent. Pitched beneath a grand maple tree, it was, as a camper wrote in *Pack and Paddle,* "frequented quite often by the camp girls in need of medication to treat their cuts and bruises, and the 'prevalent' cases of poison ivy, which were treated with a good dousing of kerosene."[24]

Stone fences are another way the past survives on the Door County landscape. A stone fence tumbles in a broken line a few yards east of Shore Road. During Meenahga's time, the land between the fence and the Cottage was wide open. Another stone fence parallels the tennis court. Both likely date to the original Evenson farm.

The steep drive used by the Zachows to deliver groceries still exists as a park service road. Near it, a ground-level septic structure is just a few feet from the gravel. Close by is the pumphouse's concrete slab where Benno Clark etched his initials in 1922. The third structure, a low-slung fieldstone foundation from the Lodge, stretches several yards north of the pumphouse, then disappears into the woods.

The area to the north, between the Lodge foundation and the intersection of Shore and Skyline Roads, accommodated two or three tents for kitchen staff as well as a remote tent for camp masters and chore boys. Along with poison ivy, piles of rubble mark the ground. Rusty barrels entombed in concrete are nearby, the remains of a five-seater johnnie. What remains of the Club may be scattered along a ridge north of the tennis court.

Today, the tennis court looks unkempt. Past the tennis court is a deep, sweeping natural hollow. This was the amphitheater for tableaux vivants and music. Beyond the hollow, the land slopes down to a level place. Where the earth is flat, campers once played baseball, basketball, and rode horseback in the riding ring.

Close your eyes. Imagine. Listen. What remains, essentially, are stories.

THE BEST STORIES

The best stories, the ones worth telling over and over again, are those that happen in a certain place under unexpected circumstances. Characters discover strengths they had all along. In real time, events seem to happen by chance, yet, in hindsight, destiny is easier to see.

The best stories tell us something about ourselves, too. They remind us how to nurture (or know when to sever) relationships, and they tell us ways to love people and things in our lives, including the land. We grow and change and see ourselves in different characters with each retelling of the tale. First, we feel like the spirited camper learning to sail choppy waters. Another time, we see our lives reflected in the St. Louis girl who left home for the first time, traveling by day and night to work in a place far away. Later, we become the indomitable park superintendent, the steadfast friend.

Kidy Mabley, a young widow working hard to give the people she loved a happy life, might speak to us. Kidy Mabley the clever toastmistress, turned out in an evening gown at the final banquet, the one who made sure everyone was recognized in song or rhyme. Kidy Mabley the daring hiker, who climbed Sven's Tower and slept under the stars. Or perhaps the character who summons us most is Alice Orr Clark. Gentle. Resilient.

Stories unearth what is worth preserving. They reveal values, some of which we ascribe to and others we do not. Either way, the story of Camp Meenahga, "the merriest place on the whole Door County peninsula,"[25] is about taking risks, surviving loss, and the true worth of friendship.

Appendix: Camp Meenahga Roster

The appendix lists all known campers, counselors, staff, and others who either attended or worked at Camp Meenahga during its thirty-three-year history. Names were gathered through oral histories, shared in personal correspondence, and collected in the pages of *Pack and Paddle* and *Pack and Paddle News.*

Abernathy, Carol	Kansas City, MO	Camper	1944, 1946–1947
Abernathy, Joan	Kansas City, MO	Camper	1941–1942, 1944–1946
Adams, Maylo	Dubuque, IA	Counselor	1922
Adrian, Margaret	Unknown	Camper	1933
Agnew, Stanton	Kansas City, MO	Camp master	1924
Aikens, Virginia	Kansas City, MO	Counselor	1929
Allen, Clara	Louisville, KY	Camper	1919
Allen, Elizabeth	St. Louis, MO	Camper	1923
Allen, Frances	Louisville, KY	Camper	1919
Allen, Joan	Longmont, CO	Counselor	1943
Allen, Katherine	Louisville, KY	Camper	1919
Allen, Lillie	St. Louis, MO	Camper	1923
Allen, Louise	St. Louis, MO	Counselor	1946
Allen, Mrs. W. B.	Louisville, KY	Counselor	1919
Alt, Mary Ellen	Manitowoc, WI	Camper	1947
Ament, Donna Kay	Beverly Hills, CA	Camper	1944
Ammerman, Charles	Kirkwood, MO	Camp master	1941–1942
Amos, Amy	Unknown	Camper	1939
Antrim, Ruth Burlingame	St. Louis, MO	Camper	1943, 1945–1946
Apple, Gene	Unknown	Camp master	1937–1938
Apple, Martha Ann	Unknown	Camper	1938
Armstrong, Katherine	Evanston, IL	Camper	1928
Arnold, Elizabeth	Fort Benning, GA	Camper	1941
Arnold, Emily	Fort Benning, GA	Camper; counselor	1941, 1944
Arnold, Mary Louise	Evanston, IL	Camper	1929

Aston, Marjorie	Rolla, MO	Camper	1934
Atha, Julia Patsy	St. Louis, MO	Camper	1943–1944
Ator, Leslie Winnifred	Western Springs, IL	Camper	1945
Atwood, Elizabeth	Ferguson, MO	Camper; Camp Spirit Girl	1924–1925
Atwood, Ellen	Ferguson, MO	Club girl	1925
Atwood, Frederica	Madison, WI	Camper	1919
Atwood, Katherine	Ferguson, MO	Counselor	1924–1925
Austrian, Alma Jane	Chicago, IL	Camper	1921–1923, 1925
Austrian, Margaret	Chicago, IL	Camper; Club girl	1921–1922, 1924–1925
Avery, Virginia	Kansas City, MO	Camper	1919–1920, 1922–1923
Babcock, Anne	Louisville, KY	Camper	1933–1934
Babcock, Blandina	Glenview, KY	Camper	1943
Bagley, Jane	Unknown	Camper	1938
Bagnell, Jane	Nelson, MO	Camper	1928
Bair, Deborah	St. Louis, MO	Camper	1946
Baker, Carlota Grace	Staunton, IL	Camper	1945
Baker, Grace C.	Staunton, IL	Adult staff	1945
Baker, Shirley	Omaha, NE	Camper	1943
Baldwin, Mayre	St. Louis, MO	Camper	1946
Baldwin, Ruth	Kenosha, WI	Camper; counselor	1937–1941
Ball, Betty	Chicago, IL	Camper	1922
Ball, Gloria	Unknown	Swimming instructor	1939
Ballard, Elizabeth	St. Louis, MO	Camper	1917
Ballenger, Janet Bond	Memphis, TN	Camper	1945
Bank, Barbara	Evanston, IL	Camper	1946
Barber, Julia	New York City, NY	Counselor	1920
Bard, Janet	Highland Park, IL	Camper	1926
Barnard, Barbara	Clayton, MO	Camper	1947
Bartholf, Beatrice	Glencoe, IL	Camper	1921–1922
Baskerville, Latham	Chicago, IL	Camp master	1918
Bass, Doris	Unknown	Camper	1933
Bass, Ruth	St. Louis, MO	Camper; Club girl	1920–1921
Baur, Edmee	St. Louis, MO	Camper	1921–1922
Bay, Barbara	St. Louis and Sikeston, MO	Camper	1920–1921
Bay, Betty	St. Louis, MO	Camper	1924–1926
Bay, Virginia	St. Louis, MO	Camper	1926

Beach, Eleanor	Kansas City, MO	Counselor	1922
Beck, Anne	Sikeston, MO	Camper	1924
Beck, Elise	St. Louis, MO	Counselor; assistant director junior camp; director junior camp	Unknown
Beck, Merrit-Paige	Baltimore, MD	Camper	1924
Becker, Barbara	Elm Grove, WI	Camper	1944–1946
Becker, Jane	St. Louis, MO	Camper	1940–1941
Becker, Joan	Elm Grove, WI	Camper	1944–1946
Becker, Mrs. A. Jack	Clayton, MO	Junior camper supervisor	1941
Becker, Patricia	St. Louis, MO	Camper; Camp Spirit Girl	1938, 1940–1943
Bennett, Beverly	Milwaukee, WI	Camper	1921–1922
Bennett, Virginia	St. Louis, MO	Camper	1920
Berg, Anita	Unknown	Camper	1916
Berg, Hans	Milwaukee, WI	Riding master	1917–1924
Berger, Margaret	Unknown	Camper	1946
Bergh, Marilyn	Omaha, NE	Camper	1943
Bergner, Grace	St. Louis, MO	Counselor	1941
Bergs, Peggy	St. Louis, MO	Camper	1924
Bergstrom, Elizabeth	Neenah, WI	Camper	1929
Bergstrom, Marjorie	Unknown	Camper	1933
Berkley, Georgia Lee	St. Louis, MO	Camper	1945–1946
Berrien, Stephanie	St. Louis, MO	Camper	1944
Bertha, Marjorie	Chicago, IL	Camper	1925
Bethel, Emily	Louisville, KY	Camper	1921
Bettman, Irene R.	St. Louis, MO	Camper	1943–1946
Bhirdo, Elizabeth	Door County, WI	Kitchen staff	1933
Bhirdo, Evelyn (Franke)	Door County, WI	Kitchen staff	1933
Bhirdo, Olive	Door County, WI	Kitchen staff	1933
Bhirdo, Sydney	Door County, WI	Chore boy	Unknown
Bick, Aloyse	Clayton, MO	Camper	1943
Bick, Barbara	Clayton, MO	Camper	1943
Bick, Marjorie	Omaha, NE	Camper	1943
Bilderback, Millicent	Champaign, IL	Camper	1939–1941, 1944
Binkley, Reba	Tulsa, OK	Counselor	1922
Bisbee, Patricia	St. Louis, MO	Camper	1933–1934

Bischoff, Marion Moreno	Clayton, MO	Camper	1945–1946
Bishop, Mary	Indianapolis, IN	Counselor	1945–1946
Bissel, Emily	Unknown	Camper	1916
Black, Bonney	St. Louis, MO	Camper	1922
Blair, Katherine	St. Louis, MO	Camper	1919–1920
Blair, Mary	St. Louis, MO	Camper	1921
Blair, Nancy	St. Louis, MO	Camper	1920–1921
Blake, Anne Lanier	Tampa, FL	Camper	1946
Blakeman, Ann	Unknown	Camper; counselor	1938–1939
Blanchard, Elizabeth	Detroit, MI	Camper	1920
Bland, Isabelle	St. Louis, MO	Camper; Camp Spirit Girl	1929–1930
Blaul, Elizabeth	Burlington, IL	Camper	1924, 1926
Block, Helen	Chicago, IL	Camper	1929–1930
Block, Marjorie	Chicago, IL	Camper	1924–1927
Block, Madeline	Chicago, IL	Camper	1918–1919
Blyth, Helen	Unknown	Camper	1930
Bock, Dorothy	Chicago, IL	Counselor	1926–1927
Bodley, Edith	Louisville, KY	Camper	1918
Bogges, Elizabeth	Louisville, KY	Camper; counselor	1920, 1926
Boggess, Katherine	Louisville, KY	Camper	1920
Bollman, Mari	St. Louis, MO	Camper	1917
Bond, Edith	Manhattan, KS	Dancing, physical training counselor	1916–1917
Bond, D. Jane	Madison, WI	Counselor	1942–1943
Bond, Mary Scudder	St. Louis, MO	Club girl	1927
Boohger, Sarah	St. Louis, MO	Camper	1920
Boulden, Ruth	St. Louis, MO	Counselor	1922–1923
Boulicault, Dione	Clayton, MO	Camper	1941
Bowe, Julie Ann	Chicago, IL	Camper	1941
Bowen, Mary Katherine	Hibbing, MN	Camper	1929–1930, 1933–1934
Bowerman, Elizabeth	Buffalo, NY	Camper	1920
Bowers, Frances	Unknown	Camper	1930
Bowman, Dr. Dora	LaGrange, IL	Doctor	1926
Boyd, Ann	Highland Park, IL	Camper	1943
Boyd, Emily	Kirkwood, MO	Camper	1927
Boyd, Martha	Appleton, WI	Camper	1934–1935

Boyer, Elizabeth	Unknown	Camper	1930
Brach, Barbara	Evanston, IL	Camper	1929
Bradley, Gertrude	Milwaukee, WI	Camper	1919
Bradley, Mary Earle	Birmingham, AL	Camper	1943
Bradshaw, Frances	St. Louis, MO	Camper	1919
Bramham, Janet	Oshkosh, WI	Camper	1921
Brand, Viginia	Kansas City, MO	Camper	1922
Brehner, Robert	Green Bay, WI	Camp master	1946
Brennemann, Barbara	Winnetka, IL	Camper	1929
Brennemann, Deborah	Winnetka, IL	Camper	1929
Brennemann, Mary	Winnetka, IL	Counselor	1927–1928
Brent, Ellison Kelly	Kansas City, MO	Camper	1943–1944, 1946
Brewer, Corrine	Chicago, IL	Camper	1921
Brewer, Frances	Columbia, MO	Counselor	1924–1926
Brewer, Louise	Chicago, IL	Camper	1921–1922
Briggs, Adeline	Madison, WI	Camper	1918
Bristle, Elizabeth	Evanston, IL	Camper	1928
Bromley, Katherine	Birmingham, MI	Camper	1920
Brosius, Genevieve	Lock Haven, PA	Counselor	1920
Broughton, Janet	Burlington, IA	Counselor	1927
Brown, Elizabeth	Unknown	Camper	1937
Brown, Evelyn	Chicago, IL	Counselor	1924
Brown, Harriet	Peoria, IL	Counselor	1924
Brown, Marjorie	Chicago, IL	Camper	1918
Brown, Nina	Indianapolis, IN	Camper	1927–1928, 1930, 1933
Browning, Connie	Winnetka, IL	Camper	1946
Bruce, Wilma	Marshall, MO	Camper	1929
Bruckner, Katherine	Dallas, TX	Camper	1918–1919
Buckley, Virginia	Joliet, IL	Camper	1946
Buell, Elizabeth	Dallas, TX	Camper	1919
Buford, Nancy Ann	Clayton, MO	Camper	1947
Bugbee, Martha	St. Louis, MO	Camper; Camp Spirit Girl	1929–1930
Buhl, Jacqueline	Highland Park, IL	Camper	1928
Bunting, Barbara	Kansas City, MO	Camper	1919–1921
Burch, Rachel	Winnetka, IL	Camper	1943
Burdick, Ruth	Unknown	Counselor	1930
Burge, Lydia	Louisville, KY	Camper	1918
Burge, May Norris	Louisville, KY	Camper	1921
Burke, Elizabeth	Kansas City, MO	Camper	1928
Burke, Jane	Champaign, IL	Camper	1940

Burnett, Ann	St. Louis, MO	Camper	1921
Burnett, Halstead	Unknown	Adult staff	1916
Burnett, Margaret	Unknown	Adult staff	1916
Burnett, Mary Ann	St. Louis, MO	Camper	1924–1926, 1928–1929
Burnham, Amanda	Cincinnati, OH	Camper	1922–1925
Burnham, Nancy	Cincinnati, OH	Camper; Club girl	1924–1925, 1928
Burr, Mary Jessie	St. Louis, MO	Camper	1921
Bush, Charlotte	Detroit, MI	Camper; Club girl	1922, 1927
Bush, Catherine Eloise	St. Louis, MO	Camper	1923
Butcher, Martha	Danville, IL	Camper	1926
Butterworth, Elizabeth	Columbus, OH	Camper	1929–1930
Byfield, Gene	Chicago, IL	Camper	1940
Byfield, Rita	Winnetka, IL	Camper	1939–1940
Cabanne, May	St. Louis, MO	Camper; Club girl	1917, 1922
Cady, Elizabeth	Detroit, MI	Camper	1924–1925, 1927
Cady, Mr. and Mrs. (Marie)	Unknown	Assistant riding masters	1930
Cale, Julian	St. Louis, MO	Camp master	1926
Calhoun, Margaret	St. Louis, MO	Counselor	1944
Calhoun, Phyllis	St. Louis, MO	Camper	1943–1944
Calkins, Marion	Madison, WI	Counselor	1925
Canavan, Constance	St. Louis, MO	Camper	1943–1944
Canavan, Minerva	St. Louis, MO	Camper; counselor; Camp Spirit Girl	1943–1945
Campbell, Elizabeth	St. Louis, MO	Camper; Camp Spirit Girl; counselor	1933–1935, 1940
Campbell, Mr. and Mrs. Gordon	Chicago, IL	Adult staff	1929
Cameron, Betty	Milwaukee, WI	Counselor	1922
Cardine, Laver	Cincinnati, OH	Camper	1921–1923
Carlson, Janet	Washington, DC	Camper	1934
Carr, Catherine	St. Louis, MO	Counselor	1927–1929
Carr, Julia	St. Louis, MO	Unknown	1944
Carr, Julia Ann	St. Louis, MO	Camper	1944–1945
Carruth, Eleanor	Chillicothe, OH	Camper	1925–1926
Carruth, Letitia	Chillicothe, OH	Camper	1925–1926
Carson, Bill	Burlington, IA	Camp master	1917

Carson, Louise Antoinette	Burlington, IA	Camper; Club girl	1919–1925, 1927
Carver, Clay	New Canaan, CT	Camp master	1946
Castle, Janet	Geneva, IL	Camper	1927–1928
Castle, Peggy	Geneva, IL	Camper	1925–1927
Castrillon, Nancy	Clayton, MO	Counselor	1946
Caswell, John	New Haven, CT	Camp master	1921–1923
Cates, Ellen	Burlington, IA	Camper	1943
Cella, Eloise	St. Louis, MO	Camper	1946
Chadeayne, Ann Revell	St. Louis, MO	Counselor	1941–1942
Chadeayne, Deborah	St. Louis, MO	Camper	1941
Chadeayne, Marilee	St. Louis, MO	Counselor	1942
Chamberlain, Elaine	Unknown	Camper	1939
Chamberlaine, Diane	Evanston, IL	Camper	1938–1941
Chamberlaine, Janice	Evanston, IL	Camper	1940–1941
Chambers, Harriet Roper	Louisville, KY	Camper	1945
Chaplin, Al	Chicago, IL	Camp master	1933
Chaplin, Alice	Clayton, MO	Counselor	1929
Chapman, Alice Louise	St. Louis, MO	Camper	1920–1921
Chapman, Alice Ruth	St. Louis, MO	Camper	1924
Chapman, Eliza	Louisville, KY	Camper	1919
Chapman, Jacqueline	St. Louis, MO	Camper	1921
Chapman, Joanna	Highland Park, IL	Camper	1924–1925, 1927
Chapman, Joy	Bloomington, IL	Counselor	1946
Chapman, Louise	Louisville, KY	Camper	1919–1920
Chapman, Lulubelle	Berlin, WI	Camper	1927
Chester, Connie	Unknown	Camper	1935
Chevrolet, Lillian	Birmingham, MI	Club girl	1926
Chilson, Nancy	Green Bay, WI	Camper	1942
Chivvis, Barbara	St. Louis, MO	Camper	1934–1935, 1937
Chivvis, Jane	St. Louis, MO	Camper	1933–1935, 1938
Chivvis, Mary Ellen	St. Louis, MO	Camper; Camp Spirit Girl	1929, 1931, 1934–1935
Christensen, Chris	Unknown	Riding master	1925–1933
Church, Eleanor Clark	St. Louis, MO	Counselor	1922
Church, Louise	St. Louis, MO	Camper	1922–1923
Churchill, Alice	Chicago, IL	Camper	1919
Claggett, Dorothy	St. Louis, MO	Camper	1917
Clarahan, Doris	St. Louis, MO	Camper	1934

Clark, Alice (Day)	St. Louis, MO	Camper; counselor; Club girl; director	1916–1927, 1944–1948
Clark, Alice Orr	St. Louis, MO	Director	1916–1948
Clark, Benjamin	St. Louis, MO	Camp visitor; camp master	1916–1926
Clark, Freda	Detroit, MI	Club girl	1923
Clark, Holly	Alton, IL	Camper	1917
Clark, Janice	Dundee, IL	Counselor	1946
Clark, Judith Margaret	Burlington, IA	Camper; Camp Spirit Girl; counselor	1937–1941, 1945
Clark, Lena	St. Louis, MO	Camper	1922–1923
Clark, Louise	Burlington, IA	Camper	1943–1944, 1946
Clark, Polly	Burlington, IA	Club girl	1924
Clarke, Barbara	Chicago, IL	Camper	1944
Clarkson, Marie	St. Louis, MO	Camper; counselor	1917–1918, 1922
Clifford, Clark McAdams	St. Louis, MO	Camp master	1927
Clifford, Alice	St. Louis, MO	Counselor	1926–1928
Clifford, Anna Margaret	Madison, WI	Counselor; Club girl	1923, 1925
Clough, Barbara	Kansas City, MO	Camper	1919
Clough, Beatrice	Kansas City, MO	Camper	1919
Coghian, Peggy	Ladue, MO	Camper	1943
Cole, Margaret	Sappington, MO	Camper	1941–1944
Cole, Wallace	St. Louis, MO	Sailing instructor	1947
Coleman, Elizabeth	Louisville, KY	Camper	1924
Collins, Anne	Ferguson, MO	Camper	1946–1947
Collins, Bernice	Unknown	Camper	1916
Comey, Margaret	Cleveland Heights, OH	Camper	1928
Conard, Mrs. B. D.	St. Louis, MO	Junior camp assistant director	1921–1924
Conard, Catherine Lee	St. Louis, MO	Camper; Club girl	1920–1924
Condie, Bertha	Ferguson, MO	Club girl	1922
Connor, Constance V. J.	Marshfield, WI	Camper	1923

Conrad, Mrs.	Unknown	Junior camp director	1922
Converse, Marys	Louisville, KY	Counselor	1941
Conway, Joan	St. Louis, MO	Camper	1918
Conzelman, Jane	St. Louis, MO	Camper	1920
Cook, Elizabeth	Tulsa, OK	Camper	1921–1922
Cooke, Cynthia A	Geneva, IL	Camper	1924, 1926
Cooley, Thomas	Detroit, MI	Camp master	1929
Corbett, Catherine	Plymouth, WI	Counselor	1924
Corley, Erwin	Clayton, MO	Camper	1947
Corlis, Catherine	St. Louis, MO	Camper	1917
Cornils, Thade "Ted"	Chicago, IL	Riding master	1934–1947
Coulter, Jean	St. Louis, MO	Camper	1945
Courtenay, Mary Ann	Louisville, KY	Counselor	1945
Cralle, Joan Lee	Louisville, KY	Camper	1945–1946
Cramer, Dorothy	Webster, MO	Camper	1917
Crane, Mary Ellen	Milwaukee, WI	Camper; counselor	1939, 1941
Craven, Lucille	Kansas City, MO	Counselor	1921–1922
Crawford, Ann	Omaha, NE	Camper	1943
Crawford, Barbara	Louisville, KY	Camper	1941–1945
Crawford, Martha	Cleveland, OH	Counselor	1926
Crawford, Mary	Louisville, KY	Camper	1944–1946
Crissey, Carol	Geneva, IL	Camper	1945–1946
Crocker, Carol	Chicago, IL	Camper	1947
Crocker, Nancy	Chicago, IL	Camper	1947
Crosby, Ada	St. Louis, MO	Camper	1924–1925, 1927
Crosby, Elizabeth	St. Louis, MO	Camper	1924–1925, 1927
Crosby, Viola	St. Louis, MO	Club girl	1927
Crowell, Janet	St. Louis, MO	Camper	1946
Cullin, Jean	Clayton, MO	Camper	1943
Cunliff, Eleanor	Clayton, MO	Camper	1943–1944
Cunliff, Martha	St. Louis, MO	Camper	1926
Cunningham, Carol	Louisiana, MO	Camper	1943
Curby, Ruth	St. Louis, MO	Camper	1921–1922
Currie, Sally Ann	St. Louis, MO	Counselor	1940–1942
Curry, Florence	Unknown	Camper	1927, 1930
Czirr, Betty Jean	Oak Park, IL	Camper	1947
Dalton, Lynn	Fish Creek, WI	Camper	1946
Dalton, Sara Lynn	Fish Creek, WI	Camper	1945

Danforth, Mary Louise	Washington, IL	Camper	1920–1921
Darlington, Carlyn	Louisville, KY	Camper	1924
Darlington, Margaret Evelyn	Cincinnati, OH	Camper; Club girl	1924–1928
Darly, Esther	Kirkwood, MO	Camper	1918
Darly, Nell	Kirkwood, MO	Camper	1918
Dauchy, Barbara	Chicago, IL	Camper	1926–1927
Davies, Elizabeth	Racine, WI	Camper	1918–1919
Davies, Nancy	La Grange, IL	Camper	1947
Davis, Adell	St. Louis, MO	Camp cook	1916–1926
Davis, Bill	St. Louis, MO	Handyman	1916–1926
Davis, Catherine	St. Louis, MO	Camper	1924
Davis, Elinor	St. Louis, MO	Counselor	1928–1930
Davis, Jane	Unknown	Camper	1930
Davis, Jean	Glencoe, IL	Camper	1942–1943
Davis, Mary	Clayton, MO	Camper	1941
Davis, Mary Carter	St. Louis, MO	Camper; counselor	1917, 1920, 1924
Davis, Mary Isabel	Pontiac, MI	Camper	1921–1922, 1924
Day, Eleanor	Indianapolis, IN	Camper	1924
Dazey, Suzanne	Unknown	Camper	1933
Dean, Anne	Unknown	Camper	1933
Dean, Dorothy	Unknown	Camper	1933
Dean, Helen	Kansas City, MO	Camper	1920
Deane, Garrett	Fulton, MO	Camp master	1940
Deateale, Carol	Louisville, KY	Camper	1944
De Camp, Cecilia	St. Louis, MO	Counselor	1921–1922
Dehn, Alice	Burlington, IA	Counselor	1944
Deibel, Julianne	St. Louis, MO	Camper; counselor	1945–1947
Deicke, Georgia Lou	Clayton, MO	Counselor	1944–1945
Deicke, June	Clayton, MO	Counselor	1945–1946
De Jacobs, Matilda	Mexico City, Mexico	Camper	1923
Dennig, Bobby	Unknown	Camper	1937–1938
Dennis, Jean	Cleveland, OH	Camper	1928
Dennis, Jeanette	Kansas City, MO	Camper	1944–1946
Dennis, Ruth	Kansas City, MO	Camper	1943–1946
Denny, Harriet	Indianapolis, IN	Camper	1927
Denny, Margaret	Indianapolis, IN	Counselor	1926–1927, 1929
Deslage, Ann	Unknown	Camper	1937
DeWitt, Joan	St. Louis, MO	Camper	1946–1947

Dexter, Helena	Milwaukee, WI	Camper	1920
Dickey, Gladys	St. Louis, MO	Camper; counselor	1917–1919
Dicks, Jean	Unknown	Counselor	1937–1938
Dickson, James	Evanston, IL	Camp master	1924
Disbrow, Marie	Kirkwood, MO	Camper	1920
Disbrow, Terry	St. Louis, MO	Camper	1944
Dittman, Jane	St. Louis, MO	Camper	1922
Dix, Mary	St. Louis, MO	Camper	1919
Dixon, Gladys	St. Louis, MO	Adult staff –swimming	1916
Doane, Olivia	Burlington, IA	Camper	1917–1918
Dobbratz, Verna	Milwaukee, WI	Camper	1922–1923
Dodd, Charles	Evanston, IL	Camp master	1923
Dodson, Eleanor	Unknown	Camper	1916
Doe, Arthur	Milwaukee, WI	Camp master	1917
D'Oench, Jean	Creve Coeur, MO	Camper	1947
Donnell, Susan	Findlay, OH	Camper	1946–1947
Doolittle, Ruth	Fish Creek, WI	Camper	1921–1922, 1924
Dorchester, Jeannette	Sturgeon Bay, WI	Camper	1943
Dorsey, Suzanne	St. Louis, MO	Camper	1934
Downes, Margaret Ellen	Oshkosh, WI	Camper	1926–1927
Droegemueller, Joan	Winnetka, IL	Camper	1943
Duen, Alleen	St. Louis, MO	Camper	1917
Dugger, Louise	St. Louis, MO	Camper	1917
Dumesnil, Ann	Unknown	Camper	1937
Duncan, Sarah	St. Louis, MO	Camper	1946–1947
Dunnagan, Helen	University City, MO	Counselor	1924
Durrie, Janet	Madison, WI	Camper	1918
Dyas, Aida	St. Louis, MO	Camper	1926–1927
Dyer, Alice	Chicago, IL	Camper; counselor	1918–1923, 1927
Dyer, Esther	Chicago, IL	Camper; counselor	1918–1919, 1921–1922
Dyer, George Turnley	Chicago, IL	Camp master	1920–1922
Dyer, Nancy	West Chicago, IL	Camper	1946–1947
Dyer, Willis	St. Louis, MO	Camper; Club girl	1918, 1927
Eames, Judith B.	Chicago, IL	Counselor	1926
Eaton, Martha	Burlington, IA	Camper	1940–1941

Edler, Louise	St. Louis, MO	Camper	1918
Edmunds, Dean	St. Louis, MO	Camp master	1918
Edwards, Louise	Unknown	Camper	1919–1920
Edwards, Mary Saffell	Lawrenceburg, KY	Camper	1940
Eichengreen, Lucille	Chicago, IL	Camper	1919
Eitel, Elva	Highland Park, IL	Camper	1928
Ellis, Betty Jane	St. Louis, MO	Camper	1927, 1930
Elwell, Anne	Western Springs, IL	Camper	1929
Elwood, Virginia	Unknown	Camper	1933
Embry, Elizabeth	Louisville, KY	Camper	1921
Embry, Marjorie	Louisville, KY	Camper; counselor	1917, 1921–1922
Endicott, Betty	Birmingham, MI	Camper	1923
Endicott, Ruth	Birmingham, MI	Camper	1923
Engelsman, Elsa	Webster Groves, MO	Camper	1921
Engelsman, Lucille	St. Louis, MO	Camper	1919
Epstein, Edna	Chicago, IL	Camper	1923–1924
Epstein, Elsa	Chicago, IL	Camper	1921
Epstein, Lucille	Chicago, IL	Camper	1921, 1923–1924
Ericson, Barbara	Unknown	Camper	1934
Erickson, Hazel	Beloit, WI	Counselor	1920
Erickson, Irene	Anoka, MN	Counselor	1922–1923
Erickson, Irene	St. Louis, MO	Counselor	1926
Erlanger, Margaret	St. Louis, MO	Camper	1923
Erlanger, Ruth	St. Louis, MO	Camper	1923
Espy, Carlotta	Savannah, GA	Camper	1921
Espy, Elsie	Milwaukee, WI	Camper	1921
Eubank, Annabelle Cowles	Shelbyville, KY	Camper	1945
Evans, Amy	Evanston, IL	Counselor	1943
Evans, Amy Louise	Grosse Pointe Shores, MI	Counselor	1945
Evans, Eugenia	St. Louis, MO	Camper; Club girl	1926–1928
Evans, Julia	St. Louis, MO	Camper	1921–1922
Evans, Mary Louise	St. Louis, MO	Camper	1926, 1928
Evans, Nancy	Unknown	Adult staff	1935
Evans, Vera	Wichita, KS	Camper	1923
Everhard, Nancy	Hinsdale, IL	Camper	1943
Evers, Mary	Unknown	Camper	1916
Evers, Sarah	Unknown	Camper	1916

Evert, Mary	Milwaukee, WI	Camper	1937–1938, 1940
Ewing, Jane	New York, NY	Camper	1928
Fairchild, Elizabeth	Omaha, NE	Camper	1917–1921
Fairchild, Helen	Ontario, Canada	Counselor	1920
Fairfield, Elizabeth	New York, NY	Counselor; Club girl	1922, 1926–1927
Fairfield, Wynne	Omaha, NE	Camper; Club girl	1917–1922
Fairweather, Frances	Chicago, IL	Camper	1927
Falk, Marian	Clayton, MO	Camper	1944
Fancher, Janet	Evanston, IL	Counselor	1947
Fantoni, Elena Margaret	Ravinia, IL	Camper; counselor	1920, 1923–1924
Farrell, Dorothy	Jacksonville, IL	Camper	1920
Farson, Frances Jane	Geneva, IL	Counselor	1925
Fatheringham, Arline	St. Louis, MO	Camper	1929
Fearing, Gertrude	Ravinia, IL	Camper	1920–1921
Fearing, Iola	Highland Park, IL	Camper	1922
Feldman, Helen	Kirkwood, MO	Camper	1917
Feldon, Nancy	Winnetka, IL	Camper	1943
Felman, Barbara	Joliet, IL	Camper	1946–1947
Felman, Nancy	Joliet, IL	Camper	1944–1946
Felman, Patricia Stephanie	Joliet, IL	Camper	1945–1947
Felten, Katherine	Chicago, IL	Camper	1924–1925
Finerty, Alleyne	Oklahoma City, OK	Camper	1921
Fischel, Susan	St. Louis, MO	Counselor	1944
Fischer, Margaret	Webster Groves, MO	Camper; counselor; Camp Spirit Girl	1941, 1943–1944, 1946
Fischer, Judy	Clayton, MO	Camper	1941
Fischer, Mary Jane	St. Louis, MO	Camper	1938–1940
Fischer, Mrs. Ira	Webster Groves, MO	Camp banker	1943–1944
Fischer, Peggy	Webster Groves, MO	Camper	1943
Fish, Janet	Webster Groves, MO	Camper	1926–1927
Fish, Marjorie	Webster Groves, MO	Camper; counselor	1920, 1926, 1928
Fishback, Ruth	Indianapolis, IN	Camper	1933–1934
Fishback, Sophie	St. Louis, MO	Camper	1917
Fisher, Barbara	Chicago, IL	Camper	1947
Fisher, Elizabeth	Evanston, IL	Camper	1928

Fisher, Katherine	Kansas City, MO	Counselor	1923
Fisher, Mary Jane	Unknown	Camper	1937
Fisher, Peggy	Webster Groves, MO	Camper	1942
Fiske, Mary Katherine	Kirkwood, MO	Camper	1943
Fitch, Barbara	Louisville, KY	Camper	1944
Fitzpatrick, Helen	Detroit, MI	Unknown	1921
Folk, Dorothy	St. Louis, MO	Camper; counselor	1921, 1924–1925
Folk, Joe	St. Louis, MO	Camp master	1924
Fons, Frances	Door County, WI	Kitchen staff	1922
Fons, Peter	Door County	Camp master	1921–1922
Fontani, Elena	Highland Park, IL	Counselor	1925
Fonyo, George	Clayton, MO	Camp master	1943
Foote, Constance	Champaign, IL	Camper	1925
Ford, Edrita	Winnetka, IL	Camper	1942–1943
Ford, Marian	Unknown	Camper	1938
Foreman, Doris	Unknown	Camper	1935
Foreman, Jean	Chicago, IL	Camper	1933–1935
Forgy, Juliabelle	Unknown	Camper	1933
Forrester, Marian	Louisville, KY	Camper	1921
Fowler, Janet	Evanston, IL	Counselor; Club girl	1923–1924
Fowler, Nancy Steel	Evanston, IL	Counselor	1923–1924
Fox, Dorothy	Clayton, MO	Camper	1920
Fox, Florence	Wichita, KS	Camper	1923
Fox, Mary Ann	Wichita, KS	Camper	1924
Fox, Patricia Stephanie	Racine, WI	Camper	1945
Frank, Samuel B.	St. Louis, MO	Camp master	1928–1929
Franke, Gertrude (Kalms)	Door County, WI	Kitchen staff	1933
Fraser, Margaret	Burlington, WI	Camper	1917
Frazier, Virginia	Wichita, KS	Camper	1921–1923
Freeman, Betty Ann	St. Louis, MO	Camper	1924–1925
Freeman, Dorthea	Pensacola, FL	Camper	1929
Freeman, Warren	St. Louis, MO	Camp master	1922, 1924
Freiberg, Charlotte	Cincinnati, OH	Camper	1924–1925
Freidman, Agnes	St. Louis, MO	Camper	1917–1919
French, Marjorie	Cleveland, OH	Camper	1929
Freschi, Phyllis	Kirkwood, MO	Camper	1947
Freund, Irene	Unknown	Camper	1930

Froemke, Geraldine Martha	St. Louis, MO	Camper	1945
Frunsch, Joan	St. Louis, MO	Camper	1947
Frumberg, Blanche	St. Louis, MO	Camper	1919
Fry, Grace	Detroit, MI	Camper	1920
Fulton, Rosemary	Manitowoc, WI	Counselor	1947
Gaessler, Ruth Marie	Ames, IA	Counselor	1943
Gage, Susan	Green Bay, WI	Camper	1946–1947
Gale, Margaret or Martha	Unknown	Camper	1938
Gallagher, Sarah	Wilmette, IL	Counselor	1921
Gardner, Ann	Unknown	Counselor	1938–1939
Gardner, Katherine	Omaha, NE	Camper	1918–1919
Garner, Margaret V	Louisiana, MO	Counselor	1943
Garvin, Helen	Omaha, NE	Camper	1917–1918
Garvin, Lucy	Omaha, NE	Camper	1919
Gasaway, Alice	Kansas City, MO	Counselor	1924
Gay, Virginia	St. Louis, MO	Camper	1946–1947
Gayton, Gracemary	Youngstown, OH	Counselor	1944
Grambill, Elizabeth	St. Louis, MO	Camper	1922
Gettys, Grace	St. Louis, MO	Camper	1920
Giese, Tootie	Unknown	Camper	1934
Gilbert, Kate	Neenah, WI	Camper	1933–1934
Gilbert, Pulla	Neenah, WI	Camper	1933–1934
Glaser, Mary Nell	Youngstown, OH	Counselor	1947
Glassberg, Ernestine	St. Louis, MO	Camper	1918
Gleerup, Grace	Madison, WI	Camper	1919
Godchaux, Justine	New Orleans, LA	Camper	1923
Goessling, Diane	St. Louis, MO	Camper	1945–1946
Goldsmith, Marian	Milwaukee, WI	Camper	1921
Goodman, Elizabeth	Chicago, IL	Camper	1921–1923, 1925
Goodman, Marian	Chicago, IL	Camper	1919
Goodwin, Mary Elizabeth	St. Louis, MO	Counselor	1945
Gordan, Mary Margaret	Marshall, MO	Camper; counselor	1925–1926, 1928, 1930
Gougian, Augusta	St. Louis, MO	Club girl	1924
Graham, Agnes	Louisville, KY	Camper	1921
Grant, Martha	Webster, MO	Camper	1917
Grassman, Leo	Madison, WI	Riding master assistant	1939

Graves, Eleanor	Madison, WI	Camper; Club girl	1919, 1925
Gray, Ethel	Unknown	Camper	1939
Gray, Helen	Unknown	Camper	1939
Grayson, Elizabeth	St. Louis, MO	Camper	1918
Greaves, Eleanor	Unknown	Camper	1916
Green, Cathleen	St. Louis, MO	Camper	1920
Green, Eleanor Gaik	Detroit, MI	Camper; counselor	1920–1921, 1923
Green, Marguerite	St. Louis, MO	Camper	1920
Green, Dr. W. E.	Detroit, MI	Doctor	1921
Greenberger, Joan	Chicago, IL	Counselor	1941
Greene, Diana	Evanston, IL	Camper	1929
Greene, Martha	Louisville, KY	Camper	1943
Greenebaum, Elisabeth	Pontiac, IL	Camper	1928–1929
Griesedieck, Ann	Kirkwood, MO	Camper	1944
Griffin, Judith H.	St. Louis, MO	Camper	1926–1927
Griffith, Dorothy Dee	Lawrenceville, IL	Counselor	1945–1946
Griswold, Anna Grant	Louisville, KY	Camper; counselor	1942–1947
Griswold, Charlotte	Louisville, KY	Camper	1940–1941
Grove, Elizabeth	Shorewood, WI	Camper	1921–1922, 1924
Guggenheim, Louise	Unknown	Camper	1935
Gundersen, Billy	La Crosse, WI	Camp master	1940
Gundersen, Signe	La Crosse, WI	Camper	1940–1941
Gustafson, Mrs. Gusty	Door County	Camp cook	1947–1948
Gustafson, Marjorie	Door County	Kitchen staff	1922
Hafner, Frances	Unknown	Adult staff	1944
Hafner, Mary Fran	Webster Groves, MO	Camper	1944
Hafner, Ruth	St. Louis, MO	Counselor	1927–1928
Hallburg, Sarah	Evanston, IL	Camper	1929
Hamel, Nancy	Webster Groves, MO	Camper	1944–1945
Hammerstein, Albert	St. Louis, MO	Camp master	1918
Hammet, Dorothy	Wheaton, IL	Camper; counselor	1920–1922
Hammett, Celeste	St. Louis, MO	Camper	1922
Hammett, Mary Louise	St. Louis, MO	Counselor	1922
Hancock, Anne	St. Louis, MO	Camper	1918
Hancock, Deane	St. Louis, MO	Counselor	1927–1929

Harbaugh, Elise	Chicago, IL	Camper	1920
Harbaugh, Marie	Chicago, IL	Camper	1920
Harbur, James	Clayton, MO	Camp master	1945
Hardin, Carol	Darien, CT	Camper	1947
Harding, Jane	Indianapolis, IN	Camper	1926–1927, 1929
Hargis, Nancy	Kansas City, MO	Camper	1927–1928
Harnett, Genevieve	St. Louis, MO	Camper	1919
Harris, Dorothy	Richmond, VA	Counselor	1922
Harris, Ruth	Webster, MO	Camper	1917
Harrison, Marcia	Highland Park, IL	Camper	1947
Hart, Annette	Kansas City, MO	Camper	1922
Hart, Marion	Unknown	Camper	1927, 1930
Hart, Mary Rodes	Harrodsburg, KY	Counselor	1940
Hart, Roberta	Milwaukee, WI	Counselor	1944
Hartley, Betty Jane	Hagerstown, IN	Camper	1927–1928
Harvey, Cora	St. Louis, MO	Club girl	1929
Harvey, Helen	Chicago, IL	Counselor	1947
Harvey, Jean	Chicago, IL	Counselor	1947
Haskell, Lucy	St. Louis, MO	Camper	1917–1918, 1921
Hastings, Natalie	Omaha, NE	Camper	1919
Hawes, Bartow	St. Louis, MO	Camp master	1920
Hawes, Jeanne	New Canaan, CT	Camper	1947–1947
Hawes, Mary Dozier	New Canaan, CT	Camper	1946
Head, Eleanor	Madison, WI	Counselor	1922, 1924
Healy, Martha	Webster Groves, MO	Counselor	1919
Healy, Mary Ann	Chicago, IL	Camper	1947
Healy, Muriel	Milwaukee, WI	Counselor	1947
Heaslett, Elizabeth	Birmingham, AL	Counselor	1945
Heath, Edith	St. Louis, MO	Camper	1937, 1940
Heath, Margaret	St. Louis, MO	Counselor	1923–1924
Heath, Susan	St. Louis, MO	Camper	1940
Heath, Virginia	St. Louis, MO	Camper	1926
Hedinger, Lloyd	Door County, WI	Chore boy	1929
Heffern, Merriam	Ferguson, MO	Camper	1924–1925
Heiskell, Elizabeth	Indianapolis, IN	Camper	1927
Hemenway, Virginia	St. Louis, MO	Camper	1922
Henkle, Margaret	St. Louis, MO	Camper; Camp Spirit Girl; counselor	1937–1942
Hennings, Ruth	St. Louis, MO	Camper	1922
Henry, Emma	Door County, WI	Pastry chef	1947–48

Henry, JoAnne	Door County, WI	Kitchen staff	Unknown
Hermann, Margaret	St. Louis, MO	Camper	1917–1918
Hermann, Vera	Unknown	Camper	1916
Herpel, Peggy	Clayton, MO	Camper	1942
Herschkowitz, Aliz	St. Louis, MO	Camper	1921
Herz, Elizabeth	St. Louis, MO	Camper	1928
Hewitt, Emily	Alton, IL	Camper	1920
Hibberd, Lestra	Richmond, IN	Camper	1925
Higbee, Caroline	Burlington, IA	Camper	1924
Higbee, Mary	Burlington, IA	Camper	1924
Higdon, Gertrude	St. Louis, MO	Counselor	1924
Hill, Carol	St. Louis, MO	Camper	1941
Hinch, Kathleen	Milwaukee, WI	Camper	1941
Hobart, Gano	Unknown	Camper	1937
Hobart, Helen	Unknown	Camper	1935
Hobart, Mary Ann	Milwaukee, WI	Camper	1942
Hobson, Elizabeth	Clayton, MO	Camper	1946–1947
Hobson, Gail	Clayton, MO	Camper	1947
Hoeffler, Joan	Hubbard Woods, IL	Camper	1919
Hoffman, Ruth	Unknown	Camper	1927, 1930
Holgate, ?	Unknown	Camp master	1938
Holler, Barbara	Clayton, MO	Camper	1943–1944
Hollister, Aimee	Beloit, WI	Camper	1917
Holloway, Rosalind	Indianapolis, IN	Camper	1927–1930
Holman, Ruth	St. Louis, MO	Camper	1922
Holmes, Eleanor	Unknown	Camper	1939
Holt, Mrs. Harry	Evanston, IL	Counselor	1922
Horchell, Katherine	Louisville, KY	Camper	1921–1922, 1924
Hornbrook, Hannah H.	Detroit, MI	Camper	1923–1925, 1927
Horner, Kay	Unknown	Camper	1939
Horr, Mary	Duluth, MN	Camper	1924
Horton, Alby	Webster Groves, MO	Camper	1944
Houx, Elizabeth	Houston, TX	Camper	1925–1930
Howard, Marilyn	Summit, NJ	Camper	1943
Howard, Martha	Unknown	Camper; counselor	1937–1939, 1941
Howard, Shirley	St. Louis, MO	Camper	1941–1942
Howell, Catherine	Kansas City, MO	Camper	1920–1921
Hoxie, Alice Lee	St. Louis, MO	Camper	1921
Hoxie, Lynn	Ferguson, MO	Camper	1943
Hoxie, Pamela	Ferguson, MO	Camper	1943

Hoyle, Louise	St. Louis, MO	Camper	1927
Hubsch, Peggy	Unknown	Counselor	1930
Huckins, Janet	Oklahoma City, OK	Camper	1921
Hughes, Harry	Ferguson, MO	Camp master	1925
Hughes, Helen	Ferguson, MO	Camper	1924–1925
Hughes, Martin	Ferguson, MO	Camp master	1925
Hughes, Warner	Ferguson, MO	Camp master	1943
Hughes, Winifred	St. Louis, MO	Club girl	1929
Hulburd, Ruth	Cleveland, OH	Camper	1919
Hume, Dorothy	St. Louis, MO	Camper	1933–1934
Hume, Peggy	Normandy, MO	Counselor	1947
Humphrey, Elizabeth	Louisville, KY	Camper	1943
Hundley, Eustis	Keytesville, MO	Camper; counselor	1918, 1923, 1926
Hunton, Edith	St. Louis, MO	Camper; counselor	1921
Hussy, Helen	St. Louis, MO	Camper	1919
Hussy, Mary Jane	St. Louis, MO	Camper	1927
Huttig, Katherine	Kansas City, MO	Camper	1920
Huttig, Margaret M.	St. Louis, MO	Camper	1945
Irwin, Marie	Clayton, MO	Camper	1942
Jack, Mary Catherine	Chicago, IL	Camper	1926
Jackes, Dorothy	St. Louis, MO	Counselor	1922
Jackson, Beatrice	Darien, CT	Club girl	1923
Jackson, Joanne	Madison, WI	Counselor	1942
Jacobs, Angie	Unknown	Camper	1933
Jacobson, Mary	Door County, WI	Kitchen staff	1922
Jacobson, Ruby	Door County, WI	Kitchen staff	1922
James, Elizabeth	St. Louis, MO	Camper	1927, 1929
James, Katherine	St. Louis, MO	Camper	1929–1930
James, Patricia	Cleveland, OH	Camper	1926–1930
James, Peggy	Unknown	Camper	1927, 1930
Jansen, Emery	Unknown	Camp master	1922
Jelliffe, Jane	Racine, WI	Camper	1925–1926
Jelliffe, Marilyn	Unknown	Camper	1937
Jennings, Sarah	Louisville, KY	Camper	1945–1947
Jensen, Maryellen (Dietz)	Kirksville, MO	Counselor	1947
Jett, Eleanor	Louisville, KY	Camper	1920–1922
Joannes, Phyllis	Green Bay, WI	Camper	1929
Job, Elizabeth	Alton, IL	Camper	1917

Johansen, Judy	Clayton, MO	Camper	1946
Johnson, Agnes (Gauger)	Door County, WI	Kitchen staff	1927
Johnson, Eleanor Chouteau	Kirkwood, MO	Camper	1944, 1946
Johnson, Hazel	St. Louis, MO	Camper	1920
Johnson, Jeanette	Toronto, Ontario	Camper	1917
Johnson, Marie Christy	Kirkwood, MO	Camper	1944–1946
Johnson, Margaret Ruth	Wichita, KS	Camper	1921–1922
Johnson, Martha	Boonville, MO	Camper	1920
Johnson, Maurine	St. Louis, MO	Counselor	1925
Johnston, Ethel	Ferguson, MO	Counselor	1923–1925
Jones, Caroline	Unknown	Camper	1938–1939
Jones, Caroline	Chicago, IL	Counselor	1946
Jones, Christine	St. Louis, MO	Camper	1920–1921
Jones, Gladys	Glencoe, IL	Camper	1917
Jones, Jane Elizabeth	St. Louis, MO	Camper	1921–1922
Jones, Katty	Unknown	Camper	1937–1940
Jones, Lucia Doris	Glencoe, IL	Camper	1920
Jones, Marguerite Nabers	Birmingham, AL	Camper; counselor	1937–1939, 1943–1945
Judson, Gertrude	St. Louis, MO	Camper	1923
Jungwirth, Joe	Door County, WI	Camp master	1930, circa
Kales, Katherine	Chicago, IL	Camper	1920
Kane, Elizabeth	St. Louis, MO	Counselor	1926–1928
Kantcheff, Victoria	Unknown	Camper	1934
Karcher, Leonor Murray	Barrington, IL	Camper; counselor	1944–1945
Kavanaugh, Doris	Unknown	Counselor	1933
Kayser, Ruth E.	St. Louis, MO	Counselor	1944–1946
Kealy, Coiana	Kansas City, MO	Camper	1922
Kelley, Catherine	Kansas City, MO	Counselor	1924–1925
Kellner, Carola	Highland Park, IL	Camper	1929
Kellogg, Caroline	Chicago, IL	Camper	1927–1930
Kelly, Kitty	Louisville, KY	Camper	1940
Kendrick, Kitty	Winnetka, IL	Club girl	1927, 1937
Kendrick, Mary	Unknown	Camper	1938
Kendrick, Nancy	Evanston, IL	Camper	1947
Kennedy, Elizabeth	St. Louis, MO	Camper	1940

Kennedy, Margaret	Unknown	Camper	1939
Kennedy, Marguerite	St. Louis, MO	Camper	1940
Kent, Moya	St. Louis, MO	Camper	1942
Kerner, Mary Alyce	Chicago, IL	Camper	1943
Kershaw, Ann	Clayton, MO	Camper	1947
Kimberly, Mary	Neenah, WI	Camper	1927–1928
Kimberly, Nancy	Neenah, WI	Camper	1927–1928, 1930
Kimberly, Susan	Unknown	Camper	1934–1935, 1937
King, Fern	Chicago, IL	Camper	1941
King, Georgia	Kansas City, MO	Camper	1927
King, Mary Elizabeth	Webster Groves, MO	Camper	1943–1944
Kinney, Jean	Cleveland, OH	Camper	1927
Kirk, Jacqueline	Highland Park, IL	Camper	1943
Kirkland, Jane	New York, NY	Club girl	1925
Kitchell, Claudette	Peoria, IL	Camper	1945
Kitchell, Virginia	Madison, WI	Camper	1919
Klien, Louise	Chicago, IL	Camper	1924
Klipstein, Julia	St. Louis, MO	Camper	1920
Kniegan, Dorothy	St. Louis, MO	Camper	1934
Knight, Ahden B.	St. Louis, MO	Camper	1926, 1928
Knoernschild, Pauline	Milwaukee, WI	Camper; counselor	1933–1934
Koerber, Katherine	St. Louis, MO	Camper	1920–1922
Koetter, Wilma	St. Louis, MO	Camper	1921
Kostka, Erwina Mary	Chicago, IL	Camper	1944–1946
Kotstrean, Nancy	St. Louis, MO	Camper	1941–1943
Kouser, Clara	Webster, MO	Camper	1917
Kraft, Mary Ann	St. Louis, MO	Counselor	1940–1941
Kramer, Leona	St. Louis, MO	Camper	1919
Kramer, Mary	St. Louis, MO	Camper	1941
Krause, Eunice	Door County, WI	Kitchen staff	Unknown
Krause, Inez	Door County, WI	Kitchen staff	Unknown
Krebs, Dr. Otto	St. Louis, MO	Doctor	1922
Kreider, Billie Jean	Unknown	Nurse	1944
Kreisman, Ruth	St. Louis, MO	Club girl	1924–1926
Krey, Jacquelyn Ann	St. Louis, MO	Camper	1945
Krieger, Dorothy	Unknown	Camper	1933
Kropp, Helen	Webster Groves, MO	Camper	1917
Kurth, Elisbeth	Elm Grove, IL	Camper	1946
Kurtz, Mary Kay Stuart	Unknown	Camper	1927, 1930

Lafon, Tammy	University City, MO	Camper	1917
Laidley, Sandra	Lake Forest, IL	Camper	1943
Lamb, Martha	Unknown	Camper	1927, 1930
Lammert, Mary Elise	St. Louis, MO	Camper	1919
Lamson, Louise	Unknown	Counselor	1924
Land, Marjorie	St. Louis, MO	Camper	1917
Landauer, Beth	Milwaukee, WI	Camper	1919
Lanier, Elizabeth	Hopkinsville, KY	Camper; counselor	1942, 1946
Lanier, Grace	Hopkinsburg, KY	Camper; Camp Spirit Girl; counselor	1934–1935, 1937–1938, 1940–1942
Lanier, Marie	Tulsa, OK	Counselor	1921, 1924
Lansing, Dorothy	Evanston, IL	Camper	1929
Lansing, Loraine	Evanston, IL	Camper	1929
Larsen, Elizabeth	Green Bay, WI	Camper	1928
Lasker, Frances	Chicago, IL	Camper	1927, 1929–1930
Lauer, Janet	Cincinnati, OH	Camper	1924–1925
Laughlin, Edward L.	St. Louis, MO	Camp master	1927
Lauter, Joan	Unknown	Camper	1938–1939
Laver, Caroline	Cincinnati, OH	Camper	1921–1923
Lawrence, Diane	Highland Park, IL	Camper	1947
Lawson, Carol	Detroit, MI	Camper	1928
Lawson, June	Detroit, MI	Camper	1928
Layman, Grace	St. Louis, MO	Camper; Club girl	1921, 1924
Layman, Laura	St. Louis, MO	Counselor	1921–1922, 1927
Learned, Mary	Sturgeon Bay, WI	Counselor	1926
Leavitt, Elizabeth	St. Louis, MO	Camper	1926–1928
Lecher, Sylvia	Milwaukee, WI	Camper	1934
LeClair, Joan	Door County, WI	Kitchen staff	Unknown
Ledford, Olive	St. Louis, MO	Camper	1924
Lee, Dorothy	Urbana, IL	Camper	1926
Lee, Julia	Fayette, MO	Counselor	1947
Lee, Katherine	Evanston, IL	Camper; counselor	1939, 1941–1942, 1944, 1947
Lee, Marjorie	Milwaukee, WI	Camper	1933–1934
Lee, Virginia	Unknown	Camper	1933
Leggett, Elizabeth Lee	Unknown	Camper	1937
Leiter, Georgette	Kansas City, MO	Camper	1920
Leland, Mary Talbot	St. Louis, MO	Camper	1947
Lemon, Elizabeth Ann	Kansas City, MO	Camper	1926

Lemonds, Elizabeth	Louisville, KY	Camper	1920
Lemp, Marian	St. Louis, MO	Camper	1917–1920
Lempertz, Elizabeth	St. Louis, MO	Camper	1920
Lennon, Mary Louise	Kansas City, MO	Counselor	1925–1926
Lentz, Patricia	Webster Groves, MO	Camper	1944
Leopold, Edith	Burlington, IA	Camper; counselor	1937–1940
Leonard, Valle	St. Louis, MO	Camper	1927
Letter, Georgette	Kansas City, MO	Camper	1919
Levis, Mary Elizabeth	Alton, IL	Camper	1921
Levis, Mary Lou	St. Louis, MO	Camper; counselor	1937–1939, 1941–1942
Levy, Alice	St. Louis, MO	Camper	1940–1941
Lewis, Elizabeth	Louisville, KY	Camper	1920
Lewis, Elizabeth Ann	Louisville, KY	Camper	1946–1947
Lewin, Constance	Kirkwood, MO	Counselor	1922
Liggett, Ann	Clayton, MO	Camper	1940–1942
Lindburg, Wilma	Unknown	Assistant riding master	1945
Lindesmith, Karen	Bloomington, IN	Camper	1947
Linehan, Lenore	Chicago, IL	Camper	1921–1922, 1924
Linn, June Addams	Chicago, IL	Counselor	1925
Little, Marjorie	St. Louis, MO	Camper	1917
Locke, Elise	Louisville, KY	Camper; Club girl	1921, 1924
Lodwick, James R.	Indianapolis, IN	Camp master	1944
Loetscher, Harriet	Dubuque, IA	Camper	1922
Logeman, Charlotte	Milwaukee, WI	Counselor	1925
Long, Annie	Troy, MO	Camper	1919
Longan, Georgette	Kansas City, MO	Camper	1926–1927
Lord, Jane	Unknown	Camper	1927, 1930
Loring, Janet	Kansas City, MO	Counselor	1943
Lothman, Anna	St. Louis, MO	Camper	1922–1923
Louden, Roberta	Fairfield, IA	Counselor	1923
Love, Nancy	Kirkwood, MO	Camper	1942–1944
Low, Betty Jane	Dayton, OH	Camper	1927
Low, Marilyn	Chicago, IL	Camper	1947
Low, Marion Ruth	Dayton, OH	Camper	1927
Low, Nancy	Omaha, NE	Counselor	1943
Low, Phyllis	Chicago, IL	Counselor	194–1947
Lubbe, Kimball	Peoria, IL	Camp master	1920

Luddington, Florence	St. Louis, MO	Camper	1922
Ludlow, Peggy	Unknown	Camper	1938
Luedinghaus, Elinor	St. Louis, MO	Camper	1918–1920
Lueth, Mary	Omaha, NE	Camper	1947
Lueth, Virginia	Omaha, NE	Camper	1947
Luten, Mary	Indianopolis, IN	Camper	1929
Luten, Wilhelmina	Indianapolis, IN	Counselor	1928–1929
Lyons, Martha	Fort Worth, TX	Counselor	1929
Mabley, Elaine	St. Louis, MO	Camper; Club girl	1916–1920, 1921–1926
Mabley, Frances	St. Louis, MO	Camper; tennis counselor; Club girl	1916–1919
Mabley, Hilda	St. Louis, MO	Camper; Camp Spirit Girl; Club girl	1916–1920, 1921–1923
Mabley, Frances Woodward "Kidy"	St. Louis, MO	Director	1916–1931
MacCarthy, Mary Ann	Clayton, MO	Camper; counselor	1933, 1940, 1941, 1944
MacMahon, Frances	St. Louis, MO	Camper	1944
Mack, Elizabeth	Milwaukee, WI	Camper	1919, 1921–1922, 1924
Mackay, Mary Margaret	Kansas City, MO	Camper	1922
Magerstadt, Ann Henrietta	Chicago, IL	Camper	1945
Maguire, Bernice	St. Louis, MO	Camper	1924–1927
Maguire, Elizabeth Jane	St. Louis, MO	Camper	1924
Maguire, Jessie	St. Louis, MO	Camper	1924–1926
Maguire, Zaida	St. Louis, MO	Camper	1924–1928
Manley, Florence	Omaha, NE	Camper	1918
Mansfield, Carol	St. Louis, MO	Camper; counselor	1927–1928, 1930, 1934, 1944–1945
Mansfield, Elizabeth	St. Louis, MO	Camper	1927–1928
Manter, Harriet	Webster, MO	Camper	1917
Many, Margaret	St. Louis, MO	Camper	1922
Mapel, Fanny	El Paso, TX	Camper	1920–1921
Mardorf, Elise	St. Louis, MO	Camper	1922
Marks, Jocelyn	New York, NY	Camper	1919–1920
Marsh, Jamie	Highland Park, IL	Camper	1922, 1924–1925
Marsh, Patricia	Highland Park, IL	Camper	1922, 1924

Marsh, Ruth	St. Louis, MO	Nurse	1942
Marshutz, Josephine	Milwaukee, WI	Camper	1924–1925
Marston, Joan Louise	Lake Forest, IL	Camper	1945
Marston, Joanne	New York, NY	Camper	1946
Mason, Adelaide	Grosse Point, MI	Camper	1925, 1927–1929
Mason, Marjorie	Grosse Point, MI	Camper	1929
Martin, Dr. Kirby	St. Louis, MO	Doctor	1921–1922
Martin, Matea	Louisville, KY	Camper; counselor	1922–1923, 1933–1934
Martin, Monea	Louisville, KY	Counselor	1934
Mastin, Dudley	Kansas City, MO	Camper	1922, 1924
Matthews, Frances Louise	Joplin, MO	Camper	1925
Matthews, Georgia	Bronxville, NY	Camper	1944
Matzinger, Agnes	Buffalo, NY	Camper	1920
Maxwell, Maxine	Kansas City, MO	Counselor	1927
May, Dorothy	Terrell, TX	Camper	1919
Mayer, Barbara	Chicago, IL	Camper	1946–1947
Mayer, Betty Jane	St. Louis, MO	Camper	1933–1935
Mayer, Patsy	Unknown	Camper	1937, 1938, 1940
Mazzone, Phillip	St. Louis, MO	Camp master; adult staff	1925–1926
McCall, Ethel	Kenosha, WI	Counselor	1925
McCarthy, Mary Ann	Unknown	Camper	1934
McCarty, Carol	Hamburg, NY	Camper	1916–1917, 1919
McCarty, Margaret	Hamburg, NY	Camper; Camp Spirit Girl; counselor	1916–1923, 1927
McCarty, Ralph	Fairfield, CO	Camp master	1938
McClelland, Lucille	Detroit, MI	Camper	1922
McClintock, Jean	Galva, IL	Camper	1924–1925
McClintock, Marion	Galva, IL	Club girl; counselor	1922, 1924
McCormack, Jean Marie	St. Louis, MO	Camper	1945
McCormick, Elizabeth	St. Louis, MO	Counselor	1942
McCulloch, Mary Sue	St. Louis, MO	Camper	1924
McCullough, June Ann	Evanston, IL	Counselor	1947
McCurdy, Jacqueline	Evanston, IL	Camper	1940–1941
McDonald, Camille	Chicago, IL	Camper	1939–1941, 1943
McDonald, Charlotte	Omaha, NE	Camper	1919

McDonald, Marianne	Chicago, IL	Camper; counselor; Camp Spirit Girl	1940–1942, 1945, 1947
McElvain, Caryl	Morris, IL	Camper	1947
McFarland, Helen	St. Louis, MO	Club girl	1925
McGee, Newell	Martin City, MO	Camp master	1922
McKay, Mary Jane	St. Louis, MO	Camper; Club girl; counselor	1921–1922, 1924, 1927–1929
McLaughlin, Jean	Wauwatosa, WI	Camper	1947
McMackin, Martha	Clayton, MO	Camper	1941
McManus, Aileen	St. Louis, MO	Camper	1921
McMillan, Anne	Clayton, MO	Camper	1944–1946
McRoberts, Eve	Clayton, MO	Camper	1944–1947
McRoberts, Ida	St. Louis, MO	Counselor	1924
McVoy, Atwood	St. Louis, MO	Camper	1928
Mead, Alison Craigie	Indianapolis, IN	Camper	1945
Medart, Mimi	St. Louis, MO	Camper	1945–1946
Meek, Helen	St. Louis, MO	Camper	1926–1929
Mengel, Alice	Unknown	Camper	1937
Meredith, Patricia	Chicago	Camper	1930, 1933–1934
Meriweather, Elizabeth	Kansas City, MO	Camper	1920
Merrell, Charlotte	Webster Groves, MO	Camper	1918–1919
Merrell, Marian	St. Louis, MO	Camper	1927
Messick, Jane	St. Louis, MO	Camper	1920–1921
McCarty, Ralph	Fairfield, CO	Camp master	1938
Messinger, Carl	Clayton, MO	Camp master	1941
Messinger, Frances	Clayton, MO	Counselor	1941
Messinger, Marianna	Clayton, MO	Camper	1942
Messinger, Polly	Clayton, MO	Camper; counselor; Camp Spirit Girl	1941, 1943–1944
Meyer, Adolpha	St. Louis, MO	Counselor	1940
Meyer, Aimee	Unknown	Camper	1916
Meyer, B. J.	St. Louis, MO	Camper	1934
Meyer, Elaine	St. Louis, MO	Camper	1927
Meyer, Vivian	St. Louis, MO	Camper	1927
Michael, Constance	Unknown	Camper	1937
Michaels, Mildred	St. Louis, MO	Counselor	1922–1924
Millard, Barbara	Omaha, NE	Camper	1923, 1925–1926
Miller, Barbara	Hinsdale, IL	Camper	1927–1928

Miller, Barbara D.	Cleveland, OH	Camper	1927
Miller, Lucy Lee	Unknown	Camper	1934, 1937–1938
Miller, Rita E.	Fox Point, WI	Camper; art counselor	1934–1935, 1940
Miller, Virginia	Naperville, IL	Camper	1921
Millikin, Emily	St. Louis, MO	Camper	1918–1919
Ming, Nancy	St. Louis, MO	Camper	1944–1947
Minor, Emily	Webster Groves, MO	Camp store secretary	1945–1946
Mitchell, Helen	Kansas City, MO	Camper	1947
Mitchell, Jean	St. Louis, MO	Camper; Camp Spirit Girl	1934–1935, 1937
Mitchell, Jerry	Clayton, MO	Camp master	1945
Mitchell, Margaret "Pat"	Kansas City, MO	Camper	1947
Moffitt, Josephine	St. Louis, MO	Camper	1919
Moffitt, Natalie	St. Louis, MO	Camper	1919
Moffitt, Olive	St. Louis, MO	Camper	1919
Mohn, Elaine	Red Wing, MN	Dancing counselor	1933–1934
Moir, Elizabeth	Burlington, IA	Camper	1918–1919
Moir, Nancy	Burlington, IA	Camper	1918–1919
Monroe, Josephine	Chicago, IL	Camper	1921
Moody, Barbara	Chicago, IL	Camper	1941–1943
Moon, Katherine	St. Louis, MO	Camper	1944–1945
Moore, Joan	Evanston, IL	Camper	1941
Moore, Joella	Charleston, MO	Camper	1920
Moore, Martha	Kansas City, MO	Camper	1920
Moore, Sally B.	Unknown	Camper	1938
Moreno, Harriet	St. Louis, MO	Camper	1922–1923
Morey, Mary V.	St. Louis, MO	Camper	1924
Morley, Elise	Birmingham, MI	Camper; Club girl	1919, 1920, 1922–1923, 1927
Morley, Mary Kathleen	Birmingham, MI	Camper; Club girl	1920–1922, 1924–1925, 1927
Morris, Marge	Unknown	Camper	1938
Morrison, Mary Caroline	Unknown	Camper	1935
Mory, Barbara	Unknown	Camper	1933
Mory, Mimi	Neenah, WI	Camper	1933–1934
Moss, Marietta	Chicago, IL	Counselor	1926
Moulton, Jane	St. Louis, MO	Camper	1926–1929

Mudd, Ann	Birmingham, AL	Camper	1943
Mueller, Elizabeth	Kansas City, MO	Camper; counselor	1938, 1940–1941
Muenstermann, Agnes, RN	Jefferson City, MO	Nurse	1945
Mumford, Mary	Urbana, IL	Counselor	1925
Mumford, Ruth	Columbia, MO	Counselor	1927
Murchison, Mary	Montgomery, AL	Counselor	1944
Murphy, Ann Dorr	Green Bay, WI	Camper	1945
Murphy, Lee	Balboa Island, CA	Camper	1942
Mutrux, Elaine	Clayton, MO	Camper; counselor	1941–1943, 1945
Nall, Martha	St. Louis, MO	Camper	1919–1920
Nintcheff, Vililia Mary	Milwaukee, WI	Camper	1934
Nash, Emma	Omaha, NE	Camper	1920
Nash, Viola	Wisconsin Rapids, WI	Camper	1921
Nast, Helen	Chicago, IL	Camper	1922, 1924, 1927
Nath, Marjorie	Highland Park, IL	Camper	1941–1942
Neidringhaus, Mary	St. Louis, MO	Camper; counselor; Club girl	1917–1920, 1925
Nelson, Charlotte	St. Louis, MO	Camper	1919–1921
Nelson, Harriet Rose	Wilmette, IL	Camper	1924
Nelson, Ida Harry	St. Louis, MO	Camper; counselor	1920–1922, 1924–1925
Nelson, Jeanette	Wilmette, IL	Camper	1920–1923
Neufeld, Amy Louise	Green Bay, WI	Camper	1945
Neufeld, Lu Ann	Green Bay, WI	Camper	1946
Nevitt, Elizabeth	Oshkosh, WI	Camper	1925–1927
Newald, Evelyn	Milwaukee, WI	Camper	1929
Newcomb, ?	Unknown	Camp master	1921
Newcomb, ?	Unknown	Kitchen staff	1922
Newman, Emily	Buffalo, NY	Camper	1920
Newman, Jane	St. Louis, MO	Camper	1921–1923
Newman, Lina	Kansas City, MO	Counselor	1924
Nichols, Mabel	St. Louis, MO	Camper	1919–1920
Nichols, Mary Bruce	St. Louis, MO	Camper	1921, 1924–1925, 1927–1928
Niedringhaus, Mary	St. Louis, MO	Camper	1916, 1921–1923
Nixon, Barbara	Alton, IL	Camper	1947
Noble, Mary Frances	St. Louis, MO	Camper	1918–1922
Noetzel, Gertrude	Waukesha, WI	Camper	1920–1921

Noland, Elizabeth	Unknown	Camper	1933
Noland, Louise	Birmingham, AL	Camper	1943
Noyes, Margaret	Evanston, IL	Counselor	1924
Noyes, Margaret or Helen	Milwaukee, WI		1932
Nulson, Mary Orr	St. Louis, MO	Camper	1941
Oatman, Isabel	St. Louis, MO	Camper	1919–1920
O'Brien, Pauline	Milwaukee, WI	Camper	1928
O'Brien, Winifred	Milwaukee, WI	Camper	1923–1924
Odegard, Evelyn	Chicago, IL	Camper	1921–1922
Olin, Barbara	Alton, IL	Camper	1946–1947
Olin, Eunice	Alton, IL	Camper	1947
Olin, Judy	Alton, IL	Camper	1946
Olmsted, Jane Anne	Clayton, MO	Camper	1941, 1943
Olson, Judy	De Pere, WI	Camper	1946
Orr, Isabel	Unknown	Counselor	1924
Orr, Katherine (Nulson)	St. Louis, MO	Camper; counselor; Club girl; assistant director	1916–1917, 1921, 1925–1928, 1933
Orr, Mary	St. Louis, MO	Camper; Club girl	1917–1918, 1921
Orr, Mary	Unknown	Adult staff	1935
Orr, Maury	Unknown	Adult staff	1935
Orwig, Harry Mercer	St. Louis, MO	Sailing camp master	1934–1941
Osborne, Marguerite	Milwaukee, WI	Counselor	1928–1929
Osterman, Claire	Milwaukee, WI	Camper	1921–1922, 1924
Oswald, Posy	Unknown	Camper	1937–1938
Overton, Mary Kate	Madison, WI	Camper	1919
Owen, Ann	Birmingham, AL	Counselor	1943
Owen, Bubs	Heflin, AL	Counselor	1944
Paddock, Dr. Richard	St. Louis, MO	Doctor	1923
Pahmeyer, Mary Louise	Clayton, MO	Camper	1947
Paine, Elizabeth	Evanston, IL	Camper	1924–1927
Paine, Helen	Milwaukee, WI	Camper	1921
Palbicke, Barbara	Chicago, IL	Camper	1943
Pangman, Hope	St. Louis, MO	Camper	1924
Parke, Jean	St. Louis, MO	Camper	1943–1944
Parker, Elizabeth	Kansas City, MO	Camper	1921

Parker, Mary	Kansas City, MO	Camper; adult staff	1921, 1945
Parkhurst, Adele	Clayton, MO	Camper	1944
Patton, Marjorie	Chicago, IL	Camper	1933
Patton, Mary Alice	Springfield, IL	Counselor	1947
Patton, Nancy	Louisville, KY	Camper	1946–1947
Patton, Joan	Chicago, IL	Camper	1944
Paulson, Newell	Crown Point, IN	Camp master	1924
Payne, Nancy	Unknown	Camper	1933, 1935, 1937–1939
Peck, Dorothy	Webster Groves, MO	Camper	1917
Peck, Eda Marie	Kansas City, MO	Camper	1919–1920
Peck, Honey	Unknown	Camper	1935
Peck, Lilly Anne	Thomasville, GA	Camper	1928–1930
Pedigo, Margaret	St. Louis, MO	Camper	1919
Peil, Adeline "Tootsie"	Baileys Harbor, WI	Camp cook	1937–1941
Pendill, Gretchen	Washington, DC	Camper; Camp Spirit Girl	1947
Perkins, Virginia	Highland Park, IL	Camper	1925, 1928–1929
Peters, Edith	St. Louis, MO	Camper	1922–1924
Peters, Marion	St. Louis, MO	Camper	1924
Petrine, Helen	St. Louis, MO	Camper	1917–1919
Pfeffer, Virginia	Lebanon, IL	Camper	1941
Phelps, Ann	Unknown	Camper	1935
Phillips, Claire	Milwaukee, WI	Counselor	1941
Phillips, Dr. Mary A.	Unknown	Doctor	1925
Phillipson, Georgia	Milwaukee, WI	Camper	1928–1930
Pick, Mary	Glencoe, IL	Camper	1943
Picker, Helen	Unknown	Camper	1916
Pickett, Camille	Highland Park, IL	Camper	1941
Pieper, Jeanette	Unknown	Camper	1935
Pierson, Natalie	Kansas City, MO	Camper	1944
Pilcher, Helen	Louisville, KY	Camper	1921
Pirrung, Henriette	Clayton, MO	Camper	1925
Platt, Margaret	Chicago, IL	Camper	1944–1947
Plek, Gladys	Highland Park, IL	Camper	1942
Plek, Mary	Glencoe, IL	Camper	1942
Polk, Cynthia	St. Louis, MO	Camper	1922
Polk, Grizelda	Unknown	Camper	1933
Post, Helen James	Unknown	Camper	1930
Prentis, Lindsay	Detroit, MI	Camper	1924
Prescott, Constance	Unknown	Camper	1919–1920

Prescott, Katherine	Kansas City, MO	Camper	1919–1920
Price, Jane	St. Louis, MO	Camper	1933–1934
Price, Virginia	St. Louis, MO	Camper	1918
Pridmore, Josephine	Wilmette, IL	Camper	1929–1930
Priest, Virginia	San Antonio, TX	Camper	1916–1917
Pringle, Irene (Pruitt)	St. Louis, MO	Kitchen staff	1945–1946
Probeck, Mary Lou	Louisville, KY	Camper	1944
Proxmire, Adele	Lake Forest, IL	Camper	1928
Prud'homme, Marguerite	St. Louis, MO	Camper	1920–1921
Pruett, Marjorie	Clayton, MO	Camper	1944
Pruett, Mary Jane	St. Louis, MO	Camper	1939–1940
Pulliam, Mary	Unknown	Camper	1937
Racey, Louise	DeKalb, IL	Camper	1924
Rand, Carla Clingman	St. Louis, MO	Camper	1945
Rand, Helen Octavia	Clayton, MO	Camper	1944–1945
Rand, Jeanette Hale	Clayton, MO	Camper	1944–1945
Rand, Sally	Unknown	Camper	1934
Randolph, Charles	Milwaukee, WI	Camp master	1921
Ranney, Esther	Unknown	Camper	1935, 1938
Ransome, Barbara	Birmingham, AL	Camper	1918
Rathman, Elizabeth	St. Louis, MO	Camper	1924–1926
Read, Katherine	St. Louis, MO	Camper	1928
Reaves, Patricia Anne	St. Louis, MO	Camper	1945–1946
Reber, Helen	Chicago, IL	Camper	1921–1922
Reber, Virginia	Wheaton, IL	Camper; counselor	1919–1920, 1922
Reeve, Natalie	Clayton, MO	Camper	1947
Reinhart, Alice (Free)	Door County, WI	Camp cook	1927
Remick, Elizabeth	Evanston, IL	Counselor	1945
Rentdorf, Helen	Lake Forest, IL	Counselor	1924
Rhodes, Jacquel	Webster Groves, MO	Unknown	1944
Rice, Elinor	Evanston, IL	Dancing counselor	1927–1930, 1933
Rice, Jeff	St. Louis, MO	Camp master	1922
Richards, Emily	Geneva, IL	Camper	1927–1928
Richards, Mary Stuart	Geneva, IL	Camper	1925–1927
Richards, Sarah	Alton, IL	Camper	1946–1947
Richardson, Thelma	Unknown	Camper	1938
Richmond, Celia	St. Louis, MO	Camper	1946
Ricker, Hetty	Milwaukee, WI	Camper	1941

Rigali, Adeline	Oak Park, IL	Counselor	1925
Rigali, Yolanda	Oak Park, IL	Club girl	1925
Ring, Ban	Unknown	Camper	1939
Ringer, Dorothy	St. Louis, MO	Counselor	1924
Ritzinger, Frances	Kirkwood, MO	Counselor	1947
Roach, Mary Jane	St. Louis, MO	Counselor	1927–1928
Robbins, Nancy	St. Louis, MO	Camper	1924–1925
Roberts, Isabella	St. Louis, MO	Camper	1946
Roberts, Patricia	Indianapolis, IN	Counselor	1934
Robinson, Elizabeth	Shreveport, LA	Camper	1924
Robinson, Mary	Webster Groves, MO	Counselor	1941
Rodgers, Helen	Unknown	Camper	1935
Rogers, Jean	Unknown	Camper	1938–1939
Rogers, Lois	Chicago, IL	Counselor	1942
Rollins, Jacquelyn	Miami, FL	Counselor	1947
Rolwing, Polly	Clayton, MO	Camper	1947
Romaine, Alton	Scranton, PA	Camp master	1920
Rosenthal, Hannah	La Porte, IN	Camper	1922
Ross, Jane	Anchorage, KY	Counselor	1943
Ross, Jean	Chicago, IL	Camper; counselor	1938, 1940
Roth, Nelda Jean	Indianapolis, IN	Camper	1927
Rothschild, Babette	Chicago, IL	Camper	1924–1926
Rothschild, Susan	Chicago, IL	Camper	1934–1935
Rounds, Julia	Chicago, IL	Camper	1919
Rouse, Winifred	Kansas City, MO	Counselor	1920
Royston, Anna May	Unknown	Camper	1930
Runyan, Carolyn	Louisville, KY	Camper	1946–1947
Russell, Evelyn	Louisville, KY	Camper	1940
Russell, Nancy	Kansas City, MO	Camper	1919–1920
Ryan, Margaret	St. Louis, MO	Camper	1925
Ryan, Mary	St. Louis, MO	Camper	1919
Ryder, Marian	Unknown	Camper	1927, 1930
Ryland, Elizabeth	Kansas City, MO	Counselor	1944
Sackett, Katherine	Louisville, KY	Camper	1918
Salmon, Nilita	Unknown	Camper	1916
Sample, Katherine	Shreveport, LA	Camper	1924
Samuel, Bettty Lee	Lake Forest, IL	Camper; counselor	1944–1945
Samuels, Agnes	Madison, WI	Counselor	1919
Sanders, Bunch	Unknown	Counselor	1939

Sanders, Leone	St. Louis, MO	Camper; Camp Spirit Girl	1917
Sauer, Wilifred	Rolla, MO	Camper	1933–1934
Savage, Sally	Indianpolis, IN	Camper	1946
Sawyer, Catherine	Racine, WI	Camper	1919
Sawyer, Helen	Unknown	Camper	1927, 1930
Sayman, Do Jean	Unknown	Camper	1927, 1930
Scarritt, Katherine "Kip"	Kansas City, MO	Camper	1947
Schackelford, Dorothy	Frankford, KY	Camper	1921
Schackelford, Susan	Frankford, KY	Camper	1921
Schaeffer, Alice Elizabeth	St. Louis, MO	Camper	1926–1928
Schaffer, Jane	St. Louis, MO	Camper	1921
Scheimmer, Geraldine, RN	St. Louis, MO	Adult staff	1947
Schermerhorn, Margaret	Unknown	Camper	1921–1923
Schumtler, Frances	St. Louis, MO	Kitchen staff	1945
Schneider, Betty Ann	Louisville, KY	Camper	1945–1946
Schneider, Jean	Tucson, AZ	Camper	1946
Schneider, Mary Ann	Tucson, AZ	Camper	1946
Schramm, Gretchen	Burlington, IA	Camper	1943–1944, 1946
Schramm, Sieglinda	Burlington, IA	Camper	1947
Schreiber, Claudelle	Louisville, KY	Camper	1944–1946
Schreiber, Susan	Oshkosh, WI	Camper	1927
Schrode, Sue	Unknown	Camper	1938
Schroth, Bettie Bush	St. Louis, MO	Camper	1945–1946
Schroeder, Fred	Sheboygan, WI	Camp master	1942, 1946
Schuessler, Helen	Alton, IL	Camper	1924–1925
Schultz, Arthi May	Kansas City, MO	Camper	1920
Schultz, Margaret	Milwaukee, WI	Camper; counselor	1918–1919
Schultz, Senta	Milwaukee, WI	Camper	1919–1920, 1923
Schuyler, Martha	St. Louis, MO	Camper	1920
Schwab, Alice	St. Louis, MO	Camper	1917–1919
Schwab, Kay	Chicago, IL	Camper	1922
Scwartzburg, Grace	Milwaukee, WI	Camper	1923
Schwartzburg, Mildred	Milwaukee, WI	Camper; Club girl	1919, 1921
Sconce, Arlene	Omaha, NE	Camper	1943
Scott, Charles E.	Indianapolis, IN	Camp master	1944

Scott, Eleanor	St. Louis, MO	Camper; counselor	1937–1938, 1942
Scott, Nancy	Unknown	Camper	1937
Scott, Valentine	St. Louis, MO	Counselor	1942
Scoville, Delight	Riverside, IL	Camper	1942
Scoville, Jeanette	Riverside, IL	Camper; adult staff	1941
Scullin, Josephine	St. Louis, MO	Camper	1921–1924
Searle, Suzanne	Winnetka, IL	Camper	1942–1943
Secor, Edith	Chicago, IL	Counselor	1929
Seelbach, Harriet	Louisville, KY	Camper; Camp Spirit Girl	1934
Seeley, Susan	Mount Pleasant, IA	Camper	1940
Selby, Virginia	St. Louis, MO	Counselor	1929
Sellmer, Jane or Jean	Montclair, NJ	Camper	1927, 1929–1930
Selz, Barbara	Chicago, IL	Camper	1934
Selz, Eleanor	Chicago, IL	Camper; Camp Spirit Girl	1927, 1932–1935
Selz, Katherine	Chicago, IL	Camper	1924–1925
Selz, Margaret	Chicago, IL	Camper	1924–1925, 1929–1930
Serat, Eleanor	Kansas City, MO	Camper	1920
Sewell, Nancy C.	Indianapolis, IN	Archery counselor	1944–1946
Shambaugh, Marietta	Cambridge, MA	Counselor	1927
Sharp, Mary Ann, RN	St. Louis, MO	Adult staff	1947
Sheerin, Laura	Indianapolis, IN	Camper	1929
Sheerin, Mary Jane	Indianapolis, IN	Camper	1929
Shell, Ellie	Unknown	Camper	1938
Sheridan, Mary Patricia	St. Louis, MO	Camper	1945
Sherman, Dorothy	Omaha, NE	Camper; Camp Spirit Girl; Club girl	1919–1922, 1925
Sherman, Jackie	Unknown	Camper	1938–1939
Sherrill, William	Evanston, IL	Camp master	1924
Shillington, Susan	Unknown	Camper	1937
Shrode, Sue	Unknown	Camper	1938
Shumway, Mary	Rockford, IL	Camper	1921
Shutt, Tebetts	Unknown	Camp master	1939
Sibley, Katherine	Detroit, MI	Counselor; Club girl	1924–1930, 1933, 1935, 1937, 1939
Simmons, Jeannette	West Des Moines, IA	Counselor	1943

Simon, Violette	St. Louis, MO	Camper	1941
Simons, Sally	St. Louis, MO	Camper; Camp Spirit Girl	1921–1922, 1924–1925
Simpson, Helen Jean	Galesburg, IL	Camper	1927–1928
Singleton, Elizabeth	St. Louis, MO	Camper	1919
Singleton, Susan	St. Louis, MO	Camper	1919–1920
Sipple, Ann	St. Louis, MO	Camper	1921
Skinker, Nancy	St. Louis, MO	Counselor	1947
Skinner, Elizabeth	Kirkwood, MO	Camper; counselor	1942–1943
Slack, Isabel	St. Louis, MO	Counselor	1922
Slater, Grace	Door County	Kitchen staff	1945
Slaughter, Carylee	St. Louis, MO	Camper	1945
Sleeth, Arline	Flat River, MO	Counselor	1920
Sloan, Berkeley	St. Louis, MO	Camper	1947
Sloan, Mary	St. Louis, MO	Camper; Camp Spirit Girl; counselor	1919–1920, 1922
Sloan, Mildred	St. Louis, MO	Camper; counselor	1918–1921
Smith, Barbara	Pelham Manor, NY	Camper	1929
Smith, Bill	Chicago, IL	Camp master	1933
Smith, Dorothy	Oklahoma City, OK	Camper	1921
Smith, Elizabeth	Pelham Manor, NY	Camper	1929
Smith, Emily	Orlando, FL	Camper	1921
Smith, Frances	Louisville, KY	Camper	1921
Smith, Jane	Kansas City, MO	Camper	1919
Smith, Mildred	Evanston, IL	Counselor	1928–1929
Smith, Mrs. James H.	Clarksville, TN	Adult staff	Unknown
Smith, Nan Stuart	Louisville, KY	Camper	1939–1942
Smith, Penelope	Kansas City, MO	Camper	1920
Smith, Tom	Memphis, TN	Camp master	1943
Smith, Virginia	Kansas City, MO	Camper	1920, 1923
Snider, Florence	Toledo, OH	Camper	1921, 1923
Snider, Harriet	Pasadena, CA	Camper	1920
Snider, Pauline	Kansas City, MO	Camper	1921, 1924
Snider, Virginia	Kansas City, MO	Camper	1919
Snyder, Marjorie	Kansas City, MO	Camper	1947
Snyder, Sally	Kansas City, MO	Camper	1943–1944
Sommers, Elinor	St. Louis, MO	Camper	1924

Sommers, Mary Louise	St. Louis, MO	Camper	1923
Speakes, Jean	Unknown	Camper	1938
Speed, Iva	Louisville, KY	Camper	1921
Speed, Susan	Louisville, KY	Camper	1942–1943
Spencer, Betty	St. Louis, MO	Camper	1918
Spencer, Fred	Highland Park, IL	Camp master	1921
Spencer, Ruth	St. Louis, MO	Camper	1916–1917
Spitzer, Nancy	Toledo, OH	Camper	1921–1922
Spitzer, Suzanne	Toledo, OH	Camper	1921
Sprague, Helen	St. Louis, MO	Camper; counselor	1942–1945
Sproule, Helene	St. Louis, MO	Counselor	1922
Squire, Emily	Cleveland, OH	Camper	1926–1927
Stallcup, Elizabeth	Sikeston, MO	Camper	1921
Stallings, Dr. Minola	St. Louis, MO	Doctor	1928
Starks, Louisa	Louisville, KY	Camper	1920
Steel, Lois	Oklahoma City, OK	Camper	1921
Steffens, Caroline	Clayton, MO	Camper	1924–1926
Steger, Roberta	Unknown	Camper	1939
Stenger, Elizabeth	Kansas City, MO	Camper	1920
Stephenson, Carl	St. Louis, MO	Camp master	1916–1918
Stephenson, Irene	Unknown	Camper	1927, 1930
Stephenson, Olive	St. Louis, MO	Adult staff	1916–1918
Stern, Elizabeth	Milwaukee, WI	Camper; Club girl	1921–1924, 1929
Stern, Helen	Chicago, IL	Camper; Club girl; counselor	1918–1919, 1923–1924
Stern, Katherine	Chicago, IL	Camper	1924–1926
Stern, Nancy P.	Milwaukee, WI	Camper; counselor	1921–1927, 1929, 1933–1935
Stern, Susan	Glencoe, IL	Camper	1940
Stevens, Beverly	Wauwatosa, WI	Camper	1945–1946
Stifel, Marie	Unknown	Camper	1916
Stirton, Jean	Chicago, IL	Camper	1926
Stix, Mary	Cincinnati, OH	Camper; Camp Spirit Girl	1924–1927
Stone, Louise	Clayton, MO	Camper	1938–1942
Stone, Reba	Clayton, MO	Camper; Camp Spirit Girl; counselor	1939–1943
Storms, Ruth	Glencoe, IL	Camper	1918

Stoughton, Ann	Unknown	Camper	1935
Straube, Jo Ann	Kansas City, MO	Camper	1943–1946
Straus, Nancy Dee	Glencoe, IL	Camper	1939–1942
Strauss, Dorothy	Malvern, AR	Camper	1929
Strauss, Marjorie	Chicago, IL	Camper	1921
Stresenreuter, Margery	Chicago, IL	Camper	1921
Strickler, Martha	St. Louis, MO	Camper	1920–1921, 1923–1924
Stroughton, Ann	Unknown	Camper	1934
Sullivan, Joanne	St. Louis, MO	Camper	1941
Sullivan, Mary Louise	Pontiac, MI	Camper	1925–1926
Sultan, Mrs. Pres	St. Louis, MO	Club girl	1924
Summers, Mary Louise	St. Louis, MO	Camper	1922
Sunderland, Alice	Omaha, NE	Camper	1920
Surridge, Nancy	St. Louis, MO	Adult staff	1921
Sutcliffe, Flora	Louisville, KY	Camper; Club girl	1920–1921, 1924, 1928
Sutcliffe, Ida Bolling	Louisville, KY	Camper; counselor	1920–1921, 1924
Sutherland, Jean	Unknown	Musical director	1916
Sutherland, Margaret	Elkins, WV	Counselor	1922
Swafford, Mary	Kansas City, MO	Counselor	1922
Swanson, Marianne	Omaha, NE	Camper	1942
Sweezey, Ruth	Unknown	Assistant riding master	1944
Swenson, Carolyn	Door County, WI	Kitchen staff	Unknown
Switzer, Harriet	St. Louis, MO	Camper	1946
Taft, Matilda Spittal	Kansas City, MO	Camper	1944–1946
Tatman, Elizabeth	Kirkwood, MO	Counselor	1926
Taylor, Dr. Ruth	Chicago, IL	Doctor	1924
Taylor, Gloria Jean	St. Louis, MO	Camper	1945–1946
Taylor, Mildred	Unknown	Camper	1938
Tebbetts, Nancy	Unknown	Camper	1937
Tedford, Elizabeth	Sharon, PA	Camper	1921
Tenebaum, Joy	St. Louis, MO	Camper	1941
Thanhouser, Marian	Unknown	Club girl	1921
Theis, Virginia D.	Webster Groves, MO	Camper; counselor	1943–1946
Theleen, Frances Jean	Kenosha, WI	Counselor	1940
Theurer, Elizabeth Ann	Chicago, IL	Camper	1935
Thickens, Lauren	Menasha, WI	Camper	1927, 1929–1930

Thomas, Elizabeth	St. Louis, MO	Camper	1921
Thomas, Helen	Milwaukee, WI	Camper	1921–1922
Thompson, Anne	Lake Forest, IL	Camper	1928–1929
Thompson, Carolyn	Clayton, MO	Camper	1941
Thompson, Ida Maney	Louisville, KY	Camper	1942
Thompson, Jane	Clayton, MO	Camper	1920
Thompson, Jane	Pontiac, MI	Camper; Camp Spirit Girl	1924, 1926
Thompson, Marion	St. Louis, MO	Camper	1920–1921
Thompson, Mary	Louisville, KY	Camper	1921
Thompson, Mary Ann	Clayton, MO	Camper	1920, 1922
Thompson, Noel	Ferguson, MO	Camper; Camp Spirit Girl; counselor	1936, 1940, 1942
Thorp, Evelyn	Fish Creek, WI	Camper	1921
Thorp, Dr. Ilma	Unknown	Adult staff	1929
Todd, Helen	New Albany, IN	Camper	1917, 1919
Todd, Laura	New Albany, IN	Camper; counselor	1917, 1919
Tourtelot, Joan	Evanston, IL	Camper	1947
Tramater, Adelyn	Unknown	Camper	1934
Traub, Barbara	Detroit, MI	Camper	1923
Trecker, Barbara	Elm Grove, WI	Camper	1946–1947
Trigg, Peggy Lou	St. Louis, MO	Camper	1945
Trostel, Elinor	Milwaukee, WI	Camper	1920–1921
Truesdale, Helen	St. Louis, MO	Counselor	1941
Tschudy, Janet	Kansas City, MO	Camper	1928
Tschudy, Katherine	Kansas City, MO	Camper	1927
Tucker, Fances Ellen	Madison, WI	Camper; counselor	1920–1921
Tuly, Mary	Louisville, KY	Camper	1918
Turnbull, Janet	Green Bay, WI	Camper	1927–1929
Turnbull, Katherine Elizabeth	Green Bay, WI	Camper	1927–1929
Turner, Gilbert	Kansas City, MO	Camp master	1925
Turner, Harriet	St. Louis, MO	Camper	1928
Tyler, Ann	Clayton, MO	Camper	1944
Ulman, Helen	St. Louis, MO	Camper	1921–1922, 1924
Upthegrove, Elizabeth	St. Louis, MO	Camper; Camp Spirit Girl	1922–1923
Vance, Larry	Unknown	Camp master	1937
Van Dyne, Ethel	Chicago, IL	Counselor	1933–1934

VanHengel, Jean	Waupun, WI	Counselor	1946
VanLaanen, Virginia	Green Bay, WI	Counselor	1946–1947
Van Orden, Luke	Baraboo, WI	Sailing master assistant	1944
Vardon, Major F. C.	Rockford, IL	Camp master	1926
Varland, Carole	Morris, IL	Camper	1947
Varland, Joan	Morris, IL	Camper	1947
Vaugh, Peg	St. Louis, MO	Nurse	1943
Vaughan, Angie	Louisville, KY	Camper	1917
Vegely, Comfort	St. Louis, MO	Camper; counselor	1916–1920
Vernaz, Mercedez	Warrensburg, MO	Camper; counselor	1919
Vickers, Joan	Evanston, IL	Camper	1920
Voight, Marjorie	Burlington, IA	Camper	1941–1942
Von Brecht, Flavia	St. Louis, MO	Camper	1918–1921
Von Gontard, Clara Hazel	Kirkwood, MO	Camper	1943
Vonnegut, Madie	Unknown	Counselor	1935
Walker, Barbara	Indianapolis, IN	Camper	1945–1946
Walker, Carol	Clayton, MO	Camper	1944
Walker, Dentyne	Unknown	Camper	1946
Walker, Jane	St. Louis, MO	Camper	1922
Walker, Nancy Catherine	St. Louis, MO	Camper	1943–1946
Wallace, Mary Kennard	Clayton, MO	Camper	1944–1945
Wallen, Elizabeth	Oshkosh, WI	Camper; counselor	1921–1923, 1925–1928
Walte, Mary Noel	Unknown	Camper	1938
Walton, Malcom	Louisville, KY	Camper	1941
Ward, Ann	St. Louis, MO	Camper	1941
Ward, Elizabeth	St. Louis, MO	Counselor; junior camp director	1924–1925
Warner, Ann	Hinsdale, IL	Camper	1941
Warner, Elizabeth	Geneva, IL	Counselor	1929
Warner, Mary	Geneva, IL	Counselor	1929–1930
Warren, Charlotte	Omaha, NE	Camper	1942–1943
Warren, Ruth (Becker)	St. Louis, MO	Camper; counselor; director	1916, 1927, 1941–1943
Watkins, Martha Letitia	Louisville, KY	Camper	1943–1947

Watt, Ann Duncan	Barrington, IL	Camper	1942
Watts, Ruth	Kenilworth, IL	Camper	1918
Weary, Susan	Highland Park, IL	Camper	1940–1943
Webb, Ida Maney	Louisville, KY	Camper; Camp Spirit Girl; counselor	1918, 1920–1922
Webb, Margaret	Louisville, KY	Camper	1920–1922
Webb, Mary Louise	Louisville, KY	Camper	1923
Weber, Doris	Highland Park, IL	Camper	1944
Weber, Elise	Milwaukee, WI	Camper	1925
Weber, Valle	Webster Groves, MO	Camper	1928–1929, 1933
Wegener, Susan Jane	Unknown	Camper	1922
Weidmer, Alice	Unknown	Camper	1916
Weinberg, Paula	Louisville, KY	Camper	1943
Weir, Sally Ann	Clayton, MO	Camper	1941
Weller, Elsie	Webster Groves, MO	Camper	1917–1918
Wells, Eloise	St. Louis, MO	Camper	1920
Wells, Herbert	Evanston, IL	Camp master	1924
Wetzel, Marilou	Highland Park, IL	Counselor	1947
White, Dr. Lester	St. Louis, MO	Doctor	1921
White, Louis Lynn	Clayton, MO	Camper	1944
White, Josephine Arnold	Clayton, MO	Camper	1943–1946
White, Lois Linn	St. Louis, MO	Camper	1946
Whitelaw, Helen	St. Louis, MO	Camper	1917
Whiting, Larry	Louisville, KY	Camp master	1942
Whitley, Laurie	Harrods Creek, KY	Camper	1944–1945
Whitley, Rodney	Louisville, KY	Camper	1941, 1944
Whitney, Ann	Alton, IL	Camper	1920
Whittemore, Barbara	St. Louis, MO	Camper	1946
Whittemore, Carr	St. Louis, MO	Camper	1921
Whyte, Ruth	Kenosha, WI	Camper	1942
Wickham, Marian	St. Louis, MO	Camper	1921–1922
Widen, Charlotte	St. Louis, MO	Camper; counselor	1938–1940
Widen, Elinor	Austin, TX	Camper	1940–1941
Widmer, Betty	Webster Groves, MO	Counselor	1947
Wiener, Erica	Chicago, IL	Camper	1921
Wight, Janette	Kenosha, WI	Camper	1941
Wilcocks, Crete	St. Louis, MO	Counselor	1925
Wilcox, Elizabeth	Burlington, IA	Camper	1926

Wilder, Josephine	Winnetka, IL	Camper	1943
Wilkerson, Jo-Ann Byron	St. Louis, MO	Camper	1945
Wilkerson, Suzanne D.	St. Louis, MO	Camper	1945
Willard, Louise	Highland Park, IL	Camper	1928
Williams, Barbara	Unknown	Camper	1935
Williams, Carole	Clayton, MO	Camper	1943–1945
Williams, Dorothy	Webster Groves, MO	Camper	1921
Williams, June	Detroit, MI	Camper; Club girl	1923, 1925, 1927
Williams, Margaret	Columbia, MO	Counselor	1926–1927
Williams, Mary Lucy	Webster Groves, MO	Counselor	1921
Williams, Mary Orr	Webster Groves, MO	Camper	1938–1943
Williams, Norman	Webster Groves, MO	Camp master	1940–1941
Williams, Vera	Unknown	Camper	1930
Williamson, Janet	Evanston, IL	Camper	1947
Willner, Ann	Homewood, IL	Camper	1942–1946
Wilson, Elizabeth	Kenosha, WI	Camper	1919
Wilson, Genevieve	St. Louis, MO	Counselor	1921
Wilson, Iris	Sappington, MO	Camper	1944
Wilson, Tamara	Sappington, MO	Camper	1944
Wilson, Theresa	Lexington, MO	Camper	1920
Winfrey, Trez	Unknown	Camp master	1933–1935
Winslow, Solveig	Madison, WI	Counselor	1924
Winter, Mabel	Madison, WI	Camper	1921
Wintersmith, Edith	Louisville, KY	Camper	1921
Wissman, Julia	Clayton, MO	Counselor	1944–1946
Wittemore, Hilda	Unknown	Camper	1916
Wolcott, Elizabeth	Unknown	Counselor	1935
Wolf, Hazel	Mount Horeb, WI	Camper	1918
Wolff, Noni	St. Louis, MO	Camper	1934–1935
Wollaeger, Antoinette	Milwaukee, WI	Camper; Camp Spirit Girl; counselor	1926–1929, 1934–1935, 1937
Wollaeger, Charlotte	Milwaukee, WI	Camper; Camp Spirit Girl; counselor	1919–1924, 1926, 1928, 1940, 1947
Wollaeger, Robert	Milwaukee, WI	Camp master	1939–1940
Wood, Dr. Eulalie	Webster Groves, MO	Doctor	1920
Woodbridge, Cecil	St. Louis, MO	Camper	1944
Woodbury, Margaret	Kansas City, MO	Camper	1926–1927, 1930

Woodring, Jean	Indianapolis, IN	Camper	1946
Woodruff, Elizabeth	Louisville, KY	Camper	1940
Woods, Helen	Kansas City, MO	Camper	1922
Woods, Lisa	Chicago, IL	Camper	1945
Woods, Lucia	Chicago, IL	Camper	1945
Woodsmall, Mary Jean	Lake Bluff, IL	Camper	1939–1941
Woodworth, Mary Caroline	Kansas City, MO	Camper	1922
Woolwine, Sally Brooks	St. Louis, MO	Unknown	1945–1946
Wormser, Elaine	Chicago, IL	Camper	1929
Worsham, Doris Louise	St. Louis, MO	Camper; counselor	1937–1938, 1940
Wright, Dorothy Page	Webster Groves, MO	Counselor	1926–1930
Wyman, Mary	St. Louis, MO	Counselor	1942
Wyman, Sarah	St. Louis, MO	Camper; counselor	1942–1945
Wyman, Susan E.	St. Louis, MO	Camper	1926–1927
Wymond, Elizabeth	Louisville, KY	Club girl; counselor	1921–1922, 1923
Young, Mildred	Chicago, IL	Camper	1919
Zimmerman, Ruth	Milwaukee, WI	Camper	1925–1929
Zimmers, Renate	Milwaukee, WI	Camper	1922

Bibliography

Beauchamp, Scott. "The Mystery of St. Louis's Veiled Prophet." *The Atlantic*, September 2, 2014. www.theatlantic.com/politics/archive/2014/09/fair-st-louis-and-the-veiled-prophet/379460/.

Bell, Richard C. "A History of Women in Sport Prior to Title IX." *Sport Journal*, March 4, 2008. http://thesportjournal.org/article/a-history-of-women-in-sport-prior-to-title-ix/.

Bernstein, Rebecca Sample. "Fish Creek Intensive Architectural and Historical Survey." Prepared for Gibraltar Historical Association, Fish Creek, WI. February 1993.

Between the Wars. "Modernity as a Cultural Style: Jazz in Black and White." Accessed July 15, 2019. http://chnm.gmu.edu/courses/hist409/jazz/jazz.html.

Billings, Molly. "The Influenza Pandemic of 1918." Human Virology at Stanford. Last modified February 2005. https://virus.stanford.edu/uda/.

Blahnik, Joel. "Adventure Island." In *Door County Almanak No. 5*, edited by Fred Johnson, 183–9. Sister Bay, WI: Dragonsbreath Press, 1990.

Burton, Frances. "Art in the Park." In *The Centennial Reader*, edited by Kathleen Harris, 27–31. Fish Creek, WI: Friends of Peninsula State Park, 2009.

Cataldi, Mauro, Francesco Borriello, Francescopaolo Granata, Lucio Annunziato, and Gianni Marone. "Histamine Receptors and Antihistamines: From Discovery to Clinical Applications." *Chemical Immunology and Allergy* 100 (2014): 214–6. https://doi.org/10.1159/000358740.

Cavanaugh, Maureen, and Pat Finn. *These Days*. "The African-American Railroad Experience." KPBS, March 23, 2010. www.kpbs.org/news/2010/mar/23/african-american-railroad-experience/.

Clark, Alice Orr. *Meenahga Camps for Girls* (brochure). St. Louis, MO: Author, 1919.

Clark, Alice Orr. *Meenahga Camps for Girls* (brochure). St. Louis, MO: Author, 1921.

Clark, Alice Orr. *Meenahga Camps for Girls* (brochure). St. Louis, MO: Author, 1935.

Clark, Alice Orr. *Meenahga Camps for Girls* (brochure). St. Louis, MO: Author, 1937.

Clarke, Edward H. *Sex in Education: or, A Fair Chance for the Girls*. Boston: J. R. Osgood, 1873. E-text prepared by Audrey Longhurst, Jeannie Howse, and the Project Gutenberg Online Distributed Proofreading Team. www.pgdp.net/.

Collins, Elizabeth M. "The Angels of Bataan." Department of Defense Live, April, 12, 2013. www.dodlive.mil/2012/04/24/the-angels-of-bataan/.

Davis, Tom. "The Names in the Orchard." In *Door County Almanak No. 2*, edited by Fred Johnson, 37–40. Sister Bay, WI: Dragonsbreath Press, 1985.

Eaton, Conan Bryant. *Rock Island: A Part of the History of Washington Township*. Washington Island, WI: Author, 1969.

Editors of *Education Encyclopedia*. "Progressive Education." *Education Encyclopedia* (online), June 10, 2019. https://education.stateuniversity.com/pages/2336/Progressive-Education.html.

Editors of *Encyclopaedia Britannica*. "Anna Botsford Comstock." *Encyclopaedia Britannica* (online), May 28, 2019. www.britannica.com/biography/Anna-Botsford-Comstock.

Editors of *Encyclopaedia Britannica*. "Hiawatha: Legendary Onondaga Chief." *Encyclopaedia Britannica* (online), June 16, 2019. www.britannica.com/topic/Hiawatha.

Editors of *Encyclopaedia Britannica*. "Tuberculosis through History." *Encyclopaedia Britannica* (online), June 18, 2019. www.britannica.com/science/tuberculosis/Tuberculosis-through-history.

Edmunds, Adeline Peil. "Memories of Camp Meenahga." In *Door County Almanak No. 5*, edited by Fred Johnson, 58–61. Sister Bay, WI: Dragonsbreath Press, 1990.

Edmunds, Adeline Peil. *The Loving Spice of Life*. Green Bay, WI: Quigley Printing, 1980.

First People. "Treaty with the Menominee: February 8, 1861." Accessed July 1, 2019. www.firstpeople.us/FP-Html-Treaties/TreatyWithTheMenominee1831.html.

Forest County Potawatomi. "Timeline of Potawatomi History." Accessed July 1, 2019. www.fcpotawatomi.com/culture-and-history/timeline-of-potawatomi-history/.

Gardner, Eric. "The Forgotten Falk Corporation." *EricGardner.net: Writings on Politics, Economics, and History* (blog), September 9, 2016. www.ericgardner.net/forgotten-falk-corporation.

Guenzel, Betsy Skinner. "Gray Walls Remember." In *Fish Creek Echoes: A Century of Life in a Door County Village*, edited by Virginia Kinsey and Edward Schreiber, 291–304. Fish Creek, WI: John and Nancy Sargent, 2000.

Hardin, Carol. "The Indian Memorial Pole." Address to the Door County Historical Society. Fish Creek, WI. 1971.

Harris, Kathleen, ed. *The Centennial Reader: A Collection of Stories and Histories*. Fish Creek, WI: Friends of Peninsula State Park, 2009.

Head, Tom. "Timeline History of the Ku Klux Klan." ThoughtCo.com, May 23, 2019. www.thoughtco.com/the-ku-klux-klan-history-721444.

History.com. "The Great Depression." History.com, June 11, 2018. www.history.com/topics/great-depression.

Holand, Hjlamar. *Old Peninsula Days: Tales and Sketches of the Door County Peninsula*. Menasha, WI: George Banta Publishing, 1946.

Hughes, Langston. *The Big Sea: An Autobiography*. New York: Hill & Wang, 1940.

Jay, Martin Evan. "Sigmund Freud: Austrian Psychoanalyst." *Encyclopaedia Britannica* (online), May 3, 2019. www.britannica.com/biography/Sigmund-Freud.

Kahler, Kathryn A. "Memories of Camp Meenahga." *Wisconsin Department of Natural Resources Magazine* (June 2016). https://dnr.wi.gov/wnrmag/2016/06/Back.PDF.

Kansas Heritage Group. "Menominee's Letters." Accessed July 1, 2019. www.kansasheritage.org/PBP/history/menomine.html

Kinsey, Virginia, and Edward Schreiber, eds. *Fish Creek Echoes: A Century of Life in a Door County Village*. Fish Creek, WI: John and Nancy Sargent, 2000.

Luke, Jim. "Bank Failures: The 1920s and the Great Depression." *Econproph* (blog), October 26, 2009. http://econproph.com/2009/10/26/fdic-managing-the-crisis-the-fdic-and-rtc-experience/.

Lundh, Jeff. "My Great Aunt Gertrude." In *Fish Creek Echoes: A Century of Life in a Door County Village*, edited by Virginia Kinsey and Edward Schreiber, 175–7. Fish Creek, WI: John and Nancy Sargent, 2000.

Murphy, Robert P. "The Depression You've Never Heard Of: 1920–1921." Foundation for Economic Education, November 18, 2009. https://fee.org/articles/the-depression-youve-never-heard-of-1920–1921/.

National Museum of American History. "What Is Jazz?" National Museum of American History, June 14, 2019. https://americanhistory.si.edu/smithsonian-jazz/education/what-jazz.

Nolen, John. *State Parks for Wisconsin*. Madison, WI: State Parks Board, 1909.

O'Neill, Tim. "A Look Back: River Des Peres Floods after Record Downpour in 1915." *St. Louis Post-Dispatch*, August 21, 2011. www.stltoday.com/news/local/metro/a-look-back-river-des-peres-floods-after-record-downpour/article_d9d3a223-e650–5efb-a55e-1815dc6d308c.html.

Paris, Leslie. *Children's Nature: The Rise of the American Summer Camp.* New York: New York University Press, 2008.

Peddle, Alice Clark Day. *Camp Meenahga, 1916–1948.* Peninsula State Park Archives, Fish Creek, WI. Unpublished manuscript, 1987.

Peddle, Alice Clark Day. "Camp Meenahga." Address to the Door County Historical Society. Fish Creek, WI. 1976.

Peddle, Alice Clark Day. "Meenahga." In *Fish Creek, the Summertime,* Vol. 1, edited by Libby Isham and Betsy Skinner Guenzel. Door County, WI, 1991.

Schreiber, Edward, and Lois Schreiber, eds. *Fish Creek Voices: An Oral History of a Door County Village.* Ellison Bay, WI: William Caxton, 1990.

Sholem, Stanford H. *Horseshoe Island: The Folda Years.* Ephraim, WI: Ephraim Foundation, 1998.

Simon, Kenneth A., and W. Vance Grant. *Digest of Educational Statistics.* Bulletin 1965, No. 4. Washington, DC: US Government Printing Office, 1965.

Suttie, Jill. "Four Ways Music Strengthens Social Bonds." *Greater Good Magazine* (January 15, 2015). https://greatergood.berkeley.edu/article/item/four_ways_music_strengthens_social_bonds.

Thorp, Duncan. "Summer Camp Time." In *Pieces of the Past,* edited by Pamela Thorp Sarett, 12–20. Unpublished manuscript, 1987.

Tishler, William. *A History of Peninsula State Park: Door County's Emerald Treasure.* Madison, WI: University of Wisconsin Press, 2006.

US Census Bureau. "Door County, Wisconsin, 2010." American Fact-Finder, July 15, 2019. https://factfinder.census.gov/faces/nav/jsf/pages/community_facts.xhtml?src=bkmk

US House of Representatives Office of History, Art & Archives. "Missouri's Ratification of the 19th Amendment." Accessed June 28, 2019. https://history.house.gov/Records-and-Research/Featured-Content/Missouri-Ratification-of-19th-Amendment/.

Van Slyck, Abigail A. *A Manufactured Wilderness: Summer Camps and the Shaping of American Youth, 1890–1960.* Minneapolis, MN: University of Minnesota Press. 2006.

Wack, Henry Wellington. *The Camping Ideal, the New Human Race: A Brief Survey of the Summer and Winter Outdoor Camp Movement in the United States.* New York: Redbook Magazine, 1925.

Wehling, Joanne Kodanko. "Kodanko Farm Girl." In *The Centennial Reader,* edited by Kathleen Harris, 84–9. Fish Creek, WI: Friends of Peninsula State Park, 2009.

Whitaker, Jan. "Tea Room History." *Jan Whitaker's Consumer Society* (blog), June 28, 2019. www.janwhitaker.net/events.htm.

Wicentowski, Danny. "First-Hand Accounts Show the Horror of East St. Louis' 1917 Race Riot." *River Front Times* (blog), June 28, 2017. www.riverfronttimes.com/newsblog/2017/06/28/first-hand-accounts-show-the-horror-of-east-louis-1917-race-riot.

Wikipedia. "James H. Howard." Last edited May 30, 2019. https://en.wikipedia.org/wiki/James_H._Howard.

Wikipedia. "New Woman." Last edited June 5, 2019. https://en.wikipedia.org/wiki/New_Woman.

Wikipedia. "The Song of Hiawatha." Last edited May 26, 2019. https://en.wikipedia.org/wiki/The_Song_of_Hiawatha.

Wikipedia. "Tableau Vivant." Last edited October 4, 2018. https://en.wikipedia.org/wiki/Tableau_vivant.

Wikipedia. "Veiled Prophet Ball." Last edited May 27, 2019. https://en.wikipedia.org/wiki/Veiled_Prophet_Ball.

Woodward, Calvin M. "The Fruits of Manual Training." *Popular Science Monthly* 25 (June 1884): 347–57.

Notes

Introduction

1. Peddle, *Camp Meenahga, 1916–1948*, 5.
2. 1922 *Pack and Paddle*, 23.
3. Clark, *Meenahga Camps for Girls* (1935), 14.
4. 1935 *Pack and Paddle News.*

Chapter 1: Up to Me

1. O'Neill, "A Look Back"; Wicentowski, "First-Hand Accounts."
2. Beauchamp, "The Mystery"; Wikipedia, "Veiled Prophet Ball."
3. Peddle, "Camp Meenahga," 2; Peddle, *Camp Meenahga, 1916–1948*, 3. The Peninsula State Park archives include separate written recollections of Camp Meenahga from Alice Clark Day Peddle. Some of the information later appeared in a 1991 two-volume report, *Fish Creek, the Summertime*. In 2000, much of the 1991 text was published in Kinsey and Schreiber's *Fish Creek Echoes.*
4. Judith Clark Stephens, interview by Kathryn Hutter, Fish Creek, WI, June 8, 2005
5. Ibid.
6. Laurence Clark Day to Peninsula State Park, January 27, 2004, 3, TS; Laurence Clark Day to William Tishler, 2002, TS.
7. 1940 *Pack and Paddle*, 25.
8. Laurence Clark Day to Peninsula State Park, January 27, 2004, 3, TS.
9. Ibid.
10. Mary Orr Lowrey, interview by Kathleen Harris, Fish Creek, WI, October 5, 2013.
11. 1940 *Pack and Paddle*, 25.

Chapter 2: Scouting for a Camp

1. Guenzel, "Gray Walls Remember."
2. Peddle, "Camp Meenahga," 2.
3. *Encyclopaedia Britannica*, "Hiawatha"; Wikipedia, "The Song of Hiawatha." Henry Wadsworth Longfellow published *The Song of Hiawatha* in 1855. The poem became broadly recognized, leading some scholars

to credit Longfellow with strengthening the cultural construct of "the noble savage." In his poem, Longfellow likely used the Ojibwe word for blueberry plant, *miinagaawanzh,* but spelled it Meenahga. Hiawatha was a precolonial historical figure who helped establish the Iroquois Confederacy. In *The Song of Hiawatha,* Longfellow created Hiawatha's lover, Minnehaha, imagining her as an arrow-maker's daughter of the Dakota people. Peninsula State Park's Minnehaha Trail is a geographical error, since the fictionalized Hiawatha visited Lake Superior, not Lake Michigan.

4. Forest County Potawatomi, "Timeline of Potawatomi History"; Kansas Heritage Group, "Menominee's Letters"; First People, "Treaty with the Menominee."
5. Eaton, *Rock Island,* 6, 8–11.
6. Davis, "The Names in the Orchard," 38.
7. Cataldi et al., "Histamine Receptors and Antihistamines," 213.
8. US Census Bureau, "Door County, Wisconsin, 2010."
9. Tishler, *A History of Peninsula State Park,* 76–80, 94; Holand, *Old Peninsula Days,* 151–4.
10. Ruth Doolittle Steinseifer, interview by Kathryn Hutter, Fish Creek, WI, December 1, 2006.
11. Peddle, "Camp Meenahga," 6; Bernstein, "Fish Creek Intensive Historical and Architectural Survey," 24, 26. During her 1916 visit, Clark stayed at the Thorp Hotel, then located at 4199 Main Street in Fish Creek. "Mrs. Thorp of the hotel was kindness itself" wrote Clark in her notebook. She also noted the "wonderful fish" served at a meal. Asa Thorp established the hotel in the 1880s. Asa's son Edgar C. "Ted" Thorp took over the business around 1895, and his son Leland managed the hotel after 1943. The original hotel burned down in 1986. Asa Thorp and several relatives are buried in a private family cemetery located within Peninsula State Park near Weborg Point. One notable grave is that of his nephew Freeman Thorp, the son of Asa's brother and a daughter of Increase Claflin. Freeman died in the sinking of the *Erie L. Hackley* in Lake Michigan in 1903.
12. Peddle, "Camp Meenahga," 4.
13. *Door County News,* "Choose State Park: Party of St. Louis Young Ladies Select Peninsula State Park as Camping Place for Summer," May 31, 1916.
14. Peddle, "Camp Meenahga," 3.
15. Clark, *Meenahga Camps for Girls* (1935), 10.
16. Tishler, *A History,* 127–8.
17. Janet Huckins, 1921 *Pack and Paddle,* 50.

18. Agnes Matzinger, 1920 *Pack and Paddle,* 10.
19. Peninsula State Park carpenter Hubert Woerfel transformed the abandoned lime kiln into the Lookout. A veteran of the Spanish-American War, Woerfel is buried in Blossomburg Cemetery.
20. Evelyn Bhirdo Franke, interview by Jessica Sheppard, Fish Creek, WI, December 6, 2003.
21. Dorothy Sherman, 1922 *Pack and Paddle,* 31.
22. Mary Orr Williams, 1943 *Pack and Paddle,* 24.
23. Elaine Mabley, 1920 *Pack and Paddle,* 22.
24. Elizabeth Lanier DeRamus, interview by Kathryn Hutter, Fish Creek, WI, January 29, 2005.

Chapter 3: Beautiful Place, Beautiful Country

1. Peddle, "Camp Meenahga." Peddle read remarks she had received from Elaine Mabley Schramm.
2. Thomas Reynolds, "Plea for the Door County Park," *Assembly Journal,* 1909.
3. *Encyclopaedia Britannica,* "Tuberculosis through History."
4. Peddle, "Meenahga," 6.
5. Clark, *Meenahga Camps for Girls* (1921), 3.
6. Hilda Mabley, 1918 *Pack and Paddle,* 14.
7. Clark, *Meenahga Camps for Girls* (1919), 2.
8. Clark, *Meenahga Camps for Girls* (1935), 5.
9. Jane Hubbard, 1929 *Pack and Paddle,* 25.
10. Paris, *Children's Nature,* 62.
11. Thorp, "Summer Camp Time," 14.
12. Wack, *The Camping Ideal,* 16, 66.
13. Nolen, *State Parks for Wisconsin,* 10, 41
14. 1918 *Pack and Paddle,* 14.
15. Bell, "A History of Women in Sport"; Wikipedia, "New Woman."

Chapter 4: Traveling to Camp

1. Grace Lanier Brewer, interview by Kathryn Hutter, Fish Creek, WI, December 28, 2004.
2. Clark, *Meenahga Camps for Girls* (1921), 23.
3. Peddle, *Camp Meenahga, 1916–1948,* 8.
4. Katherine Orr, 1917 *Pack and Paddle,* 14.
5. 1917 *Pack and Paddle,* 48–9.
6. Clark, *Meenahga Camps for Girls* (1921), 13.
7. Ibid.
8. Cavanaugh and Finn, "The African-American Railroad Experience."

9. *Door County Democrat*, “Sturgeon Bay Day,” June 29, 1917.
10. *Door County Advocate*, “Camp Meenahga Girls Arrive,” July 5, 1917.
11. 1923 *Pack and Paddle*, 28.
12. 1921 *Pack and Paddle*, 13.
13. Kinsey and Schreiber, *Fish Creek Echoes*, 53, 58.
14. *Door County News*, “Many Girls Arrive,” July 8, 1920.
15. Evelyn Bhirdo Franke, interview by Jessica Sheppard, Fish Creek, WI, December 6, 2003.
16. Mousie Stix, 1927 *Pack and Paddle*, 4.
17. Ruth Doolittle Steinseifer, interview by Kathryn Hutter, Fish Creek, WI, December 1, 2006.
18. *Door County Advocate*, “Door County’s Tourist Business: Past and Prospective,” September 19, 1919.
19. 1930 *Pack and Paddle*, 12.
20. Mimi Mory and B. J. Mayer, 1935 *Pack and Paddle News*.
21. Betsy Bueck, 1922 *Pack and Paddle*, 32.
22. 1917 *Pack and Paddle*, 16.
23. Ibid.
24. Laurence Clark Day to Peninsula State Park, January 27, 2004, 7, TS.
25. Robert Wollaeger, interview by Kathryn Hutter, Fish Creek, WI, January 28, 2005. Wollaeger’s three sisters, Valeska, Antoinette, and Charlotte, attended camp.
26. 1930 *Pack and Paddle*, 39.
27. Laurence Clark Day to Peninsula State Park, January 27, 2004, 11, TS.

Chapter 5: Camp Meenahga and the Great War

1. Peddle, *Camp Meenahga, 1916–1948*, 7.
2. Kinsey and Schreiber, *Fish Creek Echoes*, 55.
3. 1917 *Pack and Paddle*, 15.
4. 1940 *Pack and Paddle*, 26.
5. Clark, *Meenahga Camps for Girls* (1935), 15.
6. Grace Lanier Brewer, interview by Kathryn Hutter, Fish Creek, WI, December 28, 2004.
7. 1918 *Pack and Paddle*, 6.
8. 1917 *Pack and Paddle*, 28; 1918 *Pack and Paddle*, 6.
9. 1918 *Pack and Paddle*, 6–7.
10. Ibid., 6. President Wilson issued the executive order in 1916.
11. Kewpie appears several times in *Pack and Paddle*, usually in reference to younger campers. Kewpie is a variation on Cupid, the Roman god of love. Midwesterner Rose O’Neill drew merry, chubby-faced fairies. Her illustrations evolved into a popular comic strip and dolls.

O'Neill created Kewpies in 1909, the same year Peninsula State Park was established.

12. 1919 *Pack and Paddle*, 19. The word *jitney* probably originated from the French word *jeton*, referring to a coin-sized metal disk. Jitney became slang for small coins, especially nickels.
13. Wikipedia, "Tableau Vivant."
14. 1918 *Pack and Paddle*, 21.
15. Ibid.
16. Ibid.
17. *Door County News*, "Big Crowd at Park," August 8, 1919.
18. 1919 *Pack and Paddle*, 15.
19. 1942 *Pack and Paddle*, 28.
20. Peddle, "Camp Meenahga," 5. Peddle attributed these comments to Elaine Mabley Schramm.
21. Schreiber and Schreiber, *Fish Creek Voices*, 76; Harris, *The Centennial Reader*, 46. Various Door County histories include references to the Dyer sisters and their leased pioneer cabin. The sisters hosted teas, which local ladies attended, wearing hats and gloves. The Dyers also employed local youth to assist with chores. In 2016, Itsie Krause recalled cutting their grass. Former Fish Creek postmaster Anita Schultz remembered Lilia Dyer and her parasol (an old umbrella) that she carried while walking to and from the post office.
22. Landscape artist Charles Lesaar painted in oils. He had studios in San Francisco, Oakland, and Chicago. Several of his works are in the permanent collection of the Chicago Art Museum. In 1916, he married Meta Helen Schwefer. In 1918, Lesaar was accused of being a German spy, but the charge was dismissed. In ill health and separated from his wife, Lesaar died by suicide in 1941. He is buried in Blossomburg Cemetery. See *Door County Advocate*, "Man Who Worked on Totem Pole Dead—Declared Suicide by Coroner, Buried in Park," September 12, 1941.
23. 1923 *Pack and Paddle*, 38.
24. Kinsey and Schreiber, *Fish Creek Echoes*, 57.
25. Lundh, "My Great Aunt Gertrude," *Fish Creek Echoes*, 175–7.
26. From the 1920s until about 1960, Marie Gatter leased a cottage just north of Camp Meenahga in Peninsula State Park. A vast collection of owl cookie cutters, carvings, and other owl-related things filled the house. Gatter is buried in Blossomburg Cemetery.
27. Agnes Kuechler, an accomplished pianist and singer, began leasing Sven Anondsen's dilapidated cabin in the 1920s. Kuechler routinely got her Model A Ford stuck while driving up and down the bluffs—to the chagrin of various Peninsula State Park staff, who had to help free the

vehicle from the park's muddy roads. She gave piano lessons to many Door County children. Kuechler is buried in Blossomburg Cemetery.

28. Peddle, "Camp Meenahga," 4. The eagles that nested on Sven's Bluff disappeared from Door County along with other bald eagles from the 1950s to the 1990s due to the use DDT. Bald eagles then made a comeback, with about twenty pairs nesting in Door County in 2018.
29. Peddle, *Camp Meenahga, 1916–1948*, 2. The Weborg sisters taught school in Door County. Vida Weborg illustrated *Old Peninsula Days* by Hjlamar Holand. Elenora ("Ella") was described as "hawk-like" by her sister. Both are buried in Blossomburg Cemetery. Peninsula's Weborg Point came by its name when two Weborg brothers purchased the land from William Claflin. Claflin's father, Increase, and several brothers and sisters are buried in a small cemetery across from the present campground. His mother, Mary Ann, is buried near Little Sturgeon, Wisconsin, though the family moved her headstone to Peninsula State Park in the early 2000s.
30. Peddle, "Camp Meenahga," 7.
31. 1917 *Pack and Paddle*, 1.
32. Tishler, *A History of Peninsula State Park*, 194.
33. Personal correspondence from Carol Hackett, June 15, 2015
34. Peddle, *Camp Meenahga, 1916–1948*, 3.
35. 1942 *Pack and Paddle*, 28.

Chapter 6: Rise and Shine

1. Billings, "The Influenza Pandemic."
2. US House of Representatives Office of History, Art & Archives, "Missouri's Ratification of the 19th Amendment."
3. Peddle, "Camp Meenahga," 1. The Welchers had a life lease for about three hundred acres in Peninsula State Park, which reverted to the state of Wisconsin upon their deaths. Until the start of the Great War, when the United States was at war with Germany, their name was most often spelled Welcher instead of Welcker.
4. 1917 *Pack and Paddle*, 27–8.
5. Janet Hutkins,1921 *Pack and Paddle*, 19.
6. Kay James, 1920 *Pack and Paddle*, 10.
7. Elizabeth Lanier DeRamus, interview by Kathryn Hutter, Fish Creek, WI, January 29, 2005.
8. Betty Turnbull, 1929 *Pack and Paddle*, 31.
9. Maggie Woodbury, 1927 *Pack and Paddle*, 2–3.
10. Elizabeth Ann Buell and Eliza Chapman, "Tent Inspection," 1919 *Pack and Paddle*, 8.

11. Signe Gundersen Schroeder, interview by Kathryn Hutter, Fish Creek, WI, February 3, 2005.
12. 1920 *Pack and Paddle*, 19.
13. Suttie, "Four Ways."
14. 1926 *Pack and Paddle*, 18.
15. 1917 *Pack and Paddle*, 30; Tishler, *A History of Peninsula State Park*, 107–8.
16. Porgie Longan, 1926 *Pack and Paddle*, 6.
17. Barbara Becker Glass, interview by Kathryn Hutter, Fish Creek, WI, March 15, 2005.
18. Grace Lanier Brewer, interview by Kathryn Hutter, Fish Creek, WI, December 28, 2004.
19. Elizabeth Lanier DeRamus, interview by Kathryn Hutter, Fish Creek, WI, January 29, 2005.
20. Kinsey and Schreiber, *Fish Creek Echoes*, 53.
21. Elaine Mabley, 1919 *Pack and Paddle*, 9–10.
22. Eleanor Gaik Green, 1920 *Pack and Paddle*, 37.
23. Whitaker, "Tea Room History." In 2018, the former Orange Tea House cottage was sold and moved to Sturgeon Bay in order to expand parking for the Fish Creek public beach.
24. Emily Arnold, 1941 *Pack and Paddle*, 10.
25. Ruth Dennis and Kelly Brent, "Rain at Camp," 1943 *Pack and Paddle*, 25.
26. Dorothy Halverson, interview by Kathleen Harris, Fish Creek, WI, January 3, 1998.
27. Clark, *Meenahga Camps for Girls* (1937), 5.
28. Laurence Clark Day to Peninsula State Park, January 27, 2004, 3, TS.
29. Personal correspondence from Don Pringle Pruitt, August 15, 2013.
30. Lee Berkley, 1945 *Pack and Paddle*, 5.
31. Carol Mansfield Moore, 1944 *Pack and Paddle*, 30.
32. 1920 *Pack and Paddle*, 18.
33. *Door County Advocate*, "Catching Up," June 10, 1980, 8.
34. Kinsey and Schreiber, *Fish Creek Echoes*, 54.
35. Paris, *Children's Nature*, 8–9, 48–9.
36. Simon and Grant, *Digest of Educational Statistics*. Between 1900 and 1940, high school graduation rates in America rose from 6.4 to 50.8 percent.
37. *Encyclopaedia Britannica*, "Anna Botsford Comstock."
38. Paris, *Children's Nature*, 62.
39. Van Slyck, *A Manufactured Wilderness*, 20.
40. Ibid., 47.

Chapter 7: Fit as a Fiddle

1. Murphy, "The Depression You've Never Heard Of."
2. Tishler, *A History of Peninsula State Park*, 49; Harris, *The Centennial Reader*, 98.
3. Paris, *Children's Nature*, 66.
4. Clarke, *Sex in Education*, 60.
5. Bell, "A History of Women in Sport."
6. Hilda Mabley, "Athletics and the American Girl," 1918 *Pack and Paddle*, 14.
7. Elizabeth "Joe" Paine (Mrs. Stephen J. Lent) to Bruce A. Chevis, July 22, 1976, TS. Chevis was the assistant superintendent of Peninsula State Park.
8. Ibid.
9. 1923 *Pack and Paddle*, 39.
10. 1921 *Pack and Paddle*, 13.
11. 1925 *Pack and Paddle*, 11.
12. Clark, *Meenahga Camps for Girls* (1921), 15.
13. Peddle, "Camp Meenahga," 3. Peddle attributed these comments to Elaine Mabley Schramm.
14. Eleanor Beach, 1922 *Pack and Paddle*, 15–16.
15. 1917 *Pack and Paddle*, 42.
16. 1936 *Pack and Paddle News*, 2.
17. 1926 *Pack and Paddle*, 16.
18. 1928 *Pack and Paddle*, 7.
19. 1938 *Pack and Paddle*, 5.
20. 1922 *Pack and Paddle*, 11.
21. "Camp Wildwood," 1927 *Pack and Paddle*, 28.
22. *Door County Advocate*, "Island Camp Is Utopia," July 20, 1923; *Door County Advocate*, "Island Campers in Bad Storm on Lake—Yacht *Dream Girl* with Viking Ship in Tow Drenched," July 17, 1925; Blahnik, "Adventure Island," 183–9. Kinney first established Adventure Island Camp for Boys on Chambers Island but moved it to Adventure Island in 1925. Kinney's request to rename Big Strawberry Island "Adventure Island" was granted by the US Geographic Board in 1938. He ran his camp until 1952, when a Great Lakes gale wrecked the island's pier.
23. *Education Encyclopedia*, "Progressive Education."
24. Nancy Chilson, 1941 *Pack and Paddle*, 13.
25. Personal correspondence from Janice Chamberlaine Pierce, September 20, 2017.
26. 1945 *Pack and Paddle*, 9.
27. 1938 *Pack and Paddle*, 6.
28. *Door County Advocate*, "Island Camp Is Utopia," July 20, 1923
29. Woodward, "The Fruits of Manual Training," 350.

Chapter 8: Social Graces

1. *Door County News,* "In State Park," July 8, 1917.
2. Mousie Stix, 1921 *Pack and Paddle,* 26.
3. *Door County News,* "Riding Master Is a Suicide," February 27, 1924.
4. Ibid.
5. 1924 *Pack and Paddle,* 48.
6. 1930 *Pack and Paddle,* 19.
7. 1942 *Pack and Paddle,* 38.
8. Ida Manwey Webb, 1921 *Pack and Paddle,* 35.
9. Frances Ellen Tucker, 1920 *Pack and Paddle,* 6.
10. Agnes Matzinger, 1920 *Pack and Paddle,* 28.
11. Janet Fish, 1926 *Pack and Paddle,* 12.
12. Frances Louise "Jack" Matthews, 1926 *Pack and Paddle,* 69.
13. Peddle, "Camp Meenahga," 9. Peddle attributed these comments to Elaine Mabley Schramm.
14. Mousie Stix, 1926 *Pack and Paddle,* 48.
15. Peddle, "Camp Meenahga," 9. Peddle attributed these comments to Elaine Mabley Schramm.
16. Peddle, *Camp Meenahga, 1916–1948,* 2.
17. 1928, *Pack and Paddle,* 5.
18. 1939, *Pack and Paddle,* 5.
19. Tony Wollageger and Eugenia Evans, 1928 *Pack and Paddle,* 24.
20. Anna Griswold Nichols, interview by Kathryn Hutter, Fish Creek, WI, March 25, 2005.
21. Sholem, *Horseshoe Island,* 77.
22. Ibid., 68, 75. Schreiber and Schreiber, *Fish Creek Voices,* 56. According to the Folda children and correspondence from Alice Clark Day Peddle, Alma Folda's recipe for pinch pie (baked meringue topped with fruit) appeared in the first edition of *Joy of Cooking* by Irma S. Rambauer, though she is not credited.
23. Edmee Baur, 1922 *Pack and Paddle,* 19.
24. After E. F. Folda's death on January 23, 1944, Alma Folda signed a quit-claim deed to Horseshoe Island for $850.
25. Wack, *The Camping Ideal,* 1925.
26. Carol Mansfield Moore, 1944 *Pack and Paddle,* 30.
27. Mary Carter Davis, 1924 *Pack and Paddle,* 20.
28. 1926 *Pack and Paddle,* 27.
29. Evelyn Bhirdo Franke, interview by Jessica Sheppard, Fish Creek, WI, December 6, 2003.
30. 1927 *Pack and Paddle,* 39.
31. 1918 *Pack and Paddle,* 17.

32. Elizabeth Mack, 1922 *Pack and Paddle*, 29.
33. Paris, *Children's Nature*, 191–3, 205; Head, "Timeline History of the Ku Klux Klan."
34. 1941 *Pack and Paddle*, 14.
35. 1945 *Pack and Paddle*, 41.
36. Paris, *Children's Nature*, 199–200; Van Slyck, *A Manufactured Wilderness*, 184–7.
37. Carol McCarty, 1917 *Pack and Paddle*, 5.
38. Frances Ellen Tucker, 1920 *Pack and Paddle*, 5.
39. Van Slyck, *A Manufactured Wilderness*, 174, 198.
40. Burton, "Art in the Park," 31; Hardin, "The Indian Memorial Pole," 19. Hjalmar Holand conceived the idea for the pole. He asked Vida Weborg to design bands to be carved on a thirty-foot tree felled near Sentinel Trail. Kewaunee sculptor Robert Petschneider carved the original bear that was placed on top of the pole. Today, the bear is displayed at Peninsula State Park's nature center. Charles Lesaar completed carving the original pole. In 1970, a replica was erected on the park's golf course near the grave of Potawatomi Chief Simon Kahquados.

Chapter 9: Music, Writing, and Good Eating

1. Hughes, *The Big Sea*, 223.
2. Between the Wars, "Modernity as a Cultural Style: Jazz in Black and White"; National Museum of American History, "What Is Jazz?"
3. 1927 *Pack and Paddle*, 40.
4. Clark, *Meenahga Camps for Girls* (1935), 15.
5. 1923 *Pack and Paddle*, 23.
6. Jay, "Sigmund Freud."
7. 1922 *Pack and Paddle*, 36–7.
8. Peter Fons, one of twelve children, grew up on an eighty-acre homestead in northern Door County. His father, John, emigrated from Poland, first to Milwaukee and then to Door County, where he and his wife, Suzanne, farmed. Meenahga camp masters encouraged Fons in his studies and helped him secure a job in St. Louis managing the Warfield Shops, a prestigious interior design firm and tea house.
9. 1922 *Pack and Paddle*, 28.
10. 1919 *Pack and Paddle*.
11. Jane Hubbard, "Inspection," 1929 *Pack and Paddle*, 28.
12. Miriam Wickham, "The Answer," 1921 *Pack and Paddle*, 19.
13. Elena Margaret Fantoni, "Self Expression," 1920 *Pack and Paddle*, 14.
14. Posy Oswald, "The Sentinel Birch," 1937 *Pack and Paddle News*, 19.

15. 1926 *Pack and Paddle*, 8.
16. 1940 *Pack and Paddle*, 23.
17. Clark, *Meenahga Camps for Girls* (1935), 3.
18. The Camp Meenahga 1931 Model A was eventually salvaged and restored. See Kahler, "Memories of Camp Meenahga."
19. 1936 *Pack and Paddle News*, 1.
20. Peddle, "Camp Meenahga," 5. Peddle attributed these comments to Elaine Mabley Schramm.
21. Barbara Becker Glass, interview by Kathryn Hutter, Fish Creek, WI, March 15, 2005.
22. Marilyn Bergh, Louise Noland, Charlotte Warren, Jacqueline Kirk, and Peggy Coughlin, "Donut Blues," 1943 *Pack and Paddle*, 27.
23. Edmunds, "Memories of Camp Meenahga," 59.
24. Roy Gauger, interview by Jessica Sheppard, Fish Creek, WI, December 30, 2003. In the early 1900s, summer residents often brought domestic staff with them to Door County. Some employees were of African American descent. Hotels, too, hired people of different ethnicities as cooks and cleaners. Minority groups traveled to Door County for the cherry harvest as well, but in the mid-twentieth century were sequestered from whites in the "picking camps." In the mid-twentieth century, customs changed, and summer residents began employing more local people. Nevertheless, the *Milwaukee Journal* reported "no entry" signs that read "No Coloreds and No Jews" in several Door County hotels. See *Milwaukee Journal*, "Hits 'Gentiles Only' Resorts," June 28, 1949.
25. Evelyn Bhirdo Franke, interview by Jessica Sheppard, Fish Creek, WI, December 6, 2003.
26. Laurence Clark Day to Peninsula State Park, January 27, 2004, 8, TS.
27. Personal correspondence from Irene Pringle Pruitt, August 15, 2013.
28. Personal correspondence from Irene Pringle Pruitt, August 15, 2013.
29. Thorp, "Summer Camp Time," 14.
30. Ibid.
31. Peronsal correspondence from Irene Pringle Pruitt, August 15, 2013.
32. Evelyn Bhirdo Franke, interview by Jessica Sheppard, Fish Creek, WI, December 6, 2003.
33. Wehling, "Kodanko Farm Girl," 84.
34. Trez Winfrey, 1935 *Pack and Paddle News*.
35. Edmunds, "Memories of Camp Meenahga," 59.
36. Elizabeth Lanier DeRamus, interview by Kathryn Hutter, Fish Creek, WI, January 29, 2005.
37. Personal correspondence from Irene Pringle Pruitt, August 15, 2013.

38. Clark, *Meenahga Camps for Girls* (1935); Clark, *Meenahga Camps for Girls* (1919).
39. Patty James, 1927 *Pack and Paddle*, 11.

Chapter 10: The Bitter with the Sweet

1. History.com, "The Great Depression."
2. 1930 *Pack and Paddle*, 2.
3. Nina Brown, 1930 *Pack and Paddle*, 6.
4. Mary Orr Nulsen and daughter Carolyn Orr Muir, November 22, 2013, video interview and correspondence with Kathleen Harris, December 4, 2017. Saint Walpurga was an eighth-century English princess who became a missionary in Germany. Her feast day is linked to May Day and has evolved into a carnival-style celebration.
5. 1945 *Pack and Paddle*, 22.
6. C. L. Harrington to A. E. Doolittle, February 1, 1929, TS.
7. Alice Orr Clark to Arthur Doe, January 29, 1931, TS.
8. Alice Orr Clark and Fanny Woodward Mabley to C. L. Harrington, March 2, 1931, TS.
9. Alice Orr Clark to Arthur Doe, January 29, 1931, TS.
10. Luke, "Bank Failures."
11. *Door County Advocate*, "State of Wisconsin State Banking Department Notice to Creditors of the Door County State Bank, Sturgeon Bay, Wis.," October 16, 1931.
12. A. E. Doolittle to C. L. Harrington, May 15, 1940, TS.
13. L. A. Ritzman to C. L. Harrington, November 12, 1931, TS. Ritzman was president of the Noble Refining Company.
14. C. L. Harrington to A. E. Doolittle, September 30, 1932, TS; A. E. Doolittle to Paul D. Kelleter, October 5, 1932, TS. "In the new contract," wrote Harrington, "we show the amount left in the bank to be $1,162.70. There is a two-cent difference here, which doesn't really amount to anything, but it would be well to have no difference at all." Doolittle responded in a letter to Wisconsin Conservation Commission director Paul Delmar Kelleter, "I have gone over all the material I have and still find the amount of $1,162.68 is the correct balance on hand September 17, 1931. This amount is two cents lower than that on the new contract, but I cannot find anything that will make the two cents."
15. Alice Orr Clark and Fanny Woodward Mabley to C. L. Harrington, March 2, 1931, TS; Arthur Doe to Wisconsin Conservation Commission, January 4, 1932; Paul D. Kelleter to Haskell Noyes, March 11, 1932. In negotiating the lease, the Wisconsin Conservation Commission considered three things: the Commission's estimated value of the

state-owned buildings being used by Camp Meenahga ($10,000), the Commission's estimated taxes and interest on property worth $10,000 ($700–800), and the anticipated cost of septic system repairs (Internal Conservation Commission Memorandum from Matt Peterson, February 1 1932, TS). "This department has for some time been concerned about the sanitary conditions existing at the camp and as the result of an investigation made by a representative of this department, there is every indication that the sanitary conditions are so bad that they will not brook of any further delay. That is reason why this department has insisted upon the larger amount for improvements" (Paul D. Kelleter to Arthur Doe, February 3, 1932, TS).

16. Arthur Doe to Wisconsin Conservation Commission, January 4, 1932, TS.
17. Arthur Doe to Haskell Noyes, March 15, 1932, TS.
18. Alice Orr Clark to C. L. Harrington, September 1, 1932.
19. C. L. Harrington to A. E. Doolittle, September 30, 1932; A. E. Doolittle to Paul Kelleter, October 5, 1932, TS.
20. Alice Orr Clark to C. L. Harrington, October 10, 1932, TS.
21. Ibid.
22. C. L. Harrington to Paul Kelleter, March 5, 1932, TS. Harrington wrote that "their sanitary facilities are going to need a complete overhauling during the term of this contract and that will cost them more than $1,500 if they are to do any kind of a job."
23. Alice Orr Clark to Paul Kelleter, November 4, 1932, TS.
24. Personal communication with Carolyn Orr Muir, December 4, 2017.
25. *Door County Advocate*, "Riding Master of Girls' Camp Dies in Chicago," October 20, 1933. Christensen's wife and son Bernard were expert riders and accompanied him to Door County each summer. Thade "Ted" Cornils knew Christensen through his daughter, who took riding lessons at Christensen's Lakeshore Academy in Chicago. Cornils made his living as a master butcher in Chicago (he named his horse Butcher Boy) and eventually owned three meat markets on Chicago's South Side. Before emigrating from Denmark to the United States in 1909, Cornils served as groom to Baron von Gundhardt, adjutant to Germany's Kaiser Wilhelm II.
26. 1941 *Pack and Paddle*, 3, 35–7.
27. Herby Hardt, interview by Kathleen Harris, Fish Creek, WI, May 30, 2005. Hardt was the son-in-law of Thade "Ted" Cornils.
28. Alice Orr Clark to C. L. Harrington, March 23, 1934, TS.
29. *Door County Advocate*, "To Meenahga Camps Inc.," April 20, 1934.
30. Haskell Noyes to Paul Kelleter, March 5, 1932, TS.
31. Haskell Noyes to Paul Kelleter, March 17, 1932, TS.

32. Haskell Noyes to H. W. MacKenzie, September 28, 1936, TS.
33. A. E. Doolittle to C. L. Harrington, November 4, 1935, TS.
34. A. E. Doolittle to C. L. Harrington, February 12, 1936, TS.
35. Mary Ellen Crane, 1939 *Pack and Paddle*, 7.
36. 1940 *Pack and Paddle*, 8.
37. Mary Orr Williams and Margaret Kennedy, 1939 *Pack and Paddle*, 11.
38. Judy Clark Stephens to Aunt Polly, April 30, 1939, TS.
39. C. L. Harrington to Alice Orr Clark, September 24, 1936, TS.
40. C. L. Harrington to H. W. MacKenzie, October 13, 1936, TS.
41. Haskell Noyes to L. M. Hobbins, November 21, 1936, TS.
42. Alice Orr Clark to C. L. Harrington, March 1, 1937, TS.

Chapter 11: Games, Capers, and Characters

1. Edmunds, "Memories of Camp Meenahga," 60.
2. Edmunds, *The Loving Spice of Life*, 235.
3. Tishler, *A History of Peninsula State Park*, 176–9.
4. Haskell Noyes to H. W. MacKenzie, September 28, 1936, TS.
5. Tishler, *A History of Peninsula State Park*, 179.
6. Harris, *Centennial Reader*, 25.
7. 1926 *Pack and Paddle*, 13.
8. Josephine Pridmore, 1930 *Pack and Paddle*, 19.
9. Sally Simmons, 1923 *Pack and Paddle*, 13.
10. *Door County Advocate*, "Escanaba Captures Gull Championship: Rudy Carl Wins P. A. A. Championship at Fish Creek," August 10, 1945.
11. 1938 *Pack and Paddle*, 10.
12. 1938 *Pack and Paddle*, 19.
13. Gardner, "The Forgotten Falk Corporation."
14. 1938 *Pack and Paddle*, 19.
15. *Door County Advocate*, "Bulgarian Bride Declared a Suicide, Believed Over Slow Adjustment to U.S.," September 9, 1938.
16. Ibid.
17. Ibid.

Chapter 12: Foreboding Winds, Dead Calm

1. Personal correspondence from Irene Pringle Pruitt, August 15, 2013.
2. *Door County Advocate*, "Two Narrowly Escape as Truck Breaks Through Ice," February 2, 1940.
3. Elizabeth Lanier DeRamus, interview by Kathryn Hutter, Fish Creek, WI, January 29, 2005.
4. Judy Clark Stephens to Aunt Polly, July 30, 1940, TS.
5. Mike Orwig, 1941 *Pack and Paddle*, 6, 37.

6. Janice Pierce, 1941 *Pack and Paddle*, 26.
7. Personal correspondence from Janice Chamberlaine Pierce, September 20, 2017.
8. Moya Kent and Marie Irwin, 1942 *Pack and Paddle*, 15.
9. Laurence Clark Day to Peninsula State Park, January 27, 2004, 10, TS.
10. Kathy Hinch, "Air Raid," 1941 *Pack and Paddle*, 13
11. 1945 *Pack and Paddle*, 21.
12. 1939 *Pack and Paddle*, 14.
13. Bobby Houx, 1930 *Pack and Paddle*, 6.
14. Grace Lanier Brewer, interview by Kathryn Hutter, Fish Creek, WI, December 28, 2004.
15. 1941 *Pack and Paddle*, 13.
16. Mike Orwig, 1942 *Pack and Paddle*, 18.
17. Peddle, *Camp Meenahga, 1916–1948*, 5.
18. Alice Orr Clark to A. E. Doolittle, April 20, 1942, TS.
19. A. E. Doolittle to Alice Orr Clark, April 23, 1943, TS.
20. Minerva Carr Canavan, interview by Kathryn Hutter, Fish Creek, WI, January 3, 2004.
21. Personal correspondence from Irene Pringle Pruitt, August 15, 2013.
22. Marcella Gauger Desotelle, interview by Jessica Sheppard, Fish Creek, WI, December 3, 2003.
23. Personal correspondence from Irene Pringle Pruitt, August 15, 2013.
24. Ibid.
25. Marcella Gauger Desotelle, interview by Jessica Sheppard, Fish Creek, WI, December 3, 2003.
26. Alice Orr Clark to A. E. Doolittle, April 20, 1942, TS.
27. A. E. Doolittle to Alice Orr Clark, April 23, 1942, TS.
28. C. L. Harrington to H. W. MacKenzie, November 25, 1941, TS.
29. A. E. Doolittle to Robert Newberry, August 5, 1942, TS.
30. H. C. Barker, sworn testimony to A. E. Doolittle, August 8, 1942, TS.
31. Roy Grovogel, sworn testimony to A. E. Doolittle, August 19, 1942, TS.
32. Ibid.
33. E. J. Vanderwall to A. E. Doolittle, February 18, 1943, TS.
34. Alice Orr Clark to C. L. Harrington, March 16, 1943, TS.
35. C. L. Harrington to Alice Orr Clark, July 7, 1944, TS; William Beckstrom, handwritten note to C. L. Harrington, undated.
36. 1944 *Pack and Paddle*, 15.
37. Like other Angels of Bataan, Adolpha M. Meyer received the Bronze Star. Collins, "The Angels of Bataan."
38. Alice Orr Clark to William Beckstrom, October 31, 1944, TS.
39. Lois Write and Lee Karchar, 1944 *Pack and Paddle*, 45.

40. 1945 *Pack and Paddle*, 21.
41. Harriet Chambers, 1945 *Pack and Paddle*, 7.
42. Anna Griswold Nichols to Kathryn Hutter, March 25, 2005, TS.
43. Personal communication with Laurence Day, February 3, 2018.
44. Wikipedia, "James H. Howard."
45. Marianne McDonald and Jo Ann Straube, 1945 *Pack and Paddle*, 7.

Chapter 13: Suddenly, Goodbye

1. Alice Orr Clark to C. L. Harrington, November 10, 1947, TS.
2. C. L. Harrington to Alice Orr Clark, November 18, 1947, TS.
3. 1921 *Pack and Paddle*, 5.
4. 1945 *Pack and Paddle*, 36.
5. Grace Lanier, 1938 *Pack and Paddle*, 14.
6. Peddle, "Camp Meenahga," 9. Peddle attributed these comments to Elaine Mabley Schramm.
7. 1941 *Pack and Paddle*, 44.
8. Betty Campbell, 1941 *Pack and Paddle*, 35.
9. 1938 *Pack and Paddle*, 31.
10. Wita Jones, 1938 *Pack and Paddle*, 12.
11. Margaret Fraser, 1917 *Pack and Paddle*, 22.
12. Katherine Sibley, 1940 *Pack and Paddle*, 24.
13. Benno Clark, 1941 *Pack and Paddle*, 23.
14. Mary Jane Pruett, 1940 *Pack and Paddle*, 2.
15. Ernest Swift to A. F. Rankin, December 4, 1948.
16. Peddle, "Camp Meenahga," 2.
17. Ibid.
18. Clark M. Clifford to Alice Orr Clark, January 13, 1949, TS.
19. Peddle, "Camp Meenahga," 2.
20. Ibid., 4.
21. Lily Anne Peck, 1929 *Pack and Paddle*, 33.
22. Peddle, "Camp Meenahga," 2.
23. Edmunds, "Memories of Camp Meenahga," 60.
24. 1926 *Pack and Paddle*, 17.
25. *Door County Democrat*, "More Girls Arrive," July 14, 1916.

Acknowledgments

I owe thanks to many people who helped me write this book. First and foremost, I wish to thank my mother, Marian Harris, for all her love and support. Thank you to the people associated with Camp Meenahga whom I am privileged to know, including Laurence Day, Roy and Judie Gauger, Janice Chamberlaine Pierce, Dave and Carol Hackett, Lynn Matke, Bob Le Mieux, Bill Guenzel, Rick Sneeberger, and others. Thank you to Irene Pringle Pruitt, whom I was fortunate enough to make a treasured memory with as we walked the grounds of old Camp Meenahga. Thanks are due as well to the children of Meenahga campers and staff who helped me along the way. Many, including Mark Pennington, whose mother, Jean Mitchell Pennington, attended Camp Meenahga, shared treasured Meenahga mementos with me. Seeing lovely keepsakes that have been carefully saved for decades astonished me and reminded me how special Meenahga was to so many. And, of course, thank you to Alice Orr Clark and Frances Louise "Kidy" Mabley—I have done my best to honor your legacies.

Many friends helped me through the joys and challenges of writing this book. A huge thank you to each: Lynn Herman, Jessica Doell, Lance and Sue Olson, Dawn Volpe, Sharon Malloy Standbridge, Bill and Jean Casey, Dave and Bettie Chomeau, and Jerry Chomeau.

Thank you to my colleagues at the Wisconsin Department of Natural Resources. Peninsula State Park managers Tom Blackwood and Kelli Bruns have supported my work. Jean Rombach-Bartels and Bill Nelson offered excellent guidance. Kathryn Hutter, Steve Rice, Jessica Sheppard, Lauren Bremer, Renny Lea, and Sean Hickey interviewed Meenahga campers and staff, scanned documents, and proofread drafts of the manuscript. John and Gretchen Maring, Chad Slaby, Bob and Nancy Davis, and others graciously donated to support my initial research.

Others who need thanking have volunteered at Peninsula State Park over the years. I especially need to thank the steadfast nature center volunteers. Thanks also to Caitlin Tredupp, Emily Behnke, and Nina Whipple, youth volunteers who have portrayed Meenahga girls in period costumes at Peninsula State Park programs.

Thank you to Chad Frank, archivist with the Forest County Potawatomi, for sharing helpful information and insights. To Bill Tishler, author of *A History of Peninsula State Park,* thank you for your excellent research that provided a foundation for this work. Thank you to the Ephraim Historical Foundation, the Door County Library, and the Friends of Peninsula State Park. Hats off to your staff and volunteers, who have always been willing to share knowledge that helped make this book better.

Thank you to Tom Krause, editor at the Wisconsin Historical Society Press. Your keen perceptions are as impressive as your editing skills. Learning from you has been a highlight of my career. Finally, thank you to everyone at the Wisconsin Historical Society Press. You recognized that the story of Camp Meenahga needed telling, and gave me, on behalf of the Wisconsin Department of Natural Resources, the opportunity to tell it.

Index

Page numbers in *italics* refer to illustrations.

Photo by Suzi Hass

Kathleen Harris served as Peninsula State Park's year-round naturalist from 1998 to 2019. Before that, she worked as an educator at the Ridges Sanctuary in Baileys Harbor, Wisconsin, and as a county naturalist in Iowa. When she's not ambling the haunts of old Camp Meenahga, she enjoys exploring the wooded brook that tumbles across her own five-acre property with Penny, her rescue Vizsla.